Crime Scene Processing in Correctional Facilities and Prisons

Crime scenes within correctional facilities present investigators with myriad challenges, not only in working, investigating, and collecting evidence but also in obtaining reliable eyewitness accounts. As a result, they are some of the most challenging cases and environments that any investigator will encounter.

Crime Scene Processing in Correctional Facilities and Prisons addresses the unique challenges in prison, correction, and detention facilities, outlining specific procedures and techniques that will reliably improve any investigation. Issues of contaminated crime scenes can result from guards trying to regain order, few to no dedicated staff with no training or understanding of crime scenes, a lack of cooperation from witnesses and victims, and even the lack of cooperation from the on-scene incident commander – whose main objective may be to return the facility to "normal" rather than allow for the proper collection of evidence. Whatever the challenges faced, this book tackles all of them. While the processing of crime scenes entails standard procedures and practices, a correctional setting can provide anything but. As a result, the investigator must be resourceful, tenacious – yet patient – and perform their duties with objectivity and ethical integrity throughout the process.

Features:

- Serves as the only resource on the market to provide essential investigative and crime scene guidelines *unique* and *specific* to correctional facilities
- Presents the various challenges of gathering and preserving evidence and investigating crimes, in correctional settings – including federal and state prisons, jails, and detention facilities
- In addition to presenting best practices in handling evidence and investigative procedures, covers unique interview techniques, report writing, and expert testimony

Author David Doglietto, as an experienced professional with decades of first-hand experience, walks readers through the best way to perform duties to cut through the challenges and barriers and avoid the pitfalls that come with the oftentimes complex investigations in these environments. Extensive illustrations and case examples are provided within the book, as chapters present best-practice investigative practices in an environment for which there is little published resource and reference material. *Crime Scene Processing in Correctional Facilities and Prisons* is an invaluable resource for crime scene investigators, legal professionals, and the staff, leadership, and managers of correctional facilities themselves.

Crime Scene Processing in Correctional Facilities and Prisons

David J. Doglietto

CRC Press is an imprint of the
Taylor & Francis Group, an **informa** business

Designed cover image: David J. Doglietto

First edition published 2025
by CRC Press
2385 NW Executive Center Drive, Suite 320, Boca Raton FL 33431

and by CRC Press
4 Park Square, Milton Park, Abingdon, Oxon, OX14 4RN

CRC Press is an imprint of Taylor & Francis Group, LLC

© 2025 David J. Doglietto

Reasonable efforts have been made to publish reliable data and information, but the author and publisher cannot assume responsibility for the validity of all materials or the consequences of their use. The authors and publishers have attempted to trace the copyright holders of all material reproduced in this publication and apologize to copyright holders if permission to publish in this form has not been obtained. If any copyright material has not been acknowledged please write and let us know so we may rectify in any future reprint.

Except as permitted under U.S. Copyright Law, no part of this book may be reprinted, reproduced, transmitted, or utilized in any form by any electronic, mechanical, or other means, now known or hereafter invented, including photocopying, microfilming, and recording, or in any information storage or retrieval system, without written permission from the publishers.

For permission to photocopy or use material electronically from this work, access www.copyright.com or contact the Copyright Clearance Center, Inc. (CCC), 222 Rosewood Drive, Danvers, MA 01923, 978-750-8400. For works that are not available on CCC please contact mpkbookspermissions@tandf.co.uk

Trademark notice: Product or corporate names may be trademarks or registered trademarks and are used only for identification and explanation without intent to infringe.

ISBN: 9781032823119 (hbk)
ISBN: 9781032823140 (pbk)
ISBN: 9781003503989 (ebk)

DOI: 10.4324/9781003503989

Typeset in Minion
by KnowledgeWorks Global Ltd.

This book is dedicated to my teacher, mentor, and dear friend Jan Johnson, CSCSA, who somehow saw that inside of this old prison drug investigator was the making of a senior crime scene analyst. Jan gave my life new direction, and I will always be grateful for her support and encouragement. Jan was a positive influence on so many individuals in the forensics profession. Her energy and passion for crime scene investigations will be greatly missed.

"I see no more than you, but I have trained myself to notice what I see."
                                                    Sherlock Holmes

Contents

Author		ix
Preface		xi
1	The Challenge	1
2	Selecting the Correctional Crime Scene Investigator	5
3	Responsibilities	13
4	Crime Scene Response Classification System & Crime Scene Investigation Inventory	26
5	Crime Scene Processing Methodology & Checklists	34
6	Crime Scene Procedure & Protocol Considerations	44
7	The Role of the Custodial CSI in Escapes, Use of Force, and Shooting Incidents	80
8	Forensic Pathology in the Correctional Setting	108
9	Bloodstain Pattern Evidence in Jails and Prisons	128
10	Suicide Investigations in Jails and Prisons	147
11	Footwear Evidence in Jails and Prisons	155

12	Fingerprint Evidence in Jails and Prison	**176**
13	Dealing with the Evidence	**190**
14	Fire Investigations	**204**
15	Interview Techniques in the Correctional Setting	**220**
16	Essential Report Writing	**227**
17	Courtroom Testimony	**243**
18	The Conclusion	**249**
Glossary		**255**
Index		**269**

Author

Investigator David J. Doglietto M.S., CSCSA began his law enforcement career in 1988 with the California Department of Corrections and Rehabilitation. In 1993, he was assigned to the Correctional Training Facility, Soledad State Prison, in Monterey County. He spent the first five years working as a tier officer in a housing unit consisting of 312 medium-maximum security level inmates supervised by only two officers. In 1998, he was assigned as an investigative officer with the Investigative Services Unit (ISU), with primary responsibility of narcotic investigations, eventually becoming a senior investigative officer with ISU, where he continued narcotic investigations and also worked as a senior crime scene analyst, latent print technician and comparison analyst, bloodstain pattern analyst, crime scene photographer, major crimes, and homicide investigator and operated a small forensic laboratory. He is a life member of the California Narcotic Officers' Association, as well as a member of the International Association of Identification (IAI) and the International Association for Arson Investigators. He is currently a Certified Senior Crime Scene Analyst and has completed over 2000 formal hours of investigative training, with most of the training in the field of forensic sciences. He has presented workshops at the annual International Association for Identification Educational Conferences since 2012. He is the Board Chair of the IAI Crime Scene Certification Board and is a member of the IAI Forensic Certification Management Board. He is an adjunct professor at Hartnell Community College, Administration of Justice Department in Salinas, California, and has developed an Introduction to Forensic Science course for the college. Investigator Doglietto retired from the California Department of Correction and Rehabilitation in 2016. He is now an investigator and senior forensic specialist with the Greenfield Police Department in Monterey County, California.

Preface

In 1998, I left Rainier Hall at the Correctional Training Facility, Soledad State Prison, North Facility, where I had been assigned as the Third Watch tier officer for five years, for a new assignment in the Investigative Services Unit. I started as a jack-of-all-trades investigator, but eventually settled into being a narcotics investigator, an assignment I pursued with ardent vim and vigor. I was good at working narcotics, and for personal reasons, working narcotic investigations was my calling. I was also blessed with a partner, Mike Williams, who also shared my enthusiasm for narcotic investigations, especially when they involved unscrupulous staff members; and we were very good at narcotic interdiction and investigations.

In 2000, an inmate was murdered on the Central Facility Exercise Yard. He was dragged off the exercise track up against the inner-perimeter fence line, an area where the assailants had correctly guessed was blind to the armed tower officers owing to the length of the fence and a slight concave bend, and an inmate-made stabbing weapon was shoved into his neck. He walked for 45 yards toward the Canteen building and collapsed in the arms of Officer Banda, the yard officer. I was on my way to my mother's 75th birthday celebration when I had to turn around and report to the prison as the official crime scene investigator. When I arrived, a 35mm camera was thrust into my hands and I was told, "Go take some pictures." The scene was mostly uncompromised, but about to be ruined. The garden hoses that slinked across the yard had been left running and a torrent of water was working its way slowly toward the crime scene for the hour and a half that it took me to get there. No one on the yard had the water keys needed to stem the flow. I had to go into one of the cell blocks and find an inmate yard worker who had been entrusted with a key and ordered him to surrender it, with the promise that I would bring it back. I then madly shut off all the garden hoses and made trenches with my bootheels to channel the water away from the crime scene.

Although the scene was saved from the impending flood, a large section of the blood trail had been erased when a sergeant instructed a large group of inmates to move out of the crime scene, and through the blood trail. It was an inexcusable action. In spite of this, the crime scene was processed, the photographs taken, the evidence recovered, and a conviction obtained; the perceived theft of a gold chain had cost the young man his life. It was on this occasion that I realized just how inadequate my in-house training in crime scene processing had been. Worse yet, the day following the murder, the State

Department of Justice crime scene technicians had been asked to review the scene to see if it had been handled appropriately. They were at a complete loss as to how to proceed in the custodial setting and things that they thought were potential weapons, such as safety razor blades used by the inmates for giving each other haircuts and soda can lift tabs, became the focus of their attention. At this, I fully understood that when it came to major crime scenes, we correctional personnel were on our own owing to the unique aspects of a confined area that is constantly in use; and most of all was a realization that I needed more training, and lots of it.

I took advantage of South Bay Regional Training Center's 40-hour Basic Field Evidence Technician course, hosted by the San Jose Police Department, and whatever free training I could find, like the Federal Bureau of Investigations' Basic CSI course in Oakland, California. It was not until 2005 when I was assigned an in-cell murder investigation at the Central Facility, the solution of which remained in the analysis of the bloodstain patterns, that I sought out and found the foremost instructional expert, Jan Johnson of Forensic Pieces.

Jan changed my life. She became my mentor as she somehow had confidence that in this old prison narcotics investigator, there was the potential for a forensic investigator as well. She convinced me to join the International Association for Identification and she hounded me to take the certification examinations, of which, with her help and guidance, I became a Certified Senior Crime Scene Analyst. I was also fortunate to attend Professor Herbert L. MacDonell's last Bloodstain Institute in Corning, New York.

I never sat back and waited for training to come to me; instead, I sought it out, most often paid for it myself and, for a time, utilized my own vacation time to attend the classes. You find that this will be a theme in this book. It may not have been fair, but life and work are not fair, and I am a better investigator, a better person, for my efforts.

As for the book, well, after years of jail and prison investigators asking me the question, "How do you process a crime scene in a prison?" I finally decided maybe I should try to put something down in writing in a way that is easy to understand and easy to follow. It seems that most of the crime scene processing books that are on the market tend to be highly technical tomes, and that just does not work for the jail or prison investigator; not that it would be beyond their understanding, but let's face it, in the custodial setting simple is best. Furthermore, a chance meeting with the *New York Times* and *USA Today* best-selling author of "White Heat" Brenda Novak (she won me at auction for $35.00, but that is another story) convinced me that I had the ability to convey my thoughts into words. I hope this is the case. I also hope that I have been as complete as possible in relating my experiences and training to you, the reader. Something tells me, however, that six months from now I will be processing a crime scene, and something will happen that will make me say, "This should have been in the book." Should this happen, it will be noted in the second edition, with my apologies.

Preface

In this book, I use the words "correctional" and "custodial" interchangeably to represent the jail or prison setting. The words tend to be regional, and their use varies across the country, but hopefully, I have not confused anyone.

I wish to express my gratitude to my dear friend and coworker Joseph Dyels, who found all my little grammatical mistakes and imperfections and kindly blamed them on the auto-correct function. I have a new appreciation for the "Oxford comma." Joseph shares my respect for Sir Robert Peel and the true, honorable role of law enforcement in society. I would also like to express my gratitude to my buddy Edward "Ted" McDonald with whom I have taught many forensic conference workshops. Ted is an excellent instructor and a good friend, and his contributions to this book were invaluable.

The Challenge

1

There is no more challenging crime scene than that found in a prison or jail setting – whether it be a federal prison, a state penitentiary, a city or county jail, or a privately run correctional or return-to-custody facility. Among the many problems inherent with prisons and jails is that the investigator will naturally be faced with a crime scene that is already contaminated, either by the routine and constant trudging of a confined inmate population or by the efforts of staff to restore order. It is unlikely that the investigator will find any area of the prison where an inmate has not frequented at least once unless it is in an area where inmate movement is strictly prohibited. Thus, the discovery of DNA from any one incarcerated individual is not as compelling to the event as it would be in the general public. Furthermore, custodial officials rely on the philosophy of "overwhelm and suppress" to control inmate disturbances. Therefore, the investigator will have to deal with an abundance of staff stuffed into a compact area of forensic importance. In contrast, the response by an individual first responder or a pair of responders on the streets can take command of an incident and limit the amount of destruction to the physical evidence present in the scene. In the custodial setting, the focus of correctional staff is the prompt restoration of order with little concern for the evidence that the crime scene contains. Little attention is given by responding staff to footwear impressions in the scene. Inmate-manufactured weapons are quickly whisked away by responding officers in an effort to keep them away from other inmates in the area, thus rendering the latent print or DNA evidence useless; not to mention there is an increased dependence on oleoresin capsicum pepper spray in modern corrections, which adds its own unique complications to the crime scene and crime scene investigator. Even if the crime scene is contained within a cell, occupied by one or two inmates, one must consider that the cell may have been previously occupied by hundreds of inmates; in other words, each cell is a veritable cornucopia of DNA.

Another problem is that there is seldom an investigator whose sole assignment is that of a crime scene investigator. Custodial officers who are trained in crime scene investigations, who routinely work as housing unit or dorm officers, culinary officers, yard or escort officers, and tower or gun position officers are tasked with being relieved from their day-to-day responsibilities in order to respond to an incident or disturbance as a crime scene investigator or technician. The response by the crime scene investigator is often delayed resulting in the loss of perishable evidence or the inability to promptly prevent the destruction of the crime scene. Even if that officer has the specific responsibility of investigating crimes within the facility, as it was in my case, it is often that you will find the investigative staff pulling extra shifts on the mainline or being redirected to cover vacant positions as a "cost-saving measure." Therefore, there remains the possibility that the staff member who is trained in crime scene investigations might actually be a part of the effort to restore order. This officer is then required to process a crime scene in an incident in which they participated.

I cannot stress this enough: an officer who has participated in quelling the disturbance must not be expected to process the subsequent crime scene. In fact, I will go so far as to say that the officer must not process such a scene under any circumstance, owing to the potential that the defense counsel will allege improprieties in the processing of the crime scene.

This is especially necessary if the crime scene investigator used force to restore order. In this case, it is best to either appoint a substitute crime scene investigator or use the resources of a mutual aid agency. The prison officials should call upon the jail officials for assistance, vice versa, or neighboring prisons or jails in contiguous counties for trained personnel. Failing this, the prison officials should call upon other local, county, or state agencies to provide this assistance. However, although the task of crime scene processing follows the same methodologies, the environment and its conditions and circumstances may be a unique challenge to investigators who are unfamiliar with those in a prison or jail.

Another unique problem encountered by the investigator in the custodial setting is the lack of cooperation from witnesses and victims. The inmate population maintains an age-old code of not providing direct critical information to correctional personnel. If you are lucky, you might get an anonymous note or "kite" dropped in the outgoing mailbox or at the infirmary pill line, with information that will be relevant to the investigation. This note might set you on the correct course for solving the crime, but this kind of evidence may present an admissibility problem to the prosecution during subsequent courtroom proceedings. Even victims are reluctant to cooperate with the investigation, either preferring to remedy the situation with "jailhouse justice" or out of fear of being labeled an informant or "snitch." I remember an occasion many years ago when I was a housing unit officer—an inmate was discovered in his cell trying to extract a screwdriver from his abdomen. The tool/weapon was introduced into his stomach earlier in the day on the exercise yard by an inmate who "borrowed" it from an inmate maintenance worker to resolve a respect issue. The victim was determined to remove the weapon on his own, stitch up any open wound with dental floss, and go about

The Challenge

his business. Inmates will, however, sometimes cooperate with the investigator to a limited extent, and the enterprising crime scene investigator will find creative ways to garner the needed information. You just have to know what questions to ask and how to ask them. These methods will be discussed in later chapters.

Oftentimes, the other problem encountered is the lack of cooperation from the on-scene incident commander, who is either anxious to return the facility to a "normal program" or to move all of the detained inmates out of the area and back to their assigned areas (i.e., cells, dorms, work or educational programs, and so forth) before their presence in or around the crime scene can be properly documented. Furthermore, medical personnel who are assigned to work in the custodial setting, but who are more accustomed to the clinical setting, often do not separate the needs of providing emergency medical care with the responsibility to preserve and protect evidence. This coupled with the insistence of the medical department personnel to move the body of a decedent to the infirmary can cause havoc to the crime scene investigator. We will discuss this at length later as well.

The other challenges that the crime scene investigator may face are that the scenes are generally either incredibly confined, such as a 6' × 11' cell, or extremely large, such as an exercise yard larger than several football fields combined; or they are at times dimly lit, such as a housing unit or cell block; or leagues away from a power source for the Alternate Light Source or portable lighting equipment. Furthermore, as stated previously, inmates who participate in a disturbance are quickly removed from the scene and little attention is given to trace or transfer evidence, to say nothing of the difficulties in recovering items of clothing from the suspects or victims.

Finally, a recent problem that has grown to epidemic proportions at many jails and prisons, especially among inexperienced officers and supervisors, and in spite of repeated training efforts, is the tendency to treat all un-witnessed incidents as "medical emergencies" instead of potential unlawful activity. Therefore, if an inmate is found unconscious on the floor in the back of a housing unit with blood flowing from his mouth, the tier officer is more likely to treat the occurrence as a "medical episode" and call for medical personnel and a gurney to pick up the inmate and take him to the Infirmary instead of following procedures to stop all inmate movement and announce an alarm. Granted there is far less paperwork involved for the tier officer and their supervisors if the incident is treated as a medical emergency, but oftentimes the determination by the medical personnel of an assault or suspicious death is not made for hours (or days) and by that time the crime scene is no longer viable. This presents a tremendous problem to the investigation of sometimes fatal assaults, and I fear this is not unique to the facility where I worked.

Other than the problems mentioned above, the actual principles involved in the processing of the crime scene in a prison or jail are exactly the same as those in the general public. The key, however, is to limit the contamination and destruction of the scene as much as possible by quickly gaining control of the crime scene. The other key is the constant and repetitious training of all line staff in the duties of the first responder, as well as the recognition of perishable evidence and the preservation of the crime scene.

Another key to the successful processing of the custodial crime scene is to have crime scene protocols and procedures in place and to have a solid and meticulous plan that provides a scientific methodology to ensure that every crime scene is processed with consistency. The purpose of this book is to provide that methodology in a way that is easy to understand and implement and to help mitigate the problems that are unique to jails and prisons.

Selecting the Correctional Crime Scene Investigator

2

Regrettably, in civil service, mediocre pays the same as outstanding. It gets promoted as often as well.
Your author

As with any law enforcement agency, the allure to promote quickly through the ranks in the custodial setting makes it difficult to retain trained crime scene investigators. In most agencies, officers can be promoted to the rank of sergeant after only three years in grade, and sergeants to lieutenants in less time. Lieutenants tend to remain lieutenants until one of the precious few captain positions opens and the promotional examination is once again offered to fill the void. Captains are eager to become associate or chief deputy wardens or assistant superintendents with the ultimate goal of sitting in that warden or superintendent chair. Unfortunately, as any competent crime scene investigator can tell you, it takes more than three years of taking advantage of every training opportunity made available to become a proficient crime scene investigator or analyst. Sadly, there is little effort made by the various custody agencies to retain trained staff in these positions. In any para-military organization, the higher one is promoted, the more their responsibilities change from that of a worker to that of an administrator; a sergeant becomes a supervisor, a captain an administrator.

Thus, it is more likely that a sergeant will supervise a crime scene investigator than to be one. Titular endowments are nice, but they generally do not come with a more appreciative boost in salary. The ambitious sheriff or prison director would do well to consider a separate grade for the investigative services personnel: as the officer or deputy progresses in training, certification, and experience in the various disciplines of the forensic sciences, so too should their title and salary. The agency should consider a rank and compensation system that would encourage personnel to remain in forensics for extended periods of time. For example, an officer (or deputy) trained in crime scene investigations and possessing a certification as a crime scene investigator should have the designation of an investigative officer. One who attains training and certification equal to a crime scene analyst should have the designation of an investigative corporal or an investigative officer II, which can be of a pay grade equal to a corporal. An officer who has the training, certification, and experience equal to a senior crime scene analyst should be compensated according to the rank of a sergeant and designated as a senior investigator or investigative sergeant. Additional educational pay should be offered to officers who attain college degrees. This system is reasonable when one considers the exorbitant costs involved with continuous training through attrition. Owing to the perilous atmosphere and conditions regarding working among the inmate population in a prison or jail, it is difficult for officials to employ non-sworn personnel in forensic positions. However, the role of correctional crime scene investigator can be filled by sworn personnel without it being a financial burden to the agency if crime scene investigators maintain other investigative, custodial security specialist, or forensic functions such as operating an on-site forensic laboratory, doing gang investigations, or working contraband interdiction.

Agencies that do employ non-sworn personnel to perform the duties of the crime scene technician in jails and prisons should also consider a system that encourages retention, promotion, and reward for training, education, experience, and certifications.

Training for the correctional crime scene investigator should be constant, contemporary, and of the highest quality. The courses of study should include, but not be limited to, basic and advanced crime scene processing, evidence collection, and documentation; crime scene reconstruction; basic and advanced bloodstain pattern analysis; latent print development and comparison; shooting reconstruction; forensic pathology; crime scene and evidence photography; death investigations; impression evidence preservation, documentation, collection, and analysis; and report writing for the forensic specialist. The agency should make every effort to provide training opportunities to its investigative personnel using competent outside vendors. Although in-house training is appropriate in some disciplines of forensic science, it is best to seek out industry experts for quality, unbiased, and up-to-date training. Every effort should also be made to provide the investigator with peer-reviewed and industry-accepted books, journals, and periodicals. Of note would be any of the crime scene processing, reconstruction, and bloodstain pattern analysis books by Ross Gardner and Tom Bevel; Richard Saferstein's *Criminalistics: An Introduction to Forensic Science*; Edward Hueske's *Practical Analysis and Reconstruction of Shooting Incidents*; Professor Herbert MacDonell's *Bloodstain Patterns* (Second Revised Edition); the DiMaio brothers' *Forensic Pathology*; the homicide investigation books of Vernon Geberth; and Edward Robinson's *Crime Scene Photography* book, Sanford Weiss' *Handbook of Forensic Photography*, to name just a few. Furthermore, the journals and publications I find most useful are the *Journal of Forensic Identification* (the official publication of the International Association for Identification), *Forensic Magazine*, and *Evidence Technology Magazine*, among others.

Forensic association membership should be encouraged and strongly recommended. Associations for consideration are the International Association for Identification (parent or state divisions), the International Association for Bloodstain Pattern Examiners, the Association for Crime Scene Reconstruction, state, or regional homicide investigators associations (such as the California Homicide Investigators Association), or any other suitable bona fide associations for crime scene investigators. Certifications should *never* be awarded in-house. Forensic certifications should be earned through a competitive and comprehensive examination administered by the aforementioned independent and unbiased entities that do not possess a vested interest in the employee's success. I cannot stress this enough: The agency that *self*-certifies its employees in the disciplines of forensic sciences will make themselves subject to undue scrutiny and oversight; the perception being that the agency has a *vested interest* in the certification process. The costs incurred with outside agency certification are minimal compared with the legal battles, audits, and challenges that often come with in-house certification.

When selecting a correctional crime scene investigator, the hiring authority should choose an individual who is dedicated to the department and the assignment, is available when least convenient, has a good history of attendance, is meticulous in detail and actions, is ethical beyond reproach, and has exemplary writing skills. The investigator should be of good moral character, strong intellect, and possess an impeccable work ethic; qualities that regrettably seem to be very hard to find these days. In other words, candidates should be chosen because they are outstanding workers, not mediocre workers. The selection should never be a "homie hook-up" appointment, where a "friend" or "popular" officer is chosen as a career boost for promotion. Remember, the goal should be longevity.

The ideal candidate should have drive and determination and should seek out training opportunities rather than waiting for the opportunities to come to them.

It has been my experience that many people who are assigned to crime scene investigation positions tend to complain about not getting appropriate training, and then complain bitterly when they must attend training. The ideal correctional crime scene investigator will seek out training opportunities, be willing to pay for the training themselves and, if necessary, use personal time off to attend the training. It may sound harsh, but that is what I did when budgetary constraints prohibited my agency from providing the necessary funds for training, and I was a better investigator for the effort.

A good candidate for the position would also be a person who does not mind being, as I often say, a beast of burden. Crime scenes in a prison or jail seldom present themselves in an area that is accessible to a motor vehicle, and undoubtedly, the correctional crime scene investigator will have to carry all the equipment needed to properly process the crime scene for great distances; oftentimes making numerous trips. It can be exhausting work, and it can mean carrying heavy cases, boxes, and duffel bags across exercise yards or cell blocks crowded with incarcerated felons. Electric carts do make this duty more bearable, but it has long been my experience that such a conveyance will never be to hand when the need is most dire; and if it is, the battery is flat, as well as the tires.

Once the appropriate candidate has been selected and trained, no constraints should be placed upon the investigator as to the amount of time that will be dedicated to the processing of a crime scene. Every scene is different, and the scene will be done when it is done, as I say. The last thing the meticulous crime scene investigator needs is a supervisor who wants the job rushed so as not to incur overtime expenses or who is in a hurry to return the inmate population to a "normal program." The scene must be processed following a scientific methodology that must be employed every time. It is best to leave the time constraints to the investigator who is actually working the scene.

Ethics and Moral Character

General H. Norman Schwarzkopf, commander of the coalition forces during the Gulf War against Ba'athist Iraq, was once asked to define the word leadership. His response was, "Leadership is a combination of two things: strategy and character. If you must be without one, be without strategy." I agree wholeheartedly with the general because I believe what matters most is the character of a person, especially if that person has chosen a career in law enforcement, and by character, I mean the character that comes from being a person of good ethics and morality. More than three decades ago, I stood with my graduating academy class, raised my right hand, and swore this oath that was adopted in 1957 by the International Association of Chiefs of Police:

> *As a law enforcement officer, my fundamental duty is to serve the community; to safeguard lives and property; to protect the innocent against deception, the weak against oppression or intimidation and the peaceful against violence or disorder; and to respect the constitutional rights of all to liberty, equality, and justice.*
>
> *I will keep my private life unsullied as an example to all and will behave in a manner that does not bring discredit to me or to my agency. I will maintain courageous calm in the face of danger, scorn, or ridicule; develop self-restraint; and be constantly mindful of the welfare of others. Honest in thought and deed both in my personal and official life, I will be exemplary in obeying the law and the regulations of my department. Whatever I see or hear of a confidential nature or that is confided to me in my official capacity will be kept ever secret unless revelation is necessary in the performance of my duty.*

I will never act officiously or permit personal feelings, prejudices, political beliefs, aspirations, animosities, or friendships to influence my decisions. With no compromise for crime and with relentless prosecution of criminals, I will enforce the law courteously and appropriately without fear or favor, malice, or ill will, never employing unnecessary force or violence and never accepting gratuities.

I recognize the badge of my office as a symbol of public faith, and I accept it as a public trust to be held so long as I am true to the ethics of police service. I will never engage in acts of corruption or bribery, nor will I condone such acts by other police officers. I will cooperate with all legally authorized agencies and their representatives in the pursuit of justice.

I know that I alone am responsible for my own standard of professional performance and will take every reasonable opportunity to enhance and improve my level of knowledge and competence.

I will constantly strive to achieve these objectives and ideals, dedicating myself before God to my chosen profession… law enforcement.

Of course, the oath I took also required devotion to the Constitution of the State of California, and to uphold the laws of the State of California.

A solemn oath, generally voiced with venerable fealty included, is a bond not only with the community but also with the self. If you hold respect for yourself, your integrity, and your good character, you will hold true to an oath. If an oath was nothing more than a nuisance requirement to gain employment in law enforcement, let me be clear – you are in the wrong profession and have made a poor career choice. The oath and the badge are our links to a chivalrous past where knights on horseback were pure and noble. I still hold my oath quite dear, these many decades later. So much so, that the first lecture of each semester class that I teach at the local college is on ethics and what I expect of my students, especially when they choose to follow a career in law enforcement. To make my point, I ask my students to list all the things they see uniformed officers do while on duty that really make them angry. The list usually includes the following: talking on a cell phone while driving, not making full stops at stop signs, speeding, using their emergency lights to clear intersections, tailgating, illegal parking, not wearing seatbelts, etc. I then ask them to list all the things peace officers who they know personally do when off-duty that makes them angry. That list includes the earlier grievances and tinted windows[1] on personal cars, no front license plates[1], obstructed license plates, expired registration, or mechanical defects with lights. Most of all, my students are generally furious that the personal vehicles of law enforcement personnel have stickers or emblems that are associated with law enforcement as if the driver is sending a message to on-duty law enforcement officers not to pull them over, because they are one of them. I do explain why some of the things they see officers do while on duty are actually within the laws and statutes or departmental policy. However, the detailed conduct of the off-duty law enforcement officers is inexcusable. In other words, the off-duty law enforcement officers who are behaving as listed are violating all the laws that they are supposed to uphold and are using as probable cause to conduct traffic stops, make arrests, or issue citations while on duty. In my opinion, this makes that officer a hypocrite. It also means they have failed to maintain those parts of their sworn oath that say they will keep their private lives unsullied and recognize their badge as a symbol of public faith. I then ask my students to think about this when they take their oath, and that I hope when they are faced with an ethical decision, they will remember what I expect of them. Interestingly, I had a young police officer who was attempting to justify his need to excessively tint the windows of his personal vehicle, ask, "Wait a minute, do you mean to tell me all those years you worked at a prison, you never tinted your windows?" My immediate response was an emphatic, "No! When I arrived at the prison, I would park my car directly in front of an exercise yard with over a thousand inmates. My license plate was pointing directly at them. I had only factory installed tint. I would take off my cover jacket and look directly at them. If I had taken off my front license plate or heavily tinted my windows, that would have been a signal to those inmates that I was afraid of them, and they would have treated me as such once I was on that same yard. It would also be a violation of the California Vehicle Codes."

I define ethics as always doing the correct thing, especially when the consequences of doing the right thing are not favorable to your own position. Ethics are core principles that govern good or noble conduct in reference to law enforcement. In the forensic community, good ethics and moral character are those that conform to accepted standards of virtuous behavior. Virtuous testimony in court proceedings is that which is fair, unbiased, and objective. The forensic technician will never give testimony that is beyond the scope of their expertise, or upon anything that they have not given careful consideration. They will never mislead any of the parties involved in court proceedings regarding their education, training, experience, or area of expertise; nor will they misrepresent or falsify reports or conclusions, or purposely withhold observations or documentation that might otherwise favor one side over another in court proceedings. They will not provide testimony in any case where they have a personal interest. They will conduct full and fair examinations and will offer conclusions based solely on the pertinent facts related to the evidence. They will never ignore exculpatory evidence. They will never bow to political pressure, favoritism, or other influences. They will support only forensic disciplines that are generally accepted by the forensic community, have been subject to peer review, and are based on sound scientific principles. A forensic technician will never knowingly perjure themselves under oath. Perhaps the hardest dilemma faced by the ethical forensic technician is the duty to report illegal or unethical behavior by other law enforcement personnel of which they have direct knowledge to the proper authorities. A failure to do so may be tantamount to an inexcusable injustice to a person who is accused of a crime. Any violation of these core values and professional obligations may result in serious consequences that will tarnish the reputation of the technician, as well as the profession they represent.

In the landmark court decision in *Pitchess v. Superior Court* (1974) 11 Cal.3d 531, known in California as a Pitchess Motion, the California Legislature expanded upon the *Brady v. Maryland* (1963) 373 U.S. 83, stare decisis, which required the prosecution to provide as discovery to the defense any material evidence that is favorable to the defendant, to further allow criminal defendants to seek discovery from the court of potentially exculpatory information located in otherwise confidential peace officer personnel records. As you can imagine, any episode of professional dishonesty or violation of professional ethical conduct could result in an inability to provide future testimony in court proceedings.

Let me also give a fair warning about professional jealousy. Professional jealousy is the worst kind of jealousy. It is the playground of insecure workers who target individuals for the sole reason that they want to be outstanding in their profession. Unlike other jealousies that involve one or two persons, professional jealousy can have a deleterious effect on an entire agency. We should all recognize our own limitations, encourage others to not settle for a mediocre work ethic, and praise their accomplishments. Eleanor Roosevelt once said, "Great minds discuss ideas; average minds discuss events; small minds discuss people." To this, I will add a quote by Albert Einstein, "Weak people revenge. Strong people forgive. Intelligent people ignore."

Furthermore, a characteristic that seems to be absent these days is that of empathy toward others. We live in a self-important, self-centered world with little regard for the well-being of others. In the city where I live is a very nice recreation trail that is used by cyclists, pedestrians, and very slow-moving runners like me. One day while plodding along, I witnessed on the trail ahead a young boy and a cyclist facing each other, zigging and zagging in tandem, until the cyclist had no alternative but to hit the brakes hard. This, of course, propelled the cyclist off the bike over the handlebars and hard onto the tarmac, right arm first. As I arrived, the cyclist immediately asked, "Is the kid alright? My arm is broken. I know it is. I am a surgeon." Hearing the 10-year-old crying, the doctor pulled himself to a seated position, his broken right arm on his lap, put his left arm around the child, and said, "Please do not cry. It was all my fault. It was my fault. I will be ok." This sentiment impressed me greatly. How many of us would have this degree of empathy, instead of harsh words, for a crying youth who was frightened by the moment, especially with a very expensive and twisted road bicycle at our feet and a broken arm in our lap.

In closing this chapter, I will leave you with one of the many quotations left to me by my father, "Remember, there are no lifeboats on a battleship, only rafts." My father had no affinity for the sea, nor was he ever in the Navy. He was a businessman. The people he admired were the ones who never gave up. When things got hard, they got harder. "Complain all you want, but the work still needs to get done." The crew of a battleship do not just quit when the shells fall and torpedoes strike. They continue to do everything possible to save the ship and to keep the guns firing until the only thing that is left are the rafts and the water.

Note

1. California Vehicle Codes require window tint to be within a specified standard and front license plates must be displayed.

Responsibilities

3

Responsibilities of the First Responder

One of the most important people at any crime scene is the first responder. One can go even further to say that without the efforts of the first responder in recognizing the importance of the crime scene and taking the necessary measures to preserve and protect the scene and its evidence, there likely would be no crime scene to process. It is rare in the public that a law enforcement official witnesses a crime in progress. Generally, a crime is reported to a dispatcher, who, in turn, dispatches a first responder to the scene. That official then conducts a cursory investigation, makes observations, collects the facts, and makes the appropriate decisions and notifications. Crimes are rarely reported to the custodial official; and if they are, the report comes days or weeks after the incident.

In the custodial setting, crimes are generally witnessed by a staff member, who, in turn, sounds the alarm. Crimes can also be "discovered" after the event by officers who conduct security checks or stumble upon a beaten, battered, stabbed, or deceased inmate. At that time, this officer becomes not only the most important person in the incident but also the first person on the scene with the most responsibility.

It is imperative that the very first action this official must take is to immediately freeze all inmate movement. You may ask how this is done when that official may be outnumbered by dozens of inmates or more. I will tell you, having performed this task on numerous occasions, that it is done with a very loud, very commanding, and very purposeful, "GET DOWN!" generally followed by an audible alarm, whistle alarm, or a radio call announcing the incident and its location. In most incidents, this action will be sufficient to "stop" the movement of the inmates who are not actively involved in the incident. If they do not, we call this a riot, and you will need a lot more staff to quell this type of disturbance. However, stopping all inmate movement is essential because in this group of inmates who assume the prone position can be found the witnesses, additional victims, and suspects who are trying to avoid detection. The active participants, the ones who oftentimes do not assume the prone position, may have to be subdued utilizing whatever use of force option is available to the staff member and pursuant to their training and objective judgment.

DOI: 10.4324/9781003503989-3

The first responder must now quickly figure out what type of incident they are dealing with; identify victims and suspects; determine the need for medical assistance, perhaps even provide immediate life-saving measures themselves; summon additional responders; identify the area of the occurrence; ensure that fragile or perishable evidence is not destroyed by responding staff or the inmates in the area; find an area where responding staff can assemble; direct staff through the crime scene and limit crime scene contamination; notify supervisors; and begin the crime scene entry and exit log. Furthermore, some agencies require the first responder, or a relief officer, to maintain the entry/exit log after the crime scene unit has taken the scene. It is a daunting responsibility to say the least. That is why it is essential that all custodial staff receive routine training in alarm response, the duties and responsibilities of the first responder, and crime scene preservation. It is also important to have expected standards that the first responder must meet, and any shirking of these standards must be met with disciplinary action. Too often, staff members do not take their responsibilities seriously and allow either contamination of the crime scene or destruction of the evidence to occur with minimal ramifications for their behavior. This cannot be tolerated.

Furthermore, the agency must have a crime scene response classification system in effect, which dictates what scenes can be handled by the first responders and which scenes require the attention of crime scene investigators. Suggestions for this classification system will be offered later.

Officers who are assigned to accompany victims to the infirmary or outside medical facilities must be diligent in recovering items of clothing evidence either before departing the institution, while en route to the medical facility, or immediately upon arrival. These officers must be cognizant of their responsibility to document the chain of custody for these items of evidence and should always safeguard the victim's clothing from needless destruction and contamination. Each item of clothing should be placed in an individual paper bag. If the garment is blood-soaked, it is acceptable to transfer the item in a plastic bag to the evidence processing area where it can be hung in a forensic drying cabinet (Fig. 3.1). The dry garment should be folded into clean butcher paper so as not to transfer stains from one part of the garment to the other prior to being transported to the evidence processing area. Today, no agency should still be using the old mesh drying cages but should invest in forensic drying cabinets that are sterilized between uses. The plastic or paper bag used to transport the item, as well as the butcher paper, should also be processed into evidence. Shoes have incredible forensic value and are one of *the most important* items of evidence to collect yet are also the most frequently neglected item.

Officers who are assigned to escort a suspect to a holding area should also make every effort to ascertain from the first responder, supervisor, or

Responsibilities

Figure 3.1 Drying cabinets for blood-soaked items of evidence.

crime scene investigator whether or not the suspect's hands should be placed in protective paper bags. They should also prevent the suspect from using the restroom until such time as they are inspected by crime scene investigators. The escort officer should notify the crime scene investigator of any observations of offensive or defensive injuries and trace or transfer evidence that were made after the suspect was removed from the scene. The officers should collect all items of clothing, including the shoes and socks of the suspect, as quickly as possible if they have not already been collected at the scene; again, making certain to preserve the chain of custody, and taking precautions not to destroy, transfer, or cross-contaminate the items of clothing.

If a suspect is apprehended and restrained in a common or open-area crime scene, feel free to take a photograph. I have discovered that the jury most often appreciates a photograph of the suspect at the crime scene. I *emphatically* do not recommend this for crime scenes, not in jails or prisons. Our protocols allow for an inmate suspect apprehended in a common or open area scene, who does not need immediate medical attention or decontamination from chemical agents and is properly restrained to remain at the scene or near the scene until such time as his presence can be documented and the crime scene investigator has had the opportunity to inspect the individual for injuries or evidence. There should be no rush to move the suspect to a holding cell unless it is absolutely essential in order to restore order. However, if there is the potential for the suspect to damage, alter, or contaminate the scene, remove them from the scene immediately. At no time should an inmate suspect apprehended within a cell or confined area following a major incident such as a homicide, attempted homicide, battery, or sexual assault be allowed to remain in the crime scene. For that matter, at no time should a cellmate be allowed to remain in a cell following the suspected medical emergency of an inmate found within a cell or confined area. Only after investigators have determined that the incident is indeed related to a medical episode should the associated inmate be returned to the cell.

It is critical that the suspects, victims, and witnesses are positively identified using an authorized photographic identification card. Positive identification is critical to a successful prosecution, which may take place years after the incident. The officer may not remember how they identified the individual when testifying in court. Therefore, their report should clearly state how the individual was identified. Sadly, staff members often ask the suspect or witness for their identifying information and never verify the information given. Remarkably, 9 times out of 10, inmates will provide their proper identifying information, but that 10th time could be crucial to proper prosecution. Always verify with whatever photographic system the facility has in place for the identification of inmates.

Responsibilities of the Correctional Medical Personnel

Medical and fire department personnel working in the correctional environment can, unwittingly, be the worst nightmare for the correctional crime scene investigator. Do not misunderstand what I am trying to say; medical and fire personnel rate nothing more than the highest praise for their often heroic efforts to save lives and to prevent further destruction of buildings and additional loss of life, but they can also be crime scene and evidence destruction teams. In the many years that I have taught crime scene preservation classes at the institution and in the public, not once did I see a member of the medical or fire departments in attendance. Efforts to introduce a training program specifically designed for these departments were always rebuked, when in fact a training program designed specifically for these departments is exactly what is needed and highly recommended.

Granted if your crime scene is on fire, it is most desirable to let the fire department do what they do best; also granted that it is far more important to save a life than it is to preserve evidence. However, most often these

Responsibilities   17

departments find themselves involved in incidents that do not involve fires or with the imminent loss of life. It is during these occasions that the crime scene investigator wishes most that these departments could balance their responsibilities with the urgent need to preserve the crime scene and the evidence it contains. Even simple contributions such as not discarding used latex gloves into the crime scene would go a long way to prevent crime scene contamination.

Fire personnel, anxious to remove victim garments in order to affix AED pads, could well serve the crime scene investigator by carefully preserving bloodstain evidence, gunpowder burns, and bullet and edged weapon defects.

Not many years ago, I responded to the infirmary following a brutal assault with great bodily injury. An inmate had been attacked by another inmate from behind. One of the injuries sustained by the inmate was a vicious bite to the back (Fig. 3.2). The bite mark, which was not deep enough to draw blood, was a textbook impression. Unfortunately, in the three minutes that it took my partner and me to report to the infirmary, medical personnel had already sanitized the site and rubbed in an antiseptic ointment, destroying any DNA evidence that may have remained and making photography difficult owing to the glossiness of the ointment. The case was not prosecuted by the District Attorney's Office as the victim was unable to identify his attacker,

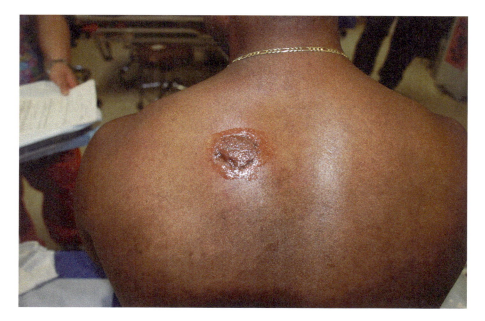

Figure 3.2 A nurse sterilized the wound and applied an antiseptic ointment prior to the collection of a DNA specimen or the proper photographic documentation of the injury by investigators.

as he was attacked from behind, and there were no other witnesses. It is not always fire or medical personnel who have destroyed a crime scene as I have had custody personnel spit sunflower seeds into the scene where a deceased inmate lay on the floor; custody staff who have picked up two weapons used in a stabbing and put them in a uniform pocket; and staff who have allowed inmate porters to clean up bloodstain evidence before my arrival in a suspicious death investigation.

Responsibilities of the Correctional Crime Scene Investigator

Gone are the days when a crime scene investigator would enter a crime scene with a cigarette in their mouth, wearing short sleeves, and their favorite pair of tennis shoes. We must remember that a suspect may leave touch DNA in a crime scene, but we too may inadvertently contribute our own DNA in the exact same place. It is suggested that we shed upward of 400,000 epithelial skin cells in a 24-hour period[1], which by my math is almost 278 cells every second you are in the crime scene. The suspect who wore gloves, a hat, a mask, and a long-sleeve shirt and spent three minutes in the crime scene will invariably contribute far fewer cells than the crime scene investigator who is not wearing a mask, has no gloves, is not wearing a head covering, is wearing a short-sleeved shirt and spends an hour in the crime scene.

One of the chief responsibilities of the crime scene investigator is to take every step possible to prevent the contamination of the scene. For example, we need look no farther than a certain South African detective who was roasted by the judge in the bail hearing for Olympian Oscar Pistorius in the shooting death of Reeva Steenkamp for contaminating the crime scene by not wearing protective shoe coverings. Suffice it to say, detectives and crime scene investigators who enter a crime scene without proper protective gear today will face the same grilling by a well-versed defense attorney.

I keep by my desk a "ready bag," which is a gear or duffel bag containing Tyvek suits, Tyvek sleeves, N-95 masks, boot covers, eyewear, head wear, and latex and cotton gloves (as a side note, I often wear cotton gloves underneath the latex gloves. The cotton absorbs the sweat and allows for easier exchange of latex gloves. It is also my habit to double glove with latex gloves so that I always have a barrier between my skin and one layer of gloves. Furthermore, when necessary, I wear terrycloth wristbands to intercept any sweat that may creep down my arms under the Tyvek coverings.). I also have a box of bleach wipes and sterile water ampoules in the bag to sanitize latex gloves or equipment before collecting DNA evidence, even though I change gloves by habit between items of evidence.

The primary ambition of the crime scene investigator should be the proper documentation of the scene; the proficient and legal collection of all items of evidence within the scene; the maintenance of the chain of custody of the evidence; and the ability to articulate the steps taken, including scientific methodologies, evidence collected, photographs captured, measurements documented, diagrams made, and to paint a visual picture of the scene to the jury, judge, and attorneys during courtroom proceedings.

When arriving at the crime scene, the crime scene investigator, technician, or analyst must first determine that the scene is safe to enter, for themselves and for their team members. The investigator should then make a quick assessment of the scene for perishable or fleeting evidence and for any hazard that might alter or damage the scene before it can be processed. Once satisfied that the scene is safe and not in danger of losing valuable evidence, the investigator must then establish the crime scene perimeter by speaking with the first responder on the scene to determine what actions they saw, what evidence they noticed, and where they discovered victims, suspects, and witnesses. It is best to establish a perimeter that is much larger than the actual scene you will be processing. You can always make the perimeter smaller, but you can never enlarge the area without being able to account for the contamination that occurred from the initial perimeter being established and the time it was expanded.

I prefer to set a double perimeter. I will string barrier tape at the actual scene—say a cell and the area in front of the cell—and then establish a larger area to keep the curious further away and to limit contamination of the areas of ingress and egress, perhaps the entire tier or even the entire housing unit if necessary. I then establish an area within this second perimeter to stage my equipment, preferably just outside the actual crime scene. I spread a sterile blanket for my equipment staging area and, if I am lucky, I may be able to procure a folding table first. When processing a scene outside of the secured prison perimeter, it is a good idea to arrange for the posting of armed officers outside of the outer crime scene perimeter to control the crowd, the curious, the media, or the return of the suspect(s), which has happened to more than a few investigators.

The investigator should immediately determine if the suspect(s) is in custody or is at large, whether the victim is deceased at the scene, if lifesaving efforts are ongoing, or if not, to ascertain where the victim(s) has been taken. Should an eyewitness be available, the investigator should briefly interview them focusing on what they saw, smelled, and heard. It should be noted that a crime scene investigator will ask different questions than a first responder. The first responder is intent upon locating the victim, additional victims, suspects, and other eyewitnesses, and perhaps a perfunctory overview of what happened. Among the information the crime scene investigator is most concerned about is what happened and where, who was in the crime scene before, during, and after the event, what weapons were used, what was touched by the suspect, what injuries were sustained by the victim, was the suspect bleeding, and in which direction did the participants arrive and depart. If possible, it is imperative that the investigator talks to any responding medical personnel who remain at the scene.

Once the initial information gathering interviews are finished, the investigator should meet with the other members of the crime scene team, should there be other members of the team, outside of the secondary crime scene. The team should be given their assignments such as scribe, photography, diagramming and measurements, evidence collection, etc. They can then don protective coverings and make their initial examination of the crime scene. At this time, the investigator or analyst will determine the appropriate path through the scene that will prevent the destruction of evidence and ensure that each member adheres to the selected route. It is essential that the crime scene and evidence are not disturbed and that nothing is touched or moved.

In one homicide investigation, I arrived at my institution following the discovery of an inmate in a first-tier inmate restroom in one of the housing units. The inmate was bleeding from a cut to his lower lip. The staff member who discovered the inmate reported the matter as a "medical distress" call and summoned medical personnel with a gurney. As I arrived with my equipment, I passed the gurney as it progressed up the corridor to the Infirmary. I could not get a good look at the inmate, but I stopped the registered nurse who was trailing and asked her to describe the injuries. She summed it up quickly with, "Laceration to the mouth and a bump on the back of his head." I proceeded to the crime scene and asked the first responder to describe where and how he discovered the inmate. The response was that the inmate was seated on the floor in the corner of the restroom with his back to the wall, bleeding from the mouth. I then examined the restroom with a forensic light (415 nm wavelength) and a magnifying glass but could not locate any blood evidence on the floor, walls, fixtures, or ceiling. After hearing that the inmate had been taken to the local hospital by ambulance, I dispatched a team member to the hospital with a camera kit. Once at the hospital, the inmate was declared to be deceased and I instructed the team member to remain at the hospital until the Coroner's Office detective arrived. In the meanwhile, another team member began a search of the entire housing unit for blood evidence, which was detected in the back of the housing unit some 95' from where the inmate was discovered. While processing the crime scene, I received a telephone call from a detective at the Coroner's Office who recommended against an autopsy as the death appeared to be from a medical condition. I expressed my concerns regarding the absence of blood in the restroom, the discovery of blood in the back of the housing unit, and the injuries to the mouth and back of the head and requested an autopsy. The detective yielded and scheduled an autopsy the following morning at 0900 hours but added that he did not detect a bump on the back of the inmate's head.

On the following morning, I arrived at the Coroner's Office where I was met by the detective who again attempted to talk me out of the autopsy. I was unyielding.

Next, the medical examiner expressed his concerns that the external examination produced no other signs of injury other than a now-detectable slight bump on the back of his head and the laceration to his lower lip, both of which he said could have happened during, "a medical episode." I told him about my brief conversation with the nurse and the evidence from the crime scene and said, "Doc, there's only one way to find out," and the autopsy was on. Needless to say, a burst spleen, three broken ribs, and multiple subdermal contusions, and the medical examiner was convinced the inmate was the victim of a beating resulting in blunt-force trauma that caused his death. During the subsequent investigation, I was able to charge five inmates with the beating death of the inmate for his failure to provide a tattoo in an agreed-upon time. If it was not for that brief conversation that I had with the nurse as she pursued the inmate-laden gurney, I would not have had the confidence to insist upon an autopsy and a homicide likely would have been recorded as death by natural causes.

Responsibilities of the Crime Scene Team

Although there are numerous responsibilities within the crime scene, it is not necessary to have a dozen technicians in the scene, unless it is an exceptionally large scene, which can be separated into grids or sections. I find that the ideal number of technicians in the prison or jail crime scene is three, or even less. Any more than that and you risk contamination and destruction of evidence. Some scenes in the correctional setting, like a cell, are too small to permit more than one or two persons to even enter the scene. There have been, of course, many occasions when I have processed scenes without the assistance of a team. This is fine, but as they say, two sets of eyes are far better than one. It is, however, necessary that all the duties of a crime scene team are met, regardless of the number of persons employed in the task of processing the scene.

Lead Investigator or Crime Scene Analyst

It is the responsibility of the lead investigator or crime scene analyst to ascertain the known details of the crime from the primary responding units, medical and/or fire department personnel, and any witnesses who remain on the scene. It is also their responsibility to get a copy of the crime scene log; to ensure that the crime scene perimeter is established; that perishable evidence is collected and that the scene and team are safe. Furthermore, it is the responsibility of the lead investigator to determine the legal authority to be at the crime scene and to work with the incident investigator and District Attorney's Office (prosecutor) personnel to obtain a search warrant, if necessary. The lead investigator will brief the crime scene investigation (CSI) team and assign tasks. Following this, the lead investigator will visually inspect the crime scene, preferably using a forensic or clean white light, looking up, down, and all around, considering the crime scene as a whole. The lead investigator will dictate conditions of the scene and point out obvious items of evidence that need to be documented and collected. The lead investigator will coordinate with officers and investigators conducting witness canvasses or had accompanied victims to the hospital or infirmary. The lead investigator will send technicians to search areas outside of the perimeter for ingress/egress evidence. The lead investigator will coordinate with the photographer to identify items of evidence and to determine the placement of evidence markers and photographic scales and will make sure that proper evidence processing, and personal protection equipment is present and used. The lead investigator will also provide for the well-being of the team by making sure that they are hydrated and that they do not spend more than 90 minutes—45 minutes in warmer climates—in a Tyvek suit without resting, rehydrating, and changing suits. They will also coordinate with analysts from other agencies who have specialized training, such as bloodstain pattern analysis or latent print development. Furthermore, one of the most important roles of the lead investigator or crime scene analyst is to provide continuous updates on the progress of the crime scene processing to the administrators who must make decisions regarding the suspension of inmate programs, feeding, and special housing, as well to the administrative assistant or public information officer who may need to make announcements to the media.

The Assistant to the Lead

The assistant to the lead investigator helps to identify evidence, drop markers, and develop a processing plan of action. The assistant's focus is the crime scene and keeping the lead investigator informed of developments when they are away from the scene. The assistant acts as a second set of eyes making sure that all the necessary protocols are being followed, that the team is using all equipment properly, that all efforts are made not to contaminate the scene and the evidence within the scene; and that the team is safe. It may also fall on the assistant to the lead to make arrangements for special equipment or for personnel who have specialized training, such as bloodstain pattern analysts, latent print development technicians, and crime scene reconstruction experts. It is also the duty of the assistant to the lead investigator to ensure that agency policies and protocols associated with CSIs are being properly followed.

The Scribe

The scribe has one of the most important roles in the crime scene team and is often the individual with responsibilities that are ignored. It is the responsibility of the scribe to document EVERYTHING in the crime scene: from the conditions in which the crime scene was found to maintaining a running time-log of events and documenting the location, description, finder, and processor of every item of evidence discovered and collected. The scribe will also document what notifications were made and to whom, while in the crime scene. The scribe also has an important role not usually regarded outside of the jail or prison crime scene. Following a major incident in a housing unit, dining hall, exercise yard, or program where numerous inmates are assembled, it is the responsibility of the scribe to document the presence and position of every inmate detained in the area. The scribe must positively identify each inmate using photographic means of identification and must accurately record the exact position of each inmate. Failure to document the presence of a suspect detained during an incident might provide them with an alibi that they might later use in court.

The Photographer

The photographer is responsible for documenting the crime scene with images that capture the visual aspects of the crime, which are needed to convey the look of the scene to investigators, attorneys, judges, and jurors, who will not have the opportunity to view the scene firsthand in the manner in which it was viewed by the first responder and the crime scene investigator. The photographer must capture overview scene establishing, mid-range evidence establishing, and close-up or evidentiary photographs of the scene and its evidence; as well as photographs that depict the relationship of items of evidence to other items of evidence and the crime scene. It is essential that the photographer captures images of the scene before any alteration has occurred. That means that they must photograph the scene prior to the placement of markers and the movement or collection of evidence. Evidentiary photographs must be taken with the film plane parallel and perpendicular to the item of evidence and with scales placed on the same plane as the item being photographed. The photographer must maximize depth of field; may need to control, add, or eliminate lighting in the scene; and must ensure that the image is sharp, centered, in focus, and fills the frame. The photographer may be required to take photographs that are representative of the natural perspective of the crime scene and of the line of vision of victims, witnesses, and first responders.

When photographing items of evidence depicted with scales or rulers, the photographer should always photograph the item with and without the measuring device. The photographer must also maintain a log, file, or contact sheet containing a description of each frame or image captured, along with its metadata.

The Evidence Collector

In a major crime scene, it is best to assign one member of the team as the evidence collector. In this regard, the chain of custody for the item of evidence can be restricted to the finder and the collector. Furthermore, in some jurisdictions the evidence collector can testify on behalf of the evidence finder during preliminary courtroom proceedings, thus eliminating the need for additional staff to be away from the jail or prison. The evidence collection officer must follow all procedures for the collection of the items of evidence, avoid contamination, and document in their report the identification of the person who found the evidence, the description of the evidence, and the location where it was found as well as its disposition.

The Diagram Technician

The diagram technician is the too-often-forgotten member of the crime scene team. It is the responsibility of the diagram technician to accurately record the dimensions and measurements of the crime scene, horizontally and, in some cases, vertically, as well as document the relative positions of items of evidence in the crime scene and the size, shape, and dimensions of the items of evidence collected. The diagram technician may be called upon to "map" the scene for bloodstain evidence analysis and therefore must have training in this regard, although it is not necessary for the technician to be a bloodstain pattern analyst. There is more on bloodstain mapping later in this book. It is my belief that diagram technicians should be taught the "old" ways of sketching and measuring a crime scene. Modern computer-assisted "mapping" systems are wonderful devices, but my opinion of technology will always be that either it will take longer to use the device on small scenes or, as technology will often do, it will fail when you need it most. The diagram technician will need to have that old-fashioned backup plan. The old-fashioned way is discussed in a later chapter.

Other Specialist

Other specialists, such as bloodstain pattern analysts, impression evidence comparison analysts, specialized latent print development technicians, forensic videographers, forensic pathologists, crime scene reconstructionist, or any other specialized forensic discipline practitioner may be requested when needed.

Note

1. (Wickenheiser, RA. Trace DNA: a review, discussion of theory, and application of the transfer of trace quantities of DNA through skin contact. J. Forensic Sci 47 (3) (2002) 442-450)

Crime Scene Response Classification System & Crime Scene Investigation Inventory

4

I prepared the following classification system for the institution where I worked; in part to acquaint line staff with their responsibilities for crime scene response, but most importantly to make them aware that there are certain crime scenes that they should not attempt to process owing to the severity of the occurrence and their lack of training and experience. Jurisdictions with strict laws allowing for the prosecution of the possession of contraband in a jail or prison may need to adjust the below-listed criteria. Again, this is only a suggested guideline that may need revision for any particular agency.

CLASS 1

Discretionary – Non-major Incident
  Criteria: There is no potential for referral for prosecution, but documentation is required for administrative purposes.
  Type: Simple battery without serious injuries, theft, drug paraphernalia, tattoo paraphernalia, possession of a cellular telephone, possession of tobacco, possession of marijuana less than 1 g for personal use, etc.
  Responder: First responder/senior officer on scene
  Crime scene: None
  Entry/Exit log: No
  Equipment and tasks: Camera kit and evidence collection envelopes/bags, gloves; report only, photographs, some evidence processing

CLASS 2

Discretionary – Non-major Incident Requiring Documentation
  Criteria: There is limited potential for referral for prosecution, but documentation may be required for administrative purposes.
  Type: Battery with injuries not likely to produce great bodily injury (GBI), possession of escape paraphernalia, unusual occurrences (cell flooding, inmate worker injury, breaches in security, etc.), staff use of force not

resulting in death or serious injury, possession of minor amounts of controlled substances or prescribed medications, weapon stock, criminal threats, etc.

Responder: First responder/senior officer on scene or crime scene investigator

Crime scene: Restricted to the area of occurrence

Entry/Exit log: No

Equipment and tasks: Camera kit, markers, scales, sketching material (if required), measuring devices, evidence collection envelopes/bags, gloves, etc.; report, photographs, and some evidence processing.

CLASS 3

Non-discretionary – Major Occurrence

Criteria: There exists a strong potential for referral for prosecution and subsequent criminal proceedings.

Type: Assault and/or battery with GBI likely, staff assault, battery or gassing, possession of a weapon, large-quantity drug possession, attempted escape, grand theft, etc.

Responder: Crime scene investigator

Crime Scene: Primary, natural ingress and egress areas

Entry/Exit log: Yes

Equipment and tasks: Camera kit, markers, scales, measuring devices, sketching material, evidence markers, PPE, forensic kit, evidence collection materials, fingerprint kit, etc.; report, photographs, evidence processing, diagramming, blood or bodily fluid evidence collection, documentation, etc.

CLASS 4

Non-discretionary – Major Incident

Criteria: There is a high probability of referral for prosecution and subsequent criminal proceedings as well as scrutiny by the government officials, politicians, and private or government oversight committees.

Type: Homicide, attempted homicide, suicide, riot, arson, escape, staff use of force resulting in death or serious injury, etc.

Responder: Crime scene analyst and crime scene investigator(s)/specialists

Crime Scene: Primary, secondary, natural ingress and egress areas, and staging area

Entry/Exit log: Yes

Equipment and tasks: Camera kit, markers, scales, measuring devices, sketching material, evidence markers, PPE, footwear protection, sterile blanket, forensic kit, bloodstain kit, butcher paper, fingerprint kit, lighting, tripod/monopod, evidence collection materials, shooting reconstruction materials, Alternate Light Source, forensic lights, bloodstain and crime scene mapping materials, etc.; report, analysis, photographs, evidence processing, diagramming, blood or bodily fluid evidence collection, documentation, mapping, enhanced evidence detection techniques, etc.

CLASS 5

Mass Casualty and Man-Made Disaster

Criteria: There is a high probability of referral prosecution (State and Federal) and subsequent criminal proceedings as well as scrutiny by government officials, politicians, and private or government oversight committees.

Type: Acts of terrorism (riot resulting in mass loss of life and destruction of property), natural and man-made catastrophic events with numerous casualties, etc.

Responder: Crime scene analyst, crime scene investigators, outside agency assistance (FBI, Homeland Security, State Department of Justice, District Attorney Investigator, County Sheriff/Coroner's Office, FAA, etc.)

Crime scene: Primary, secondary, natural ingress and egress areas, staging areas, media areas, and evidence processing areas.

Entry/Exit log: Mandatory

Equipment and tasks: Camera kit, markers, scales, measuring devices, sketching material, evidence markers, PPE, sterile blanket, forensic kit, bloodstain kit, butcher paper, fingerprint kit, lighting, tripod/monopod, ALS, forensic lights, shooting reconstruction materials, bloodstain and crime scene mapping materials, hazardous material equipment, etc.; report, analysis, photographs, evidence processing, diagramming, blood or bodily fluid evidence collection, documentation, mapping, enhanced evidence detection techniques, etc.

Duties and Responsibilities

I firmly believe that crime scene investigators and analysts should be informed of what duties and responsibilities are expected of them. Rather than dedicating a large portion of this chapter in this regard, I recommend instead a valuable resource that has already been written, and that is Section 8.7 of the Forensic Certification Management Board Operations

Manual of the International Association for Identification, under scopes and competencies related to tasks. You can find this information at www.theiai.org/FCMB/OpsManual. This should provide a useful guide in drafting policies for your agency.

CSI Inventory

Although it is not always necessary to respond to every crime scene with a pack-mule train equipped with every conceivable product from the forensic supply catalog, there are some basic items that must be available to the crime scene investigation team; the rest can be near to hand. I have found that it is best to assemble the needed equipment in "kits" or hard cases that can be transported easily to the scene. Below listed is an inventory of items needed by category:

Evidence Marker Kit
- Alphabetic evidence marker placards
- Numeric evidence marker placards
- Datum markers
- Evidence flags – metallic
- Evidence flags – nonmetallic

Measuring and Diagramming Kit
- Fiberglass tape measure – 300' (two)
- Fiberglass tape measure – 100' (two)
- Retractable steel measures – 50' (two)
- Measuring sticks (such as Super Sticks™)
- 90-degree angle
- Cartographic, lensatic, or magnetic compass
- Notepad – lined
- Notepad – graphed
- Plumb bob
- Sketching utensils

Shooting Scene Kit
- Trajectory rods
- Lasers
- Clamps
- String
- Stands
- Zero-edge protractor
- Plumb bob
- Angle finder
- Photographic scales – alpha/numeric

- Photographic inch scales
- Cartridge casing evidence boxes
- Bullet evidence boxes
- Sodium rhodizonate (presumptive test for lead)
- Dithiooximide (presumptive test for copper)
- GSR kits
- Digital calipers
- Pocket level

Bloodstain Mapping Kit
- Measuring Pocket Rods™ (two to four w/base plates)
- Super Sticks™
- Photographic scales – alpha/numeric
- Photographic metric scales
- Price stickers (round)
- Tape
- String
- Stands
- Digital calipers
- Magnifying glasses
- Phenolphthalein (refrigerated when not in use) or Leuco-crystal malachite green
- Hexagon OBTI immrunochromatographic rapid test (refrigerated when not in use)

Evidence Collection Kit
- Evidence envelopes
- Evidence bags – small/medium/large
- Coin envelopes
- Evidence boxes – small (jewelry)
- Evidence boxes – medium (knife)
- Evidence boxes – large (handgun)
- Evidence boxes – extra large (rifle)
- Evidence boxes – shoe & pizza
- Evidence jars & canisters
- Electrician's ties – wires
- Butcher's paper rolls & dispenser
- Sterile tweezers
- Sterile scalpels
- Evidence tape

Evi-Vac™ & filters

Impression Evidence Casting Kit
- Dental stone casting material
- Water
- Frames
- Tongue depressors
- Photographic footwear scales
- Exemplar collection kit (Bio Foam™ or similar)
- Extruder w/tubes
- Gel lifters & ink roller

Alternate Light Source Kit
- Portable ALS light system
- Barrier filters
- Photographic scales
- Magnifying glasses

Latent Print Development Kit
- Feather brushes
- Finishing brushes
- Magnetic brushes
- Sterile brushes
- Sterile magnetic brush shrouds
- Powders (black, Supra-nano™, bi-chromatic, florescent, magnetic, etc.)
- Sterile powders (single use)
- Cyano-acrylate fuming wand
- Cyano-acrylate portable fuming chamber
- Lift tabs/tape
- Magnifying glasses
- Sterile scalpel
- Sterile tweezers
- Ninhydrin
- Small Particle Reagent (dark & light)
- Sticky-side tape
- Preservation cards

Blood Evidence Enhancement
- Amido Black
- Coomassie Blue or Leuco-crystal violet
- Bluestar™/Luminol™
- Sterile water
- Spray bottles

Forensic Camera Kit
- DSLR, mirrorless, or full-frame camera
- Infra-red imaging camera
- Lenses
- Flash
- Flash off-camera cords
- Flash diffusers
- Off-camera shutter release
- Appropriate filters
- Colored filters for use w/ALS
- White balance – photographic gray cards
- Memory cards
- Extra batteries & charger
- Tripod (w/reversible center post)
- Monopod

Photographic Lighting Kit
- Large standing studio lights
- Soft boxes (all sizes)
- Reflectors
- Extension cords
- Copy stand

Evidence Recovery Kit
- Hammer
- Hand saw
- Angle grinder
- Cordless drill/driver with an assortment of bits and driver tips
- Pry bars
- Probing rods
- Slim-Jim
- Spatula
- Drywall knife
- Halligan bar
- Wrecking bar
- Reciprocating saw w/blades
- Socket sets
- Pliers
- Vise Grips™
- Needle nose pliers
- Tweezers
- Screwdrivers of various sizes and lengths
- Ladders and stepladders

Crime Scene Response Classification System & CSI Inventory

Personal Protective Equipment Ready Bag
- Tyvek suits w/boots & hoods
- Protective glasses
- N-95 masks
- Cotton gloves
- Latex or polyurethane gloves
- Latex sleeves
- Terrycloth wristbands
- Bleach/distilled water (10% bleach to water solution)

DNA Collection Kit
- 100% cotton sterile swabs
- Poly-cotton blend sterile swabs
- Sterile water ampoules
- Swab protective collars
- Buccal swab cheek sponges
- Evidence tape
- Sterile tweezers

This list represents only the basic equipment generally needed by the crime scene processing team. Experience and curiosity will always contribute to any crime scene technician's shopping list.

Bear in mind that many of the items described above may require inventory accountability and control because of their potential to be used either as weapons or escape tools if possessed by an inmate.

I do not recommend the use of smart cellular telephones in the crime scene for capturing images. On occasion, however, I have found myself using the compass feature on my telephone, but that is about the only application I use. If you have found forensic applications that are useful to processing your crime scene, use them within the scopes or your agency protocols; however, be careful not to contaminate the scene with your phone, or vice versa.

Crime Scene Processing Methodology & Checklists

5

I drafted the following crime scene processing checklist for the institution where I worked. This methodology and checklist were based on my personal experience and on the methodologies that are presented by numerous forensic authors, such as Ross Gardner in his book *Practical Crime Scene Processing and Investigation* (CRC Press 2019, Chapter 2, pp. 79–85), with some modifications to adapt to the correctional environment. Agencies should research numerous methodologies before selecting one that is applicable to their needs. It should be noted that the crime scene processing methodology checklist presented here is only the minimum requirement for the crime scene investigation team to follow.

Step 1: Initial notification and response – The first step to crime scene investigations in prison or jail is the quick documentation of the manner of notification and the means of response to the incident; noting the date, time, and method of call to service as well as the manner of conveyance. During this step, it is also a good idea to formulate the most expedient, but safe, route to take and to have a plan for where you will park, assemble your team, and stage your equipment. It is also recommended that a brief description of the incident be obtained from personnel either in contact with first responders or who are present at the scene so that a mental picture of the type of equipment needed can be achieved.

Step 1 checklist:
- Document the time, date, and method of call to service (radio, telephone, etc.)
- Document the manner of conveyance utilized to respond (by foot, vehicle, etc.)
- Select a response route
- Select assembly and staging areas
- Document weather and lighting conditions

Step 2: Conduct initial observations and deploy additional resources – It is necessary to take immediate control of the crime scene and to clear the area of nonessential personnel. Once this is done, and the observations are made, it is important to detect and safeguard perishable or fleeting evidence. This is a good time to note the time of arrival on scene; the weather conditions of the scene including winds, precipitation, temperature, and barometric pressure; odors that may be present; the available ambient lighting at the scene, and the need for supplemental lighting. If life-saving efforts are ongoing, it is recommended that photographs be taken to document the efforts of the medical responders. This documentation can be useful in fending off litigious actions alleging negligence. The photographs may also be useful to convey alterations to the scene during the medical response. If the victim has been removed from the scene, it is imperative to determine their location, dispatch a photographer to capture images of the injuries before they are bandaged or wrapped, and collect their clothing. After conferring with first responders and collecting the entry/exit information, the crime scene investigator should make their initial observations, noting environmental conditions and visible items of evidence. It should also be determined if the suspect is in custody or at large. If in custody, a visual inspection of the suspect should be made paying close attention to trace and transfer evidence. The clothing and shoes of the suspect should be collected and properly processed into evidence. The clothing of the victim(s) should also be collected, but it is recommended that these items not come in contact with the clothing of the suspect. Once the crime scene has been properly classified, an appropriate crime scene perimeter should be established. Ensure that adequate security is provided for scene safety. Establish a route through the crime scene that will be the least destructive to the evidence. Assign responsibilities to the crime scene team and don appropriate personal protective equipment. Following this, the initial walk-through of the scene may be conducted. No evidence should be disturbed or removed at this time. It may be necessary to utilize a clean white light at a low oblique angle to detect physical evidence. Following the initial walk-through of the scene, the lead crime scene investigator should provide rudimentary details of the scene to the detectives and investigators. The lead crime scene investigator should also make notifications to superiors regarding an estimate of the time it will take to process the scene, the equipment needed, and additional resources if necessary.

Step 2 checklist:
- **Control the scene!** Take control of the scene and remove all non-essential personnel
- Make initial observations of the scene, victim, and suspect
- Note obvious items of evidence
- Note perishable or fleeting evidence and make an effort to preserve and protect the same

- Note life-saving efforts or artifacts associated with life-saving efforts
- Note environmental conditions
  - Time of day
  - Weather conditions
  - Temperature
  - Lighting conditions
  - Odors
- Determine classification of the crime scene
- Make observations of impression evidence (footwear, tire impressions, etc.)
- Establish or adjust crime scene perimeters if not already done
- Ensure that adequate scene security is established
- Determine ingress/egress routes of suspect(s)
- Interview first responders and available victims and/or witnesses
- Ensure garments and footwear of living victims and suspects have been properly collected
- Determine equipment needs
- Determine staffing needs and crime scene team make-up
- Determine need for additional resources & outside agency assistance
- Don appropriate personal protective equipment
- Establish a path through the crime scene that is least destructive to the evidence
- Utilize clean white light at low oblique angles to examine the scene
- Make the initial observations of the scene, the evidence contained therein and establish the order and means of processing
- Make no alterations to the scene or the evidence it contains at this time
- Notify investigators of apparent information that may be useful in determining the identity of the suspect or the elements of the crime
- Notify supervisors/administrators of preliminary findings and processing plan

Step 3: The decedent – As the body of a person known to be dead falls under the jurisdiction of the County Coroner's Office or Medical Examiner's (ME) Office, or as applicable, the scene should be secured, with only rudimentary photographic documentation of the decedent conducted prior to the arrival of a representative of the Coroner's or ME's Office. Other than circumstances where an agreement exists between the institution and the Coroner or ME that allows for non-intrusive evidence gathering or enhancement techniques, such as Evi-Vac™ trace evidence vacuum, Skin-Print Black™ latent print detection technique, swabbing the neck, hands, and arms for DNA, no inspection of the body should occur until the arrival of representatives from these entities. Efforts to identify the decedent will assist the Coroner or ME, provided these efforts are nonobtrusive to the crime scene. The decedent should not be fingerprinted at the scene. This should be accomplished following the autopsy in an effort to preserve what forensic evidence may be present on the hands, fingers, or under the fingernails of the decedent. Inspect the decedent along with the Coroner's or ME's representative once they are on the scene. Pay attention to body position, clothing, obvious signs of injury, petechiae, lividity, rigor mortis, and anything unusual or out of the ordinary. Coordinate the removal of the body and establish a time for the autopsy. Whenever possible, the body should remain at the scene until it can be documented, and all items of evidence are recovered. This, however, is at the discretion of the Coroner's or ME's Office representative. It must be remembered that in some states, such as California, it is a misdemeanor to move or disturb the body of a person known to be dead without permission of the Coroner, ME, or their appointed representatives. Determine the removal and disposition of the clothing worn by the decedent. Once the decedent has been removed from the scene, make a careful examination of the area beneath the body.

Step 3 checklist:
- Document the position and condition of the body in the crime scene (notetaking and photography)
- Make datum points for diagramming
- Note life-saving artifacts (if applicable)
- Nonobtrusive evidence collection (Evi-vac or Skin-print black, if applicable)
- Collect DNA swabs from hands, neck, etc. (if applicable)
- Document the body with the Coroner's or Medical Examiner's office representative
- Collect clothing items and determine evidence custody (agency or Coroner/ME)
- Supervise removal of the body from the crime scene by Coroner's or ME representative
- Coordinate the autopsy details
- Examine the area beneath the body for evidence

Step 4: Photographing the crime scene – The designated crime scene photographer should begin (or continue) photographic documentation of the scene. Following established protocols, the photographer should capture overall images (scene establishing), relational images (evidence establishing), and evidentiary images (close-up). Microphotography is best captured at the forensic laboratory. The photographer should first photograph the entire crime scene without scales and markers prior to the addition of these items. When photographing the exterior of a building, the photographer should photograph the exterior corners, sides, entry, and exits with identifiers such as street signs, address numbers, building name, etc. When photographing the interior of a building, the photographer should photograph rooms from the corners toward the center of the room and from the flat walls toward the opposite wall; taking care to overlap each frame by several feet. The photographer should remember to record the floor and ceiling of the room. All items of evidence must be photo-documented prior to their removal or collection. Take care not to photograph items brought to the crime scene by the CSI team (forensic lights, forensic equipment kits, etc.). It is best that these items remain outside of the crime scene until the photographic documentation is completed unless needed for photographic purposes. Personal items belonging to members of the crime scene team like coffee cups, thermoses, sodas, water bottles, food, or any other item of personal convenience must never be brought into the crime scene. Avoid photographing crime scene personnel unless it is required to accurately depict the object being photographed or in demonstrating a forensic procedure. Evidentiary images should be taken with the goal of filling the frame with the object parallel and perpendicular to the lens. The use of scales in evidentiary photography should be on the same plane as the top of the object being photographed. Compose the photograph, fill the frame, and be aware of the lighting and shadows and what is in the background.

Step 4 checklist:
- Select appropriate camera and lens
- Set white balance
- Select appropriate flash and lighting
- Select appropriate filters
- Select appropriate camera settings
- Photograph the lead card
- Photograph injuries of victim(s) and injuries (or lack of injuries) of suspects(s)
- Photograph overview of crime scene without and with markers
- Photograph identifiers (street signs, building names, addresses or cell numbers, etc.)
- Photograph images establishing the relationship of items of evidence in the scene (without and with markers)
- Photograph individual items of evidence (without and with markers and scales)

Crime Scene Processing Methodology & Checklists   39

- Photograph evidence enhancement (latent print development, bloodstain detection and enhancement, etc.)
- Photograph perspective photographs if necessary
- Photograph exit images documenting the scene following processing
- Keep a photograph log if required by policy
- Properly record images directly onto electronic media for evidence storage and download images into an evidence computer

Step 5: Documentation of the crime scene – The entire scene should be documented by the designated diagram technician in a narrative, sketched, and written form prior to the removal, disturbance, or collection of any item. The scene should be described in detail beginning outside of the scene and moving inward toward the center of the scene. The narrative should include the building, room, furniture, fixtures, environmental conditions, and all pertinent items of interest. The diagram technician should create a rough sketch of the scene including room dimensions, position and dimension of furniture, and all items of evidence. The diagram technician should determine the compass direction of true or magnetic north and indicate on the map that the sketch is not to scale. Large outdoor scenes may need to be laid out in a grid pattern or searched utilizing one of the approved methods (grid pattern, line, spiral, etc.) prior to sketching. All items of evidence should be measured in their fixed position prior to being collected. At times it is necessary to move items in order to measure or map a crime scene. For this reason, it is essential that the entirety of the crime scene be photographed, before and after the placement of evidence markers, prior to being measured and sketched.

Step 5 checklist:
- Document all pertinent information regarding the scene and its contents
- Itemize all apparent items of evidence
- Determine placement of evidence markers, scales, and labels
- Create a rough sketch of the crime scene using a compass to determine directions
- Determine diagramming technique (baseline, triangulation, triangulation or the baseline, etc.)
- Select permanent datum points

Step 6: Bloodstain pattern mapping – Mapping, marking, measuring, documenting, and presumptive testing of bloodstain patterns should be performed by the crime scene analyst or a crime scene investigator experienced in bloodstain pattern analysis. The documentation of bloodstain patterns should be conducted following the removal of the body. Bloodstain mapping is generally accomplished in the last stages of the crime scene processing and should only be conducted by trained personnel using the appropriate scales and markers. Swabbing bloodstains for DNA typing is accomplished during this step. In shooting scenes, bloodstain mapping should be accomplished before trajectories are determined and bullets are recovered from walls, furniture, ceilings, etc.

Step 6 checklist:
- Map bloodstains by target and pattern
- Document, photograph, and measure mapped stains
- Conduct presumptive testing
- Collect control swabs and bloodstain specimen swabs
- Determine the area of convergence and point of origin (if applicable)

Step 7: Conduct the first assessment – Following the thorough visualization of the crime scene and all pertinent items of evidence contained therein, and following the identification, photographing, documentation, and sketching of the crime scene, the CSI team should gather and review notes and observations before continuing with the crime scene processing.

Step 7 checklist:
- Assemble the CSI team and review notes and observations to determine the progress of the scene processing and verify no step has been left out
- Determine if additional equipment is required
- Determine if additional specialized units should be summoned (latent print technicians, forensic digital imagery specialist, crime scene reconstruction specialist, etc.)
- Determine if information developed during the processing of the scene would be helpful to detectives and investigators
- Brief supervisors and administrators regarding the progress of scene processing
- Assess the need to rest and hydrate the team and need to change PPEs

Step 8: Collection of evidence – Once all items of evidence have been documented, photographed, and sketched, it is now appropriate to begin removing, identifying, inventorying, and establishing a chain of custody for items of evidence being collected. As each item is collected, it should be examined for additional physical evidence.

Any additional items discovered when the item was moved should be documented, sketched, and photographed. Each object should be handled in accordance with established protocols with consideration for subsequent forensic analysis and processing. Should your agency see fit, it is acceptable to appoint one CSI member as the evidence collection technician. This person can collect all items of evidence, noting the identity of the original person of discovery for the chain of custody, and process all items into evidence. In this regard, the chain of custody is limited to one or two individuals and only one person is required to testify in preliminary court hearings in some jurisdictions. The drawback to this practice is that it may create some problems should that person transfer, be terminated, or resign.

Step 8 checklist:
- Examine each item of evidence for additional physical evidence
- Handle one item of evidence at a time using established protocols
- Package evidence and initiate a proper chain of custody

Step 9: Conduct the second assessment – Following the collection of all known items of evidence, it is now a good time to inspect the crime scene using a forensic light source or Alternate Light Source for overlooked evidence such as body fluids, trace fibers, hairs, etc., not detected by white light. Depending on the circumstance, this examination may be performed following the first assessment of the crime scene or before. Following this, it is an appropriate time to process the crime scene for latent prints. With each new discovery, the crime scene investigator must repeat the above steps in the processing methodology. The CSI team (ideally led by a crime scene analyst or above) should ensure that all areas have been searched and that no areas were overlooked. Advanced forensic chemical examination techniques (Bluestar, luminol, Amido-black, Coomassie Blue, Hungarian Red, Aqueous Leuco Crystal Violet, etc.) or external ballistic examinations should be considered at this time. Exit photographs should also be taken at this time.

Step 9 checklist:
- Inspect the scene using forensic light or Alternate Light Source (if not already completed)
- Process scene for latent prints
- Determine if additional examination should be considered
- Ensure that all areas of the scene have been searched and all evidence has been gathered

Step 10: Scene periphery – The scene perimeter and outlying areas, which should have been checked during the initial observations, should be thoroughly checked again. Information developed during the processing of the crime scene may lead to additional discoveries peripheral to the crime scene. Additional photographs should be taken of these areas if applicable.

Step 10 checklist:
- Search areas peripheral to the crime scene (if not already completed)
- Confer with detectives and investigators to determine if any information was gathered from interviews that should be considered before concluding the periphery search (such as direction and route of escape, mode of transportation, etc.)

Step 11: On-scene debriefing of the CSI team – The on-scene debrief consists of accounting for all investigators, evidence, and equipment. The team should briefly discuss equipment or procedural problems encountered during the processing of the crime scene. This is a good time to discuss any issues that might be challenged later in court.

Step 11 checklist:
- Assemble and account for all team members
- Account for all items of evidence
- Account for all equipment
- Make notations regarding re-supply, equipment replacements, or acquisitions

Step 12: Securing or releasing the scene – A determination should be made by the appropriate investigative personnel, with consideration to the opinions of the CSI team and crime scene analyst, to either release the crime scene to the responsible custodial authority or secure it for follow-up examination. The CSI team should have at their disposal locking devices that will allow them to "dead-line" a cell using a key or mechanism that prevents unauthorized entry. It is highly recommended that a cell that is the scene of a homicide or suspicious death should remain sealed until after the autopsy. At times, it is impossible to secure areas of the institution that are vital to the operation of the facility such as dining halls, culinary or scullery areas, educational programs, or maintenance facilities. If arrangements cannot be made to have other areas cover the responsibilities of these areas, the CSI team should prioritize their efforts to thoroughly process these areas first. In the custodial setting, scene contamination can be an issue once a cell or common area has been released and occupied by the inmate population.

Step 12 checklist:
- Determine if the scene should be held for further investigation or released
- If held, determine a suitable method for restricting entry (sealing, door boots, etc.)
- Make necessary notifications regarding the status of the scene (Unit staff, Control Room, administrators, etc.)

Step 13: Processing the evidence and report writing – At this time, all items of evidence should be appropriately packaged for long-term storage and placed in approved evidence lockers. Determinations should be made as to the disposition of the items of evidence and whether additional forensic examination is warranted. A chain of custody should be maintained, along with an inventory of all items processed into evidence. Reports, finalized sketches, photographic logs, crime scene entry/exit logs, and crime scene notes should be prepared and collected for review and submission. Equipment should be sterilized and provisioned for the next crime scene call-out.

Step 13 checklist:
- Transport evidence to a processing facility
- Dry saturated garments in forensic driers following established protocols
- Determine disposition of evidence (such as long-term storage, advanced forensic examination, etc.)
- Determine proper packaging of evidence items
- Determine disposition of evidence items that need to be submitted to forensic laboratories (such as ballistics, DNA typing, drug confirmatory analysis, etc.)
- Ensure chain of custody is established
- Sterilize all equipment using a solution of 10% bleach and water (such as tripods, lighting equipment, measuring devices, etc.)
- Re-supply crime scene kits

Step 14: Formal debriefing – A formal debriefing should be held within 48 hours of the processing of the crime scene with the CSI team, crime scene analyst, senior crime scene analyst, and investigators to discuss the important aspects of the crime scene investigation. This is a good time also to review protocols and procedures, as well as any concerns regarding the functionality, supply, or need of equipment to be used at future crime scenes.

Crime Scene Procedure & Protocol Considerations

6

It is best for the investigative authorities, in conjunction with the administration, at each jail and prison to have in place protocols and procedures that are customized to fit the specific needs and layout of their facilities. Protocols, procedures, and methodologies are what allow us to do what we do in a manner that is acceptable to the courts. Therefore, I cannot stress the importance of these documents enough. Please feel free to utilize the information from the following pages as the basis for the protocols and procedures for your facility.

Crime Scene Preservation

"Every criminal investigation must have a foundation that is based upon facts that can later be proven in court. If the evidence is not located or *properly preserved*, the entire case will be in jeopardy and may be dismissed by the magistrate under Section 871 of the California Penal Codes."

It is the responsibility of the initial first responding personnel to take the necessary steps to preserve the crime scene for physical and trace evidence. This responsibility should be undertaken instinctively by the officer without delay or the need for a supervisor to issue instructions. The priority of the first responder is to save lives and to prevent additional injury or loss of life. Medical care must be administered immediately to victims if life-saving measures are to be applied.

This should be done, however, with the least amount of destruction as possible to physical evidence on the victim or in the crime scene. If a person is known to be dead and no life-saving measures are to be employed, the decedent *must* remain in the position they were found and a determination should be made by medical personnel with as little contact with, or disturbance of, the crime scene as possible. If it is necessary for medical personnel to enter the crime scene prior to the arrival of crime scene investigators, the first responder must establish a path into the crime scene that will prevent the destruction of fragile evidence such as bloodstain patterns, footwear and tire-tread impressions, hairs, and fibers.

There are five primary responsibilities of the first responder:

- Gain control of the occurrence as quickly as possible and to "freeze" all inmate movement.

- Determine whether the victim is alive or dead and the necessary action to be taken.
- Apprehend the suspect(s), if they are still present, or broadcast the suspect information to other responding units.
- Safeguard the scene and detain reporting parties, witnesses, or suspects.
- Immediately notify supervisors and summon crime scene investigators.

The only evidence that should be collected by the *first responder* is eyewitness statements, dying declarations of the victim or spontaneous utterances of a suspect, and fleeting or perishable evidence that will be lost if not immediately collected.

The first responder should not examine or touch the contents of the crime scene unless the evidence is perishable or transient and will be lost if not immediately recovered. Weapons used in the commission of a crime in the custodial setting should *only* be collected if the area *cannot* be contained and there is a possibility that the item might be used by the suspect against peace officers or other persons. In this event, the weapon must be retrieved paying particular attention *not* to disturb fingerprint, blood, or hair and fiber evidence and, if possible, to prevent contamination. The weapon must *never* be returned to the crime scene if it is removed by the first responder. The first responder should, however, make a visual assessment of the crime scene and safeguard the area by isolating the immediate area, and the decedent if present, including any visible evidence, from nonessential personnel. The initial first responder should establish a crime scene using whatever method is at their disposal. This would include crime scene tape, barriers, or other officers posted in a manner to keep nonessential personnel out of the crime scene until such time as crime scene tape can be deployed.

The crime scene should be large enough to encompass avenues of suspect ingress and egress, and any area that might contain evidence. If the crime scene perimeter is too large, a smaller crime scene may be established by crime scene investigators, if necessary, but only after a complete and thorough search of the area for evidence has been conducted. The outer perimeter will remain a crime scene to keep nonessential personnel and media further away from the actual crime scene. The first responder is also responsible for placing personnel in positions to guard the crime scene area and to document on a chronological log all persons entering and leaving the crime scene and *their purpose for doing so*. If the first responder has taken a suspect into custody and detained the suspect within the crime scene in the custodial setting, it is acceptable that the suspect remains in situ until such time as their presence can be photographed, providing the suspect is not in immediate need of medical attention, does not pose a threat to the safety and security of the institution, is not in need of decontamination from the use of chemical agents, and will not, by his actions, alter or destroy the crime scene or the evidence it contains. This is not recommended for suspects who are apprehended in public. If the suspect has been removed from the crime scene, they should *never* be returned to the crime scene because there could later be allegations that the scene was contaminated by the suspect during the second visit and not during the initial crime. Officers transporting the suspect should never question them regarding the crime. If the suspect insists upon volunteering information or makes spontaneous statements of guilt, the officer should listen, remember, and make accurate notes of any statements made, without further interrogation, and immediately notify the crime scene and criminal investigators of the content of the statements.

Remember, a spontaneous statement is made without the prompting of law enforcement personnel. Therefore, a spontaneous statement is blurted out without any questioning or enticement whatsoever from the law enforcement officer.

The report of the first responder must accurately reflect all the actions taken by that officer including the time that they arrived, the condition of the scene, the steps taken to establish, preserve and protect the crime scene, victim description, suspect and witness information and statements made, and staff notification procedures. The chronological log of personnel entry and exit must also be included in the incident report.

Dealing with In-Custody Death Protocol Considerations

Make this clearly understood, the body of a deceased inmate, or any other person, belongs to the Coroner's Office or Medial Examiner or their designated employee. To go a little bit further:

California Government Code Section 27491.2

a. The Coroner has jurisdiction of the body.
b. For purposes of inquiry, the body of one who is *known to be dead* ... shall NOT be disturbed or moved from the position or place of death WITHOUT permission of the coroner or coroner's appointed deputy. Any violation of this subdivision is a *misdemeanor*.

I am sure most states or jurisdictions have the same or similar statute to prevent the unnecessary tampering of the body of a person who is known to be dead.

And yet, medical department personnel continue to insist upon moving the body of a deceased inmate to the infirmary so that the doctor can make a pronouncement of death. Is there any reason why the doctor cannot go to the scene and pronounce death?

It is one thing if there is the remotest chance that emergency life-saving measures can save the life of the inmate, but if lividity or rigor mortis has set in and the on-scene medical personnel have not initiated emergency procedures, then the person is known to be dead, and therefore the body must remain in the position and condition in which it was found. As I say with gallows humor to my students, "If the head is separated from the body and every time you administer rescue breathing it sounds like you are playing the ocarina, he's dead and there is nothing you can do to bring him back. The body must stay where it was found." The potential for destroying critical traces and transferring evidence by moving the body on a gurney that has not been sterilized since it was manufactured to an infirmary that is teaming with DNA contamination is tremendous. Even placing a sheet or blanket over the body that has not been properly sterilized could jeopardize the recovery of critical evidence. The criteria for not performing emergency medical care are simple; if any of the following conditions are present, life-saving measures should not be employed: rigor mortis, lividity, decapitation, decomposition, and exsanguinations. Departments should maintain protocols that excuse officers from performing emergency life-saving measures if any of the above conditions are present. Providing emergency life-saving measures to a person who is known to be dead is destructive to the crime scene, and the potential evidence it contains.

For years, we had a nurse employed at our facility who would always close their eyes, fold their arms, and place them on the chest of a deceased inmate. I was never able to convince her to stop this practice. Instead, I would always try to beat her to the scene and get my photographs as quickly as possible.

This may present a problem, however, to the incident commander in the custodial setting, especially if the death was caused by staff members trying to prevent escape or regain and control an area following a disturbance, or if rival inmate factions are involved, as the presence of the body can stimulate the ire of the inmate population and lead to further riot or rout. The use of portable curtains or barricades can help to reduce tensions and the timely appearance of the Coroner's Office or Medical Examiner personnel can also assuage their anger. This is also where good communication skills between a CSI designee and the inmate population can be immensely helpful.

I do know of one facility, many decades ago, where an inmate who was shot and killed as he attempted to scale the perimeter fence was left tangled in the razor wire until such time as sufficient ladders and equipment could be assembled to lower him to the ground. I suppose the macabre spectacle could serve as a reminder to the onlooking inmate population of the perils of escape as they gawked from their prison cell windows at the proceedings. Perhaps it was not practical to construct a barrier screen, or by doing so would create a security risk by restricting the visibility of the elevated gun positions. The sensibilities of onlookers and consideration for the victim should, however, merit an effort to conceal the body behind some form of screen. I have been present at many homicide scenes in the public setting and I am always amazed at the parents who bring very small children, some even related to the victim, as close to the scene as possible, even hoisting them up on their shoulders for a better view. Screens are expensive, burdensome, difficult to assemble, and must be thoroughly sanitized after each use, but necessary to allow personnel to conduct required investigations with a modicum of privacy. It may also be necessary to provide a screen that prevents the observation of the decedent by drones, which are commonly becoming unwelcome invigilators.

Protocols should be in place to notify the Coroner's or Medical Examiner's office and Prosecutor's office of all in-custody deaths. Autopsies should be performed for inmate deaths that were not expected and not under the care of a physician. No determination of death should be made by the officials at the facility until such time as the manner, mechanism, and cause of death are determined by the Coroner or Medical Examiner. Until such time, the occurrence should only be listed as "In-Custody Death."

Crime Scene Investigators should limit the efforts to recover evidence from the body of a decedent to those that are not obtrusive until such time as the Coroner's or Medical Examiner's office official can arrive on the scene. The investigator should then work in concert with the official to collect all physical, trace, and transfer evidence from the body of the decedent. It is important that the clothing of the victim be collected at the crime scene as body fluids and blood may continue to purge from the body while in the body bag. For this reason, DNA swabs should also be collected from the hands (palmar and dorsal), forearms, and neck of the decedent before placement in the bag. Efforts to obtain identification of the deceased should also be limited to means that do not disturb the body. Fingerprints should never be taken until such time as a determination has been made regarding the performance of an autopsy and should not be collected until after the autopsy. This is to preserve whatever evidence might remain on the fingers and also to verify that the autopsy was performed on the correct person. Some jurisdictions also require positive identification of the inked fingerprint impressions collected from the deceased with the known fingerprint cards found in their custody files before that person is removed from the official inmate population count.

Positive identification of the decedent inmate is a serious matter owing to the fact that an incarcerated individual will be removed from an official count by that death, and the death will be recorded as an official government occurrence. Protocols regarding this responsibility should be maintained by every jail and prison. Each facility should employ a technician trained as a fingerprint comparison analyst. Fingerprint impressions should be collected from the decedent following the autopsy, or after a decision has been made that an autopsy will not be performed. The technician should collect several sets of impressions using a post-mortem fingerprint kit.

The protocols at my former institution required that three sets of prints were to be collected. I find, as a comparison analyst, that of the three sets of impressions collected, I can generally assemble one full set with sufficient ridge definition for comparison. Ridge builder lotion or Lansberry's liquid can be used to improve the quality of the inked prints taken from the decedent. In more extreme cases, the coroner's office personnel can assist the technician by injecting fluids under the finger pads or other techniques depending upon the circumstances. The collected impressions should be compared to the exemplar fingerprint cards found in the official records belonging to the decedent inmate. Photographs of the decedent inmate may also be collected and compared alongside known facial photographs but should not be relied upon as the only means of positive identification. Tattoos, unique marks, and scars should also be compared to those known to be possessed by the inmate; again, not being the sole means of identification.

Crime Scene Photography Suggested Protocols

All photographs taken at a crime scene are subject to discovery in court. **This includes every photograph taken with your cellular telephone.**

Objectives of crime scene photography:

- To record the condition of the scene before alterations occur
- **To record the location and position of evidence items before being collected**
- To document the point of view of the responding officers, investigators, suspects, and witnesses
- To document the spatial relationships of pertinent items.

Photographs provide visual images and have the distinct advantage of showing physical objects in a way similar to what the human eye sees if they are properly composed and focused. Photographs of the crime scene capture its visual aspects, which are needed to convey the appearance to investigators, attorneys, judges, and jurors.

<u>Note:</u> *Photography is not a substitute for notes and sketches but is part of the overall crime scene investigation!*

Photographs are also a crucial visual record of the conditions at the scene for investigators during follow-up investigations and for investigators and analysts who are reconstructing various aspects of the crime. When combined with notes and sketches, photographs assist the crime scene specialist in painting an accurate picture of the crime scene during courtroom testimony. This contributes to the credibility, memory, and testimony of the person giving the testimony.

Photographing the Crime Scene

How Many Photographs?

There is no set number of photographs that must be taken at any crime scene. Every scene will present itself differently and additional information will need to be documented as the investigation progresses. The best policy is to always take too many photographs rather than too few as the opportunity to take photographs is usually limited to the time and conditions at the scene. The position of items of evidence can never be reproduced to exactly how they were found in the scene, therefore photographs must be taken before anything is moved or disturbed.

Conditions at the Scene

The crime scene may be as small as a cell or cover an area as large as a prison exercise yard. The photographic conditions at the scene may vary considerably depending on the weather, time of day, and lighting. These conditions will determine what photography technique to use, whether it is painting with light, bulb exposure, flash photography, or using ambient or artificial light. Always ask yourself the following questions before determining which technique to use. These questions will help obtain the best photo documentation of the crime scene:

- What is the purpose of photographing this scene?
- Does the item have any relationship to the overall scene?
- Does the item have any relationship to the other items in the scene?
- Will the item be properly exposed, focused, and composed?
- Will there be any reflections off windows or mirrors that will wash the photograph, or will there be a hot spot from a flash or artificial light?
- Is there sufficient lighting to take the photograph?
- Can the camera be placed in a position that will make it possible to take the photograph?
- Can the photograph be explained to a jury?
- Is the correct equipment being used for the scene?

Crime Scene Photography

Crime scene photography must be an accurate representation of the crime scene and the items of evidence it contains. The photographs must be considered an accurate representation of what the photographer, responding officers, and crime scene investigators observed and documented. These photographs must be correctly exposed and have maximum depth of field. The photographs must be composed, free of distortion, and in focus.

Perspective Photographs

Oftentimes, the photographer will be required to take a series of photographs that are to represent the perspective of eyewitnesses, victims, first responders, or investigators. When doing this, you should always use a tripod or monopod set to the height of the eyes of the observer to be documented. The photographer should use a good depth of field and set the focal length between 38 and 50mm, depending on the brand of camera being used, which is closest to what the normal eye sees. You may have to use a tripod that allows you to position the camera at the proper level of a car door window frame or steering wheel to replicate the position of the witness's eyes. Natural perspective photography, however, requires the photographer to stand at full height with the same focal setting.

Overall Crime Scene Establishing Photographs

The purpose of overall photographs is to establish the location of the crime scene and enable others to be able to visualize the scene as it was found. Overall photographs must not be taken from a distance that is too far to accurately visualize the area but should be from a distance that will include avenues of ingress and egress (Fig. 6.1). Remember that all photographs are considered an official record of how the scene was at the time of the investigation. Do not allow anyone to move anything prior to or during the photographic process.

Do not allow anyone to introduce items to these areas either. Never photograph crime scene processing equipment inside of the scene, unless it is necessary to accurately reflect a technique used to enhance, visualize, or collect the item of evidence. Prior to actually taking the photographs, make a mental plan of the photographs you are going to take, the method by which you are going to take them, and the possible problems you might encounter while taking the photographs. Be sure to use a methodical approach to taking the photographs that includes all aspects of the scene. First, take overall photographs without evidence markers being placed in the crime scene. Then, take the same photographs again after the markers have been placed. This will prevent the allegation that the markers are covering vital pieces of evidence in subsequent courtroom proceedings.

52 Crime Scene Processing in Correctional Facilities and Prisons

Figure 6.1 Not too far away that the image cannot be discerned, yet far enough that the viewer can see the majority of the image.

Lead Card

The first frame of a series of photographs should include a lead card (Fig. 6.2). The purpose of this card is to identify the photographs taken with a particular incident or investigation. This card should include the case number, victims and/or suspects, location, date and time, and the name of the photographer. A new lead card should be used every time there is a change in the scene, location, date, suspect/witness information, or photographer information.

Figure 6.2 The lead card identifies the photographs taken with a particular incident or investigation.

Outside and Inside Perimeters

When it comes down to it, there are only three stages of crime scene photography: long-range overview photography outside the perimeter, mid-range photography within the crime scene perimeter, and close-up photography of individual items of evidence.

1. Outside perimeter of the crime scene
   Take photographs to establish the location of the scene. This could include a street sign, a building name, a housing unit name, a cell number, some type of identifying landmark, or all of the above.

   Take photographs of the surrounding area from a natural perspective, with the photographer standing at full height. Depending on the type of scene, this could include cell blocks, access roads, fence lines, parking lots, outbuildings, and ingress and/or egress routes. Sometimes this may require additional photographs shot overhead using a fire engine ladder or a lift truck. A drone, helicopter, or airplane may be necessary to take aerial photographs of an entire facility or exercise yard. This may require mutual aid assistance from neighboring law enforcement agencies, fire departments, or the Highway Patrol.

2. Inside perimeter of the crime scene
   The photographs should be taken so that others can visualize the scene. For each room or area:
   - Begin with a view of the entrance. Start with the outside of the room and work your way toward the center.
   - Photograph the crime scene in the condition in which it was found when you arrived.
   - Take four-corner and four-flat photographs of each room. This means taking a photograph of each corner of the room and the four flat walls of the room to show its layout. Adjust the lens to a wide angle setting when taking these photographs, usually somewhere between 28mm and 50mm. Make sure to choose a setting to capture all of the room, including the ceiling and floor. In large rooms, it may be necessary to take additional photographs from other locations and overlap the photographs for complete coverage.
   - Continue with other areas that are in proximity to the scene.
   - If an item of evidence was removed from the crime scene prior to the arrival of the crime scene investigator, it should *never* be returned to the crime scene in order to prevent contamination of the evidence or crime scene. A clean evidence marker should reflect the area where the item was found, and a detailed narrative should be included in the report.

Mid-Range Evidence Establishing Photographs

When the overall photographs are completed, photographs should be taken from a closer range to show the layout of the smaller areas of the scene. These photographs also allow for the relationship between items of evidence to be established.

3. Close-up or evidentiary photographs

Close-up Evidentiary Photographs

Close-up photographs of items of evidence taken at the crime scene depict the item as it looked at the time it was discovered, documented, and recovered. However, evidentiary-quality photographs should be taken in the laboratory under ideal conditions. In both instances, the item should be photographed first without a scale or marker and then with a scale or marker in place. The scale or marker should never touch the item of evidence. When using a scale, it should be placed on the same plane as the item of evidence whenever possible. In the field, the camera must be mounted to a tripod for close-up photography. It is best to use a copy stand in the laboratory.

The camera must then be adjusted so that it is *parallel* and *perpendicular* to the surface of the item being photographed. Make sure a ruler or scale is included in the photograph. Remember to photograph the scale on the same plane as the item of evidence. You may have to raise the scale to be at the same level as the item of evidence or furrow a depression if photographing impression evidence (Fig. 6.3). Also, place

Figure 6.3 The scale is raised to be on the same plane as the top of the headstamp.

a photograph identifier label in the photograph if possible. This contains information such as the incident number, date, victim or suspect names, and evidence item number. It is best to fill the frame with the object, scale, and photograph identifier.

Scales and Markers

Using a scale in the photograph eliminates any speculation as to the size of the object. However, it is imperative that the item is photographed with the camera parallel and perpendicular to the object as any deviation may alter the perception of the object's size through distortion. Only scales, rulers, and markers that are appropriate for the purpose of photography should be used. Never use a ruler that is broken, bent, or has writing upon its surface that is not relative to the item being photographed. I still remember many years ago testifying in court as an expert on inmate-manufactured weapons when I was handed a photograph of a weapon. Not only was the weapon photographed on a bright yellow background, but the ruler used by the photographer was inscribed, "Casper – SUR XIII." Apparently, the photographer found the ruler in the cell where the weapon was recovered and added it in the frame for scale. I can only imagine what the jury thought as they studied the photograph. It is best to use an American Board of Forensic Odontology #2 L-scale for the documentation of injuries or small items of evidence.

Larger photographic L-scales should be used for footwear or tire tread impressions, as well as other impressions in snow, dust, dirt, or mud. These scales include the appropriate markings to facilitate enlargement and comparison. They also include photographic circles that indicate whether or not the camera is parallel and perpendicular to the item being photographed. Metal scales and rulers may not be suitable when using a camera-mounted flash as they may reflect the flashback toward the camera. Adhesive scales are useful when photographing fingerprints or items being swabbed for DNA. Not only are they on the same plane as the object, but they also remain in the scene following collection and therefore are a reference for measuring, sketching, or mapping.

Photographing Injuries

It is imperative that the injuries received by victims of violent crimes be photographed whenever possible. Therefore, it may be necessary to respond to incidents in a manner that allows one photographer to respond to the area where the living victim has been transported, such as the infirmary, and another photographer to respond to the crime scene. All injuries should be documented, if possible, prior to the application of bandages or wrappings

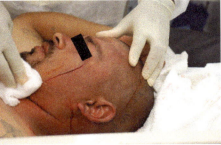

Figure 6.4 Prejudicial photograph on the left and clinical photograph on the right.

and photographed with and without a scale. Although it is advisable that the photographer must capture the injury as quickly as possible, certain photographs depicting especially grotesque deformities or excess bloodshed may not be admissible in court owing to the likelihood that the photographs will play on the emotions of the jury. Therefore, it is necessary for the photographer to take clinical photographs of the injury after the wound has been cleaned and prior to bandaging (Fig. 6.4). I recommend taking both photographs as it is the judge who will ultimately make the final determination of admissibility. It is important to remember that the photographs will be presented to the jury during courtroom deliberations and may be made a matter of public record. Therefore, it is advised that discretion be used while photographing injuries occurring in proximity to genitalia or body parts prurient in nature. When photographing the injuries of a victim, it is strongly suggested that the photographer instructs the injured person not to smile, smirk or, if possible, grimace. It is particularly hard to convince a jury that the victim has suffered a life-changing injury when they are smiling ear-to-ear.

Photographic Suspects

Suspects in the custodial setting should be photographed for injuries that are consistent with their engagement in felonious conduct. This may require the suspect to disrobe to undergarments and present themselves in a manner conducive to external examination. The photographer should document any discovered injuries or the lack of injuries in the following manner:

Overall photograph from head to foot anterior view
Overall photograph from head-to-toe lateral view left
Overall photograph from head-to-toe posterior view
Overall photograph from head-to-toe lateral view right

Both hands extended dorsal view
Both hands extended palmar view
Arms lateral and medial views
Legs lateral and medial views
Head anterior, lateral, and posterior views
Torso anterior and posterior views
Injuries with and without scale

Digital Image Protocols

Although the current trend is to store all agency photographs on a cloud server, it is not always the best policy, especially if the server compresses the files and the photographs are needed for forensic comparison purposes. Therefore, examination quality images captured by the digital camera for comparative purposes should be downloaded to a "stand alone" computer or in-house server used specifically for the purpose of the storage of photographic images. It is advisable that this computer should employ an air/wall gap network system. This computer should have software that allows for the viewing and storage of photographic files and the ability to save the images, preferably in the JPEG, TIFF, or RAW image formats. The computer should also have installed software that allows for visual watermark embedding to prevent alteration and to add authentication. The computer may have the ability to add or subtract contrast, brilliance, or other visual enhancement tools, but **MUST NOT** have software installed that allows for the distortion, alteration, metamorphosing, and/or addition of special effects to the images. This software should be maintained on a computer specifically designated for photographic enhancement and not on the computer used to store the original images. Once the image has been downloaded into a computer file, it should also be stored in an unaltered form to an archive media. It is hard to predict what method of digital media storage and retrieval we will have in the next 20 years, but I imagine everything will be stored in a cloud-based platform. It is essential that all digital images that are stored in a computer hard-drive or cloud must be backed-up in a media format that is safe and follows the rules of chain of custody.

Internal chain of custody logs will be maintained for all original memory storage devices. A copy of the photographs may be maintained in the investigative file but must be labeled as such. All digital images are subject to the rules of discovery in court proceedings and a frame-by-frame log sheet must be completed and submitted as a written report. "Contact sheets" or thumbnail prints (proof sheets) may be generated for all the digital images and can be considered as report writing aids and kept in the investigative file. If reproductions of the images are desired for incident packages or administrative reports, all images captured must be reproduced and included with the documentation.

All images captured by the digital camera will be recorded as evidence. *Digital images **WILL NEVER** be deleted from a camera at any time, unless they have first been transferred to the Digital Image Evidence Computer.* Should an image be of a nature insufficient for clarity or adequate representation of the subject matter, it will still be recorded, and a second image of the subject matter captured.

Digital images will be saved in their original unaltered format. If it is necessary to enhance an image using a software product, this will be clearly documented in the notes and will be done using a copy of the original image. Images can be enlarged, cropped, brightened or darkened, or have contrast added or subtracted, but the original image must be stored in the manner it was recorded by the camera at the time the image was taken, and the enhanced image saved as another file under the title "enhanced" along with the type of enhancement performed (i.e., image name or number-enhanced-contrast added). This file name will be documented in the notes and presented as an enhanced image in courtroom proceedings.

Finally, please, NEVER use a cellular telephone to take photographs of the crime scene, and there are so many reasons why you should not. I will say that I have on occasion taken over 350 photographs of a crime scene and wish I had taken more. I guarantee the technician who uses their cell phone will take a dozen photographs and call it a day. Cell phones also lack sufficient depth-of-field for evidentiary photography.

Video Evidence Suggested Protocols

Objectives of video evidence:

- Record the condition of the scene before, during and immediately after incidents
- Record the location and position of all individuals involved in the incident
- Record exculpatory information
- Record statements of victims, witnesses and suspects

Video provides visual images and has the distinct advantage of showing physical objects and occurrences in a way similar to what the human eye sees. Video of the incident captures the visual aspects of the occurrence, which is needed to convey the look of the event to investigators, attorneys, the judge, and jurors.

Video is not a substitute for photography, documentation and sketches, but is part of the overall incident investigation!

Video is a crucial visual record of the incident for investigators during follow-up investigations. When combined with photographs, notes and sketches, the video will assist the crime scene specialist in painting an accurate picture of the incident during courtroom testimony. Video cameras can be useful in providing exculpatory details to the prosecution and defense during courtroom proceedings. Therefore, it is necessary to have a permanent record of not only the camera documenting the incident, but also the peripheral areas providing those areas are also covered by video cameras.

Video Cameras

Most prisons and jails utilize fixed and flexible cameras throughout the facility and on occasion also use hand-held video cameras to conduct surveillance, observe special yard and housing activities, inmate movement, disturbances and to conduct video-documented interviews.

Digital Video Images

All video images captured by the fixed and flexible digital video cameras must be downloaded to a computer used specifically for the purpose of the storage of digital video images. This computer should have software that allows for the viewing and storage of video files and the ability to save the images to external electronic media (i.e., thumb-drive, hard-drive, or cloud). Although it is not necessary for all video images captured by these cameras not related to the incident to be saved for extensive periods of time, it is required that any incident captured by video cameras are to be downloaded onto the electronic media and processed into evidence as soon as the images are discovered.

Video Evidence Procedures

When an incident is discovered to have been captured by video cameras, the digital images must immediately be downloaded onto an electronic media device, server, or cloud. It is advisable that the digital images are also stored on electronic media and placed in evidence with a gummed-address label bearing the incident date, camera, and time, along with the names of the individuals involved if possible. *It is essential to record not only the cameras capturing the incident, but also the peripheral cameras for exculpatory purposes.*

Video Evidence Documentation

All electronic media evidence must be processed into evidence. An incident report must be completed and submitted with the crime reports. A second copy of the event may be retained in the investigative file if necessary.

Diagramming and Crime Scene Sketching Suggested Protocols

A sketch of the crime scene is important for the following reasons:

- It provides a two-dimensional pictorial representation of the crime scene and the relationship of evidence *prior to* collection*, which can be used later to produce a three-dimensional computer-generated image of the scene.
- It complements photographs and the written report.
- It provides factual data for crime scene reconstruction.
- It provides a visual aid for investigators and for courtroom proceedings.

Scenes in which diagrams are typically prepared include, but are not limited to:

- Homicides
- Suicides
- Stabbing/Slashing
- Sexual assaults
- Shootings
- Use of force involving less-lethal and lethal force options
- Escapes
- Assaults with great bodily injury
- Arson

Prior to the Start of the Diagram

- Discuss with the crime scene analyst what should be included in the sketch. Also discuss the type of sketch that would best capture the scene.
- Assess the scene, proportions, and scope.

*If the evidence has already been collected from the scene, make sure that evidence markers remain in place; each depicting or representing an item of evidence or key element of the crime scene.

Things to Remember

- Determine true or magnetic north and indicate it on the paper using an arrow. The direction north will typically point toward the top

of the page unless the scene outlay dictates otherwise. If there is an error in placing the directional marker when photographs are taken, the error can be corrected on the diagram provided the mistake is noted in the submitted reports.
- When taking measurements, be sure to measure to the nearest fraction. Crime scenes are generally measured in inches and feet; however, bloodstains and bullet defects are measured in metrics to allow for mathematical equations.
- Global Positioning Systems, especially those found on cellular telephones are generally only accurate to 5 or 6 m (about 16′ to 19′ or so). Therefore, in large open or outdoor areas where it is difficult to locate a permanent fixed position to use as a reference datum, it may be necessary to find one or several distant objects and then use compass directions and fiberglass tape measures to create your datum. In the event that the incident will merit a revisiting of the outdoor scene, it may be necessary to drive metal spikes into the ground indicating the datum. In this way, the returning investigator can use a metal detector to locate the datum. Unfortunately, driving a metal spike in the ground may present a security risk in an exercise yard, as the spike may later be discovered by the inmate population and subsequently used as a weapon. Therefore, it may be necessary to utilize permanent structures (towers, outbuildings, fence lines, etc.) to create triangulations based on known compass directions that can later be re-established. In some cases, it may also be necessary to request the assistance of an agency equipped with systems like the Faro or Leica ScanStation or similar laser scanning system.
- Whenever possible, utilize architecturally verified plot plans or diagrams with a scale. If this is not possible, be certain to include the caption "Not to Scale" on each sketch.
- Use standard measuring equipment:
  - Ultrasonic measurement meter
  - Steel measuring tape
  - 100 ft. fiberglass measuring tape
  - Walker wheel ("Roll-a-tape")
  - 300 ft. fiberglass measuring tape
  - Evidence markers
  - Clipboard with graphed paper
  - Ruler
  - Straight edge/triangle
  - Compass

Measuring & Sketching the Crime Scene

Fortunately, most jails and prisons have dimensional plans for everything from individual cells to buildings, warehouses, and exercise yards that are known to the maintenance plant manager and are available on plot plans that may be in a PDF format. This makes it possible for the investigative staff to have at their disposal pre-printed templates that can be carried into the crime scene, allowing for the details to be drawn directly onto the template. As you find, however, the true dimensions of any area will differ slightly from those provided on the architectural plan, so it is best to take your own measurements. Therefore, you must always take and document the overall measurements of the scene as well as the relative measurements for the items of evidence in the crime scene. Always remember that the measurements should not only include length and width but also the height of objects like desks, bunks, lockers, etc.

The most common sketches used in the custodial setting are the "bird's eye view" (Fig. 6.5) where you are viewing the scene as if you were looking down from the ceiling; "elevation view" where you are looking at a side view such as a door or wall; "exploded view" (Fig. 6.6) where it looks like you

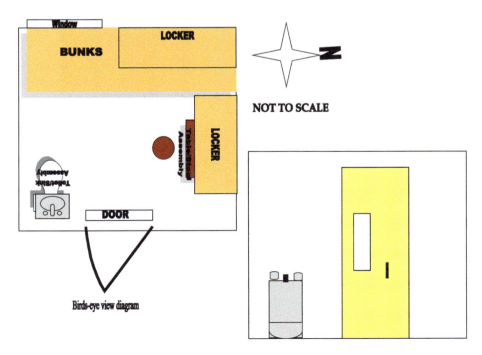

Figure 6.5 Bird's eye view diagram.

Crime Scene Procedure & Protocol Considerations

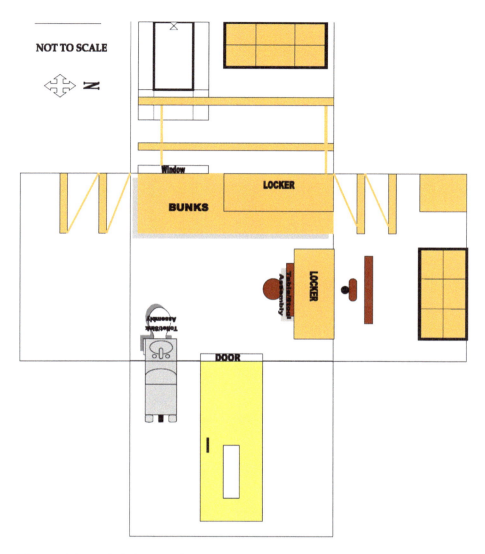

Figure 6.6 Exploded view of a cell.

opened a room as if you laid the walls flat on the ground; and "plot plan" or "aerial view" (Figs. 6.7 and 6.8A and B) where you must document an inmate's movement across a large area.

I am a big fan of ScenePD6™ and use it extensively for indoor and outdoor scenes (Fig. 6.9).

64 Crime Scene Processing in Correctional Facilities and Prisons

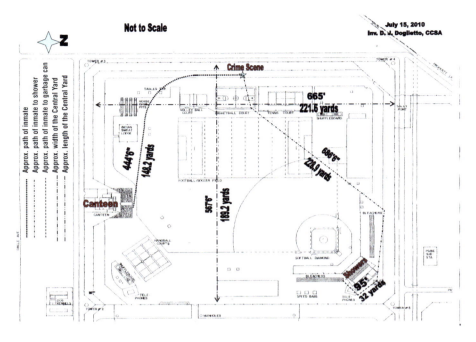

Figure 6.7 Plot plan or aerial view of an exercise yard.

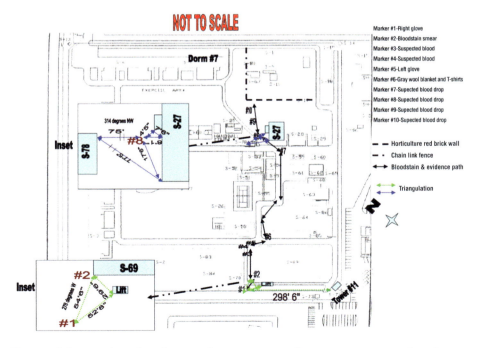

Figure 6.8 A and B Plot plans with over. Try to obtain pre-existing plot plans that display scaled measurements. (*Continued*)

Crime Scene Procedure & Protocol Considerations 65

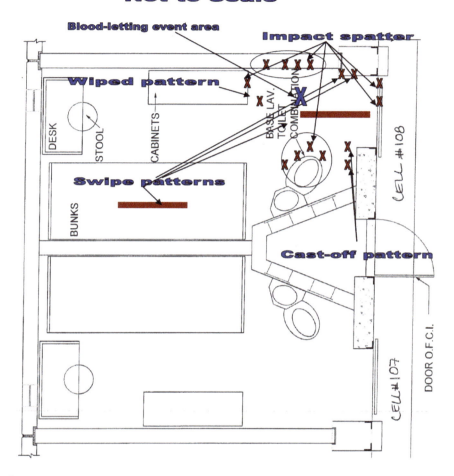

Figure 6.8 (*Continued*)

66 Crime Scene Processing in Correctional Facilities and Prisons

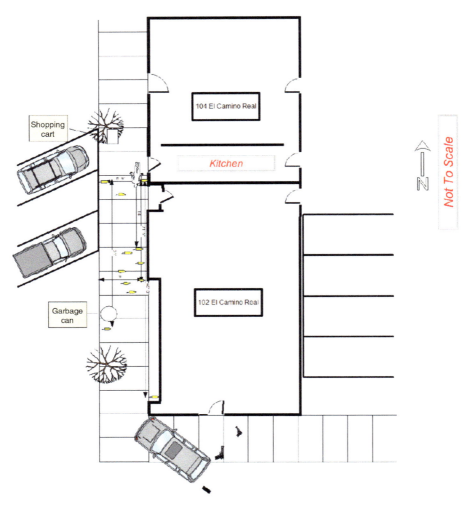

Figure 6.9 ScenePD 6 Pro diagram.

Crime Scene Procedure & Protocol Considerations

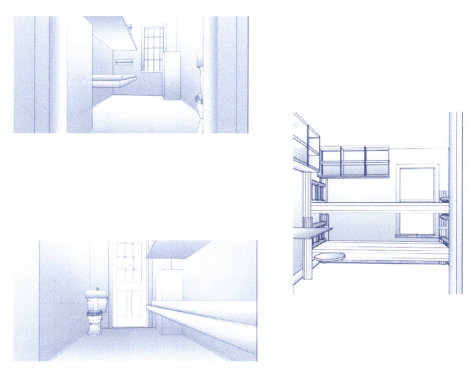

Figure 6.10 Poser 6™ and Punch Pro™ software programs.

Computer-generated diagrams created using Poser 6™ and Punch Pro™ software programs (Fig. 6.10). The diagrams may not be perfect, but they will work. Those who are tech-savvy might try SketchUp™ or Blender™ as well.

Baseline, Rectangle, and Triangulation Methods

Although the baseline method works best with large, outdoor scenes, it can also be used in a large building, such as a warehouse, or in an enclosed exercise yard, such as an Administrative Segregation exercise yard. In order to use this method, you must have at least one fixed point that will not change (fire hydrant, latrine, the corner of a building, etc.) and a compass heading. If you do not have a fixed reference point, you can use a portable GPS unit and place a stake or marker at the GPS coordinates. Roll out a fiberglass measuring tape along this line and leave it in place. This line becomes your baseline or "X" axis. Facing away from your fixed point, you may have items of evidence lying either to the left or right of the line. Those items lying to the left can be measured back to the baseline on a "+Y" axis and those items lying to the left can be measured back to the baseline on a "-Y" axis (Fig. 6.11).

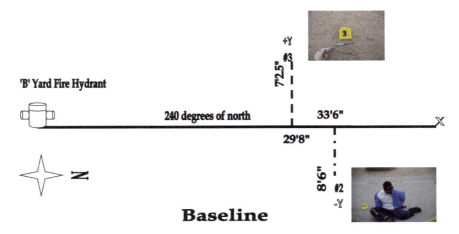

Figure 6.11 The baseline method.

Remember, the purpose of measuring and sketching the crime scene is so that any person can go back to the scene and recreate it with accuracy. Therefore, it is critical to have a compass heading for the baseline.

The rectangular measurement method is best for items of evidence that do not have a distinct shape and are found in areas that have a defined shape and fixed points, such as a cell, gymnasium, office, Administrative Segregation Unit exercise yard, etc. Run two fiberglass or metal tape measures along two adjoining walls or fences so that they meet at the corner. Then measure from the center of the object back to each tape measure (Fig. 6.12).

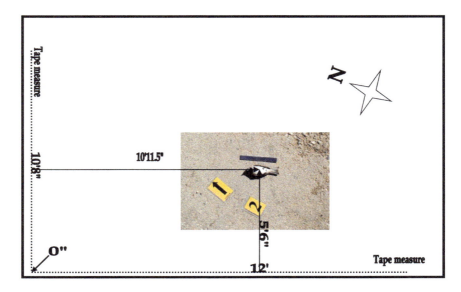

Figure 6.12 The rectangular method.

Crime Scene Procedure & Protocol Considerations   69

Whenever possible, I import (cut & paste) photographs from the crime scene directly onto my finished diagrams. This is an extremely helpful tip for those of us who cannot draw.

The triangular measurement or triangulation method can be used for items of evidence that have a distinctive shape and for items that do not have a distinctive shape but are found in an area that has a defined shape and fixed points. This is likely the most accurate measurement of the three methods listed. Items with a distinctive shape will have at least two three-point (triangle) measurements, although three would be preferred. Items without a distinctive shape will have at least one (triangle) measurement to the center mass of the object. Just as with the rectangular method, you must first determine the fixed points and stretch your tape measures so that they meet in the corner with both starting at 0 inches, then take three-point measurements back to the object (Fig. 6.13).

Again, for items that do not have a distinct shape, you need only one three-point measurement to the center of the object.

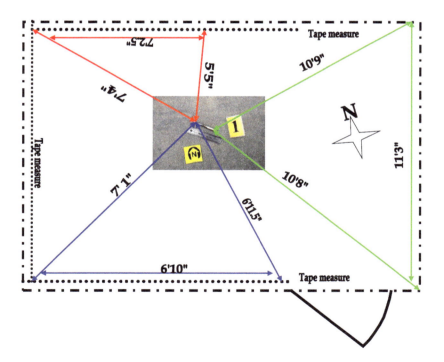

Figure 6.13 The triangulation method.

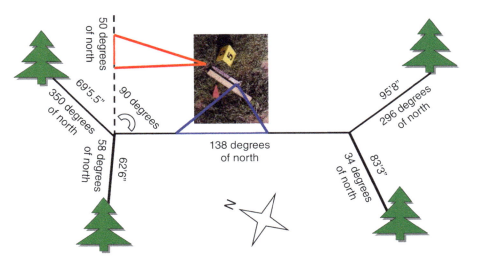

Figure 6.14 The triangulation on a baseline method.

There may be occasions where the fixed points for your crime scene are too far away to be useful for establishing a baseline or have a distinct boundary for either the rectangular or triangulation methods, you may have to combine the baseline and triangulation methods as illustrated below (Fig. 6.14). You'll need a very long tape measure and a compass.

Anyone who has been in as many full-fledged riots as I have will know well that it is the most exhilarating, yet terrifying experience combined. Especially those that occur on a large exercise yard where the potential exists for hundreds of combatants and dozens of incapacitated victims. Of course, the primary responsibility of staff is to contain the riot, control the riot and restore the peace to the facility; and of course, to put out the fires. In the aftermath, the correctional crime scene technician will likely find themselves using the grid-pattern sketch method. To use this method, the crime scene investigator will select a fixed point (corner of a building, edge of the yard, fire hydrant, etc.) and start laying out a workable grid pattern using pegs and string until the entire crime scene has been laid out. Each grid should be measured and marked accordingly. Every effort should be made to keep items of evidence within the grid; this prevents confusion later in testimony and reconstruction. Measurements can then be made either using the rectangular or triangulation method within each grid (Fig. 6.15).

Crime Scene Procedure & Protocol Considerations 71

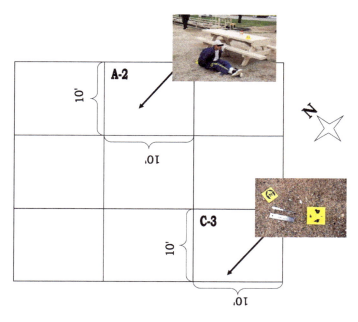

Figure 6.15 The grid method.

Sketching Forms

Forms may be used to assist the investigator with recording measurements and for a rough-draft sketch, such as the baseline form as depicted in Fig. 6.16. This report should be attached to the final report as an investigative note-taking aid.

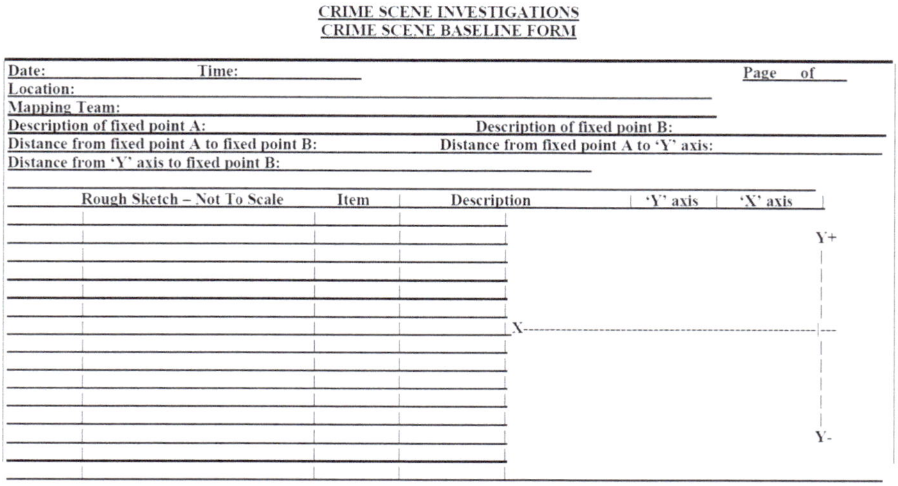

Figure 6.16 Crime scene baseline form

Datum

Having attempted to reconstruct a shooting scene with the notes taken by patrol officers who processed the scene, let me say that you have to be very specific about how you document those fixed points or datum that you used to begin and end your measurements. Your report cannot simply say, "the shell casing was 50 feet from the north-west curb." The north-west curb happens to be very long; begging the question: From where on the north-west curb did you take your measurement? Had the officers measured from one end of the curb to the datum, or fixed point, then from the other end of the curb to the datum, and provided a compass direction to the item of evidence, I could have recreated the scene with ease. So, whatever point you decide to use as the datum must have a measurable fixed point that can be recreated by anyone returning to the scene with your measurements. Many of us carry smart cellular telephones these days. Even an old prison investigator like me who remembers the days of having to have a pocket full of quarters to use at a convenient pay phone that might be near the scene (ok, it was a pocket full of dimes) now carries the latest iPhone. But the reason I do carry that phone is because of its compass. Call me pedantic, but I have noticed that no two cellular telephones will agree on a true north direction. That is why I actually carry three compasses on my person: one on my cellular telephone, one on my watch, and a very nice lensatic compass in my equipment bag.

If you are going to place your cellular telephone in a crime scene, be sure, however, that you carry with you sterilized rectangular butcher paper cut-outs to put underneath your phone so that you can place it in the crime scene without fear of contaminating either the scene or your phone. Carry enough of them so that you are placing a clean sheet down each time you move your phone. And, please, remember to sterilize your phone before you take that next call.

I cannot stress just how important it is to include the compass heading for your measurements. If a crime scene reconstructionist must return to the scene and recreate your work, it is impossible for them to accurately reprise your measurements unless you inform them of the exact position of your datum and the direction they must travel with the baseline and triangulation measurements.

The Rough Sketch

I will be the first to admit that I am not an artist. I can manage something just marginally better than a stick figure. This fact does not excuse me from trying to create at least a rudimentary sketch of the scene. These rough sketches can be extremely useful when writing reports and for creating the final sketches that will be submitted for courtroom proceedings. I find them especially helpful in shooting scenes where multiple shell casings remain in the scene. Oftentimes, it is difficult to appreciate the relationship of the shell casings to the other objects in the scene if you are reliant only on the photographs taken of the scene. Photographs are not good at depicting the distance between evidence items. A sketch, especially a bird's eye view sketch, with proper measurements is far more useful. It is, however, imperative that the investigator retains the rough sketch with their field notes as they are discoverable evidence. I scan my field notes and rough sketches into PDF files and save them in electronic form.

I am reminded of a story told to me by a Southern California police officer who in his rookie days responded to a missing child call at a small strip mall. While waiting for a detective to arrive on the scene, the officer decided to sketch the parking lot of the mall, including all the parked vehicle information. Later when the case was determined to be a homicide, it was his rudimentary sketch, that included a white van belonging to a known pedophile that had departed the scene shortly before the arrival of additional officers and detectives, which produced the lead that allowed the detectives to recover the forensic evidence needed to convict the offender. It is the little efforts that we consider to be inconsequential that oftentimes produce the best results.

Gassing Incident Crime Scene Suggested Protocols

California Penal Code Section 4501.1(a): Any person confined in the state prison who commits a battery by gassing upon the person of any peace officer, as defined in Chapter 4.5 (commencing with Section 830) of Title 3 of Part 2, or employee of the state prison is guilty of aggravated battery and shall be punished by imprisonment in a county jail or by imprisonment in a state prison for two, three or four years.

4501(b): For the purpose of this section, "gassing" means intentionally placing or throwing, or causing to be placed or thrown, upon the person of another, *any human excrement or other bodily fluids or bodily substances or any mixture containing human excrement or other bodily fluids or bodily substances that result in actual contact with the person's skin or membranes.*

In an effort to preserve sufficient evidence for incidents involving the "gassing" of employees, the following steps must be followed:

Collection

- All items of evidence directly associated with the throwing of human excrement or other bodily fluid must be collected. Therefore, it is imperative that the *cup, bowl, or receptacle* used by the inmate to propel the substance must be collected and processed into evidence.

- Any excrement or bodily fluid that may have missed the victim yet remains on the floor, ceiling, wall, cell door, or bars must be swabbed in the manner outlined in this book and processed into evidence.
- Any excrement or bodily fluid that resulted in actual contact with the person's skin should be swabbed in the manner below outlined and processed into evidence.
- That item of uniform belonging to the victim that was struck by the excrement or bodily fluid must be processed into evidence in the manner below outlined.

Swabbing

The "gassing" incident evidence collection kit contains packets of sterile swabs, sterile water ampoules, swab preservation collars, evidence tape, and evidence envelopes to be used to swab areas of evidence struck by human excrement or other bodily fluids.

1. Don latex gloves (double-gloved if possible).
2. Tear open the sterile packet at the very end and remove both swabs being careful not to touch either the cotton ends or anything with the cotton ends. Retain the empty packet.
3. Remove one sterile water ampoule and break off the tip being careful not to touch anything with the exposed tip.*
4. Grasp both swabs in your hand so that the tips are of an equal length.
5. Drop the water onto the swab tips. Never touch the swabs with the ampoule.
6. Swab the specimen covering as much of the cotton tip as possible.
7. Slide the protective collars from the ends of the sticks up to the cotton tip, avoiding touching the inside portion of the collar with any unprotected part of your hand.
8. Break off a small portion of the bottom of the stick part of the swab and return both swabs to the same sterile packet.
9. Utilize a forensic swab-drying cabinet, when possible, to prevent degradation of the sample by bacteria.
10. Fold over the end of the packet and tape the packet shut with evidence tape and place the packet into a paper evidence envelope (one packet per evidence envelope).
11. Label as necessary and process the items into evidence.

* If the specimen being collected is of a sufficient liquid content or is moist enough not to require pre-saturation of the cotton tip with sterile water, you may skip this step.

Crime Scene Procedure & Protocol Considerations   75

Skin contact

When possible, if human excrement or other bodily fluids are discovered on the skin of the employee, collection of that specimen would greatly enhance the likelihood of successful courtroom proceedings. Therefore, every effort should be made to collect the fluids using a sterile gauze pad and gloved hands. Once the specimen has been sufficiently collected, the gauze pad should be returned to the sterile envelope from which it was removed and processed into evidence following the above-outlined procedures.

My facility did not require officers to place their initials on items of evidence, especially garments that may be tested for DNA evidence. Placing initials on the garment may either contaminate the sample or provide a contamination challenge in court. Instead, garments that are of *evidentiary importance to a criminal investigation* should be processed in the following manner:

- Lay the garment out flat on a clean sheet of butcher paper (shiny side up).
- Be sure to use sufficient sheets of butcher paper to cover the entire garment.
- Find a suitable place to affix with string a completed evidence (toe) tag (such as the buttonhole of the shirt sleeve, belt loop of a pair of pants, etc.).
- Place a sheet of butcher paper on top of the garment (shiny side down).
- Fold the paper in a manner that ensures that the garment is being folded into paper and not onto itself.
- Fold the butcher paper small enough to fit into an evidence bag.
- Seal the seams with evidence tape.
- Print and sign your name, with the date along with the suspect information and date on one side of the outside of the folded butcher paper and affix a chain of custody sticker to the other side.
- If it is necessary to instruct the forensic analyst where it is necessary to look for the specimen on the garment (i.e., collar, pocket, sleeve, etc.), do not mark the garment itself. Instead, draw a picture of the garment on the outside of the folded package and mark on the picture the area where the analyst should inspect.

Gassing evidence kits should be prepared and made available and easily accessible in every housing unit, medical infirmary, Office of the Watch, and Control booths. The kits should contain the following items:

Gassing Incident Evidence Collection Kit Inventory

10 – Sterile cotton swabs
2 – Sterile gauze sponges
3 – Small evidence vials
2 – Large evidence vials
4 – Applicator shields (collars)
2 – Hazmat bags
2 – Evidence envelopes
2 – Med. Evidence bags
2 pr. – Large latex gloves
Misc. - Tongue depressors
Misc. – Evidence tape strips

In the county in which my facility is located, the District Attorney will not prosecute a gassing event unless there is sufficient physical evidence and/or competent eyewitness testimony. In one incident that was not prosecuted, two officers removed an inmate from his cell and escorted him in restraints to a secure shower stall. There were no other inmates out of their cells at the time and the inmate was the only one being escorted to the shower stall, which was not in an area surrounded by other celled inmates. The escorting officers placed the inmate in the shower and closed the grill gate. One of the officers instructed the inmate to place his handcuffed hands through the port in order to remove them. As the inmate placed his hands through the port, he drew a large mouth full of spit. The officers, expecting a gassing, both turned their faces away from the inmate. The inmate spat on the officer who was closest to him, striking him on the neck. The officer immediately ran to the sink and washed off the inmate's saliva. The inmate was removed from the shower and re-housed in his cell. The officers submitted their reports, which were forwarded to the District Attorney's Office. As I said, the District Attorney declined prosecution noting that neither officer actually saw the spittle leave the inmate's mouth. Even though the subsequent investigation reflected the absence of other inmates, the trajectory of the spittle and the sworn testimony of the officers, the one thing that was missing was the actual spittle. Had the officer had the wherewithal to collect the saliva with a sterile gauze sponge, prosecution would have been assured.

Sexual Assault Investigation Protocols

Although not as common as Hollywood would have us believe, sexual assaults do occur in the custodial setting, with inmates and staff alike being the victims. In the early years of the 21st century, incidents of prison rape received the attention of the United States Congress when it passed the Prison Rape Elimination Act. According to the National PREA

Resource Center, "The Prison Rape Elimination Act (PREA) was passed in 2003 with unanimous support from both parties in Congress. The purpose of the act was to 'provide for the analysis of the incidence and effects of prison rape in Federal, State, and local institutions and to provide information, resources, recommendations, and funding to protect individuals from prison rape'" (prearesourcecenter.org, 2016). It, therefore, goes without saying that sexual assault in prison or jail is a serious matter that merits serious investigation.

Most states, including California, have laws or regulations that prohibit the inmate population from having consensual sexual acts between either themselves or with employees, volunteers, vendors, or contractors. Thus, even consensual sexual acts may need to be investigated as a sexual assault, following the same protocols and procedures.

The State of California has complicated this issue by passing Assembly Bill 999 (AB999) in 2014. In an effort to reduce sexually transmitted diseases, AB999 mandates the California Department of Corrections & Rehabilitation to make condoms available to the inmate population. Although the department is not predicting an increase in sexual assaults owing to the availability of condoms, the potential for such acts exists.

Also complicating the issue is the likelihood that an inmate victim may not report a sexual assault for days, if not weeks, following the event. Suspects might also force their inmate victims to wash themselves in the cell sink (bird bathing) or tier shower or to destroy potential evidence by flushing biologically soiled items down the cell toilet.

Inmates who are caught *in flagrante delicto* in a cell might require the application of extraction removal techniques that may also complicate the investigation or contaminate the scene.

Inmates engaged in sexual encounters or assaults who are discovered by custodial staff must be immediately separated and isolated. The victim of a sexual assault must be treated with empathy and compassion. The victim should be instructed to disrobe while standing on top of clean butcher paper. Each item of clothing should be gently placed on top of another clean sheet of paper and folded in the manner prescribed in this book. It is essential not to shake the clothing before placing the item on the paper. Once folded and tape sealed, all items of clothing should be processed into evidence. Clothing that contains biological evidence should be placed in a forensic freezer for long-term storage. Clothing that contains trace or transfer evidence should be placed in temperature-controlled long-term storage. Once disrobed, the victim should be provided with clean clothing. The butcher paper upon which the inmate was standing should be carefully folded and processed as evidence. Personnel who are participating in the collection and processing of this evidence must wear protective equipment to include a Tyvek suit, latex gloves, N-95 mask, protective eye wear, and head covering.

Observable injuries should be documented and photographed. Fingernail scrapings and clippings should be collected, as well as pubic hair combings. The victim should be examined by medical personnel who are specifically trained in sexual assault examinations.

Sexual assault victim evidence kits should contain at least the following:

- Instructions and protocols
- Evidence collection envelopes and bags
- Swabs for collecting specimen from the lips, cheeks, thighs, vagina, anus, and buttocks
- Blood collection tubes
- A comb used to collect hair and fiber from the victim's body
- Clear glass slides
- Nail pick for scraping debris from beneath the fingernails
- Nail clippers for collecting fingernail samples
- Documentation forms
- Labels
- Evidence tape and seals

The above listed protocols should be followed with regards to the suspect of a sexual assault, being certain to label the sexual assault evidence kit as having been collected from the suspect.

It is important to note that information obtained by a medical professional or covered entity regarding sexual assaults may be disclosed to law enforcement under the Privacy Rule of the Health Insurance Portability and Accountability Act of 1996, under Section A, 5 - Reporting to Law Enforcement.

If the sexual assault occurred within a cell or confined space, it is essential that the area is secured until it can be examined by a crime scene investigator. The investigator should document the area using notes and photography before conducting their examination. The investigator should don appropriate protective equipment before entering the scene. Once in the scene, the investigator should make visual observations of the area looking for biological, or trace and transfer evidence. Signs of a struggle should be noted and documented. The investigator should examine the scene using an alternate light source (ALS), with the appropriate barrier filter, and with the use of a magnifying glass. The preferred frequency for biological evidence examination with the ALS is 445–470 nm with an orange or yellow barrier filter. Biological evidence on fixed objects should be documented and swabbed. Bedding should either be carefully placed on clean butcher paper and collected into evidence as prescribed or vacuumed using the Evi-Vac system before being collected. Used condoms should be collected using extreme

Crime Scene Procedure & Protocol Considerations

protective precautions. Pick up the condom using a pair of sterile tweezers. Place the condom on clean butcher paper. Loosely fold the paper around the condom and place it in a paper evidence bag. The condom should be placed in a forensic drying cabinet atop the original paper wrapping. Once dry, the condom and wrapping should be placed in a forensic freezer for long-term storage. Clothing, towels, and sheets collected from the scene should be placed in a temperature-controlled evidence locker for long-term storage. Biological stained items or specimen, and the sexual assault evidence collection kits should be placed in a forensic freezer for long-term storage.

Protocols and procedures are required for every aspect of crime scene processing and the subsequent forensic analysis of the evidence collected from the scene. This chapter provided recommendations for only some of these aspects. It is my hope that sufficient information in subsequent chapters will provide the necessary information to assist your agency with drafting these guidelines.

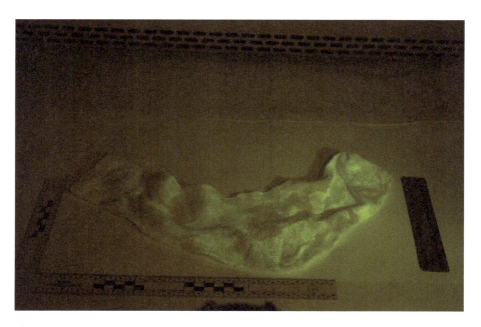

Figure 6.17 A semen-stained sock examined using ALS at 450nm w/yellow barrier filter.

The Role of the Custodial CSI in Escapes, Use of Force, and Shooting Incidents

The Role of CSI During Escapes

There is no word that will make any custodial official cringe more than the word "escape." Just the mere suggestion of the word will send jail and prison officials into an orchestrated disturbance control plan that includes an immediate lockdown of the facility, emergency count of the inmate population, accountability of staff, and deputies and correctional officers scrambling to find places where the perimeter of the facility may have been breached or compromised. In the event that an inmate has managed to free themselves from confinement and evade detection, the primary attention of the custodial officials, other than ensuring no other escapes occur, is to put as many available personnel as possible into the community to recover the offender. Oftentimes, those who are entrusted with the investigation of crimes in jail or prison are among the first to be dispatched to apprehend the fugitive. Sadly, the need to preserve evidence for the subsequent prosecution of the criminal offense of escaping is commonly overlooked (Fig. 7.1).

It is essential that a crime scene investigation team be immediately dispatched to the area of the prison where the escape occurred to collect evidence that establishes the criminal charge of escape, either successful or attempted. Blood evidence should be detected, documented, and collected. Tools and escape paraphernalia, such as inmate-manufactured rope or cutting devices, should be collected and processed into evidence.

Cut sections of the fence should be collected into evidence as well to be compared microscopically with the tools that may have been used to cut them. Escape routes from areas of confinement to areas of escape should be detected and documented. Footwear impressions should be detected, documented, and collected. The cell or bunk area of the escapee should be searched for evidence. Correspondence or miscellaneous paperwork that would be useful in determining the direction of travel, accomplices, and motive should be reviewed and collected into evidence. Recorded telephone conversations should be processed into evidence. Outgoing and incoming mail should be scrutinized. Cellmates and inmates associated with the escapee should be interviewed, and their cells and property searched for

Custodial CSI in Escapes, Use of Force, and Shooting Incidents 81

Figure 7.1 The would-be escapee's sock stuck in the razor wire.

clues pertinent to the intentions of the escapee. The scourge of the contraband cellular telephone that has manifested itself in all jails and prisons is the greatest risk to the safety and security of the public and the institution. Should it be determined that the escapee is in possession of a contraband cellular telephone, it is critical for the investigator to establish contact with the service provider as quickly as possible to establish a ping order and to deliver an order to preserve records and to subpoena billing records and call-detail information.

Quite recently, the facility where I worked had three attempted escapes from the Minimum Support Facility in as many years. To date, the score remains fence = 3, inmates = 0. However, in all three attempts, a sufficient quantity of blood was left on the fence and razor wire. In the last attempt, blood was detected on the inside perimeter between the dormitory and fence line, on the fence and razor wire, and on the outside of the fence line. As blood was detected on the outside of the fence line, facility staff were convinced that an inmate had successfully escaped, and their efforts were directed toward a search of the outer perimeter of the facility. However, when I arrived on the scene, I quickly determined that the blood on the outside of the fence line was, in fact, cast-off from a blood-letting event at the top of the fence. I also noted the blood transfer impression of a hand on the exterior of a dormitory window.

It was clear to me that the blood-letting event occurred as a result of the inmate making contact with the razor wire and not before; it was then transferred to the window when the inmate returned to his assigned housing. I therefore recommended that dormitory staff should strip search all inmates in the dormitory. The potential escapee was promptly found, with his thumb nearly severed and his arm suffering from several, deep incised cuts. I mention this incident because even though the culprit was detected quite quickly, the attempted escape was still fully processed as if he had actually managed to get over the razor wire, a task easier said than done. The scene was documented, photographed, sketched, diagrammed, measured, bloodstains documented, and swabbed, along with all the aforementioned searches and recoveries. As a side note, razor wire is quite effective when not firmly affixed to the fence line. Our maintenance department personnel are experts at stringing razor wire, leaving it supported only by several strands of barbed wire (as seen in the above photograph). As the escapee attempts to pull their body weight over the wire, it collapses sufficiently to flail back and forth, thus delivering a savage assault on its victim. The recipient of the thrashing depicted in the photograph was so badly injured that upon inspection, one would have sworn he had been shot multiple times by the alert tower officer who detected the attempted breach of the wire, which was not the case.

The Role of CSI in Use-of-Force Incidents

It is of late that there is a persistent need by custodial officials to defend themselves against the allegations of the excessive or unnecessary use of force. Therefore, it is essential for all use-of-force incidents, outside of routine handcuffing, to be treated as if a charge of criminal use of force will be levied. Failure to do so would subject innocent personnel to undue scrutiny and burden prison or jail administrators with the task of defending themselves against cries of corruption. It is imperative that sergeants and lieutenants supervising the use-of-force incident must err on the side of caution and request the assistance of crime scene investigators to process the scene. Inmate injuries, or the lack of injuries, should be documented and photographed as outlined in earlier chapters. Batons, pepper spray canisters, or departmentally issued firearms should be examined, documented, photographed, and processed into evidence. Staff injuries must also be documented and photographed in the manner earlier prescribed. Furthermore, if staff were grabbed or grappled by an inmate, the area of contact should be swabbed for touch DNA evidence. Video surveillance of the incident, if available, should be preserved and placed into evidence.

I processed a crime scene for a local law enforcement agency, through mutual aid, resulting from an assault on police officers requiring the

Custodial CSI in Escapes, Use of Force, and Shooting Incidents

Figure 7.2 Infrared imaging of a dark blue uniform shirt.

application of force on a 17-year-old offender. During the confrontation, one supervisor and two officers were badly injured; the supervisor having been stabbed several times. The juvenile offender had also stabbed and beaten his elderly grandparents. While processing the scene, I collected the supervisor's shirt and vest as evidence. Later, I conducted a forensic examination of the dark blue uniform shirt. In order to enhance the visualization of the bloodstains and stab defects in the material, I decided to utilize the infrared imaging forensic camera. While imaging the garment, I noted what appeared to be sweat or saliva transfer, potentially from the offender, on the dark shoulder patches (Fig. 7.2). This evidence would support the statements of the officers that the supervisor was grappling in close quarters with the offender.

I mention this incident to point out that although it is imperative to collect suspect and victim clothing, it is also equally important to conduct a forensic examination of the garments for evidence that is often times latent in nature.

The Role of CSI in Shooting Incidents

The one advantage we have in the custodial setting over those working crime scene investigations in the general public is that when there is a shooting, we usually know who fired the shot and from where it was fired.

Although it is not a common occurrence in jails or prisons, shooting incidents do occur and the crime scene investigator needs to be prepared to process them.

Warning Shot Incidents

Warning shots are perhaps the most common shooting incident likely encountered by the correctional crime scene investigator and, although no one was actually shot, it is an incident that still merits investigation. The crime scene investigator must determine the approximate position of the officer who fired the shot and document their view using perspective photography. The trajectory to the impact site, as well as the distance, should also be documented. The shell casing should be recovered and processed into evidence. If possible, the bullets should also be recovered. It is not necessary to process the firearm into evidence following a warning shot incident.

Less-Lethal Shooting Incidents Within the Secured Perimeter

It is important that all use of force involving weapons that deliver a bullet or projectile, whether lethal or less lethal, be documented regardless of the amount of injury sustained by the shooting victim. The 40 mm eXact iMpact and block projectiles have been an absolute godsend to the correctional industry. They deliver one or multiple projectiles fired accurately to quell disturbances effectively without causing the loss of life. The injuries sustained tend to be painful reminders of the incident, but completely survivable. Unfortunately, as crime scene investigators, we tend not to fully document these applications of force, the result being that the ever-litigious inmate population, taking advantage of our lack of interest, file lawsuits alleging unnecessary or excessive use of force. By failing to fully document the occurrence, we are leaving our officers at an unfair advantage in defending themselves in courtroom proceedings. Therefore, it is vital either for due diligence or to protect our officers for the proper use of force to document these incidents as if they were deadly uses of force.

Deadly Force Shooting Incidents Within the Secured Perimeter

In the event a deadly or lethal force shooting occurs, the crime scene investigator will follow procedures similar to those in the general public. The crime scene investigator will determine the approximate position of the officer and document their view using perspective photography. Trajectory analysis should be conducted, if possible, stringing the trajectory from the determined position of the firearm to the impact position on the victim. It is important to remember to determine the trajectory of the bullet, and not to the final position of the victim, but to the estimated position of the victim at the time the shot was fired. Tripods positioned at the shooter's position and that of the victim will assist the investigator in determining the horizontal and vertical angles of impact, as well as the use of zero-edge protractors, angle-finders, levels, and plumb-bobs. Generally, the use of lasers in the custodial setting is not as effective as the age-old stringing method, as distance, outdoor conditions, and elevation make it difficult to document the path of the laser. Bloodstains at the scene, especially those projected in nature, may assist the investigator in determining the direction of travel of the bullet.

The correct terminology for an impact site of a bullet is either bullet hole or bullet defect. It is important to remember that a bullet that passes through an object leaves a defect that is considered to be perforated in nature. A bullet that enters an object but remains within the object or embedded within the last material impacted is considered to be penetrated in nature. Therefore, if the bullet passes completely through the victim, thus exhibiting an entrance and exit defect, it is important to make every effort to find and recover the bullet. Trajectory rods are only useful if a bullet has left a sufficient guide by which the rods can determine the angle of impact. Thus, if a bullet perforated a low wall, leaving an entrance and exit defect, or two points of verifiable reference, or left a significant crater in the ground, the trajectory rod will accurately provide vertical and horizontal angles of impact. As a caveat, every semester I warn my students at the college to let the trajectory rod tell them the direction of travel. Under no circumstance should the investigator force the trajectory rod in the direction from where they think the bullet has come. The recovered bullet must be processed into evidence, with every effort made to prevent contamination, bearing in mind the potential for transfer evidence. The fired shell casing should also be documented and collected into evidence. The scene must be documented as prescribed in this text. The firearm should be rendered safe and placed into evidence following established protocols. The clothing of the victim should be collected into evidence and processed in a manner to preserve bloodstained evidence.

Generally, when lethal force is used in the custodial setting, it is a matter of last resort and dire need. The consequences are as profoundly felt as in any officer-involved shooting. Therefore, it is imperative that the crime scene investigator consider the protocols established for officer-involved shooting incidents and consult with the appropriate governing entity, prosecutor's office, or similar entity, regarding the need for a fair and unbiased investigation provided by an outside investigative effort before proceeding. The same should apply for shootings that occur involving custodial staff outside of the secured perimeter. However, one must remember that the need to preserve perishable evidence outweighs the need for an impartial agent to be dispatched for evidence processing. Therefore, it is important to preserve or collect fleeting or perishable evidence immediately and then maintain the scene until such time as assistance can arrive. More information regarding shooting incident investigations follows in this chapter.

Shooting Scene Investigations

Although rare, shootings do happen at jails and prisons, usually from elevated positions such as towers, walls, or gunner's boxes. Gone are the days, we hope, of the movies of Edgar G. Robinson and Jimmy Cagney where a "guard" leans over an elevated rail above a dining hall full of rambunctious "convicts" and empties a full drum of .45ACP from a Thompson Model 1927A1; however, even a single shot from a Ruger Mini14 in .223 caliber requires the attention of a knowledgeable crime scene investigator. Interestingly, aside from the brief mention of shooting reconstruction during basic crime scene investigation training, little effort is given to providing the crime scene investigator in the correctional setting with proper shooting scene processing, analysis, and reconstruction training. This is an oversight that must be corrected because of the high potential for shooting incidents to occur not only within the secured perimeters of the facilities but also during transportation, escape details, hospital guarding, and the odd incidents of armed persons on jail or prison grounds. Regrettably, I cannot teach everything that is needed to process a shooting scene in this one chapter. I do recommend Edward Hueske's *Practical Analysis and Reconstruction of Shooting Incidents*, 2nd edition, CRC Press as an excellent supplement to hands-on training courses. I will, however, give the reader some useful information that will assist you with your report writing, starting with the terminology of shooting incident investigations preferred by Mr. Hueske.

Terminology

Angle of deflection: The angle between the muzzle of a firearm at discharge to the target impact
Angle-finder: A device used by crime scene investigator to determine the vertical angle of impact of a bullet
Angle of ricochet: The angle of the altered path of a bullet or shot pellet from an impacted surface

Ballistics: The forensic study of bullets or other projectiles in flight

Battery: The condition of a weapon when it is ready to fire

Bolt action: A firearm with a breech that is in line with the bore and requires manual manipulation to load, cock, fire (typically the release of a firing pin), and extract a cartridge and cartridge case

Bore: The internal aspect of a barrel beyond the chamber

Breech: The opening in a firearm where cartridges are loaded into the chamber

Bullet: The projectile component of a cartridge

Bullet core: The mass of a bullet beneath the jacket (if present)

Bullet defect: A suitable term for a bullet or pellet hole

Bullet jacket: The metallic outer skin of a bullet

Bullet wipe: A combination of grease and soot surrounding the margins of a bullet defect caused by the progression of a bullet

Caliber: The cross-sectional diameter of the interior of a barrel from land to land. This is also the cross-sectional diameter of a bullet

Cartridge: The complete components of a round of ammunition including a cartridge casing, primer, propellant, and bullet. A cartridge should never be defined as a "bullet" in your report

Cartridge case: The metal or paper container that holds the propellant, bullet, and primer

Center fire cartridges: A cartridge that has a primer pocket in the center of the headstamp where a primer is seated

Chamber: The cavity attached to the barrel that is constructed to fit a particular cartridge, into which is loaded in order for it to be fired. Revolvers will have multiple chambers

Chamber marks: The transferred striations, impressions, or indentations on a cartridge casing from the imperfections within the chamber walls. These marks are significant for individual characteristics

Clip: A device used to load ammunition into a magazine

Close contact shot: A shot fired with the muzzle of the firearm pressed against a target

Concentric fractures: Circular fractures of glass radiating outward from a bullet impact

Conchoidal fractures: Fracture lines that are visible in a broken glass when viewed from the side that allows for the determination of the direction of the applied force

Cylinder gap deposit: The deposition of soot on surfaces of a firearm where a gap exists between the cylinder and the barrel. This is most commonly associated with revolvers

Dithiooxamide test: A presumptive test for the presence of copper using Dithiooxamide (DTO) as a reagent

Double action: A firearm with a trigger mechanism that cocks and releases the hammer without the need for manual cocking

Double-barrel: A shotgun with barrels arranged side-by-side or over-under

Ejection: The removal, whether manual or automatic, of the fired cartridge casing from the breech to facilitate a reload

Ejection pattern: A clustering of ejected fired cartridge cases that may assist in determining the direction a firearm was discharged from a given position

Ejector marks: Small marks left on the soft metal of a cartridge case or shotshell as it is being ejected from the breech

Exterior ballistics: The forensic discipline associated with bullets upon leaving the barrel of a fired firearm

Firing pin: The mechanism that strikes a primer and causes a discharge of the cartridge

Firing pin impression: The three-dimensional impression left on the primer by the firing pin

Flash suppressor: A device attached to the muzzle of a firearm to reduce flash upon firing

Forcing cone: A transition between the chamber and the barrel that aligns the bore with the chamber

Function testing: The process of testing a firearm to determine operability

Gas operated: A firearm that utilizes gas from the discharge of a cartridge to cycle additional cartridges into the breech and chamber

Gauge: In a shotgun, the gauge is the number of pellets or shot by size that equal to one pound

Grooves: The helical grooves in the interior of the barrel that prove stabilizing spin on a fired bullet

Gunshot residue: Residue associated with the primer and propellant upon firing

Hammer: The mechanism that delivers energy to the firing pin

Handgun: Any weapon that is designed to be held by hand without support

Internal ballistics: The forensic science that deals with the firearm prior to the bullet exiting the barrel

Intermediate range: A shot fired when the muzzle of the weapon is held away from the body at the time of discharge yet is sufficiently close to cause powder "tattooing" and stippling

Keyholing: A bullet impact that resembles a keyhole the result of a bullet that tumbles or wobbles in flight

Laminated glass: Glass made by the process of layering glass with layers of resin

Lateral angle of deflection: The deflection of a bullet to the right or the left from its original trajectory as the result of a ricochet

Lever action: A firearm that uses a lever to open, close, or cycle cartridges into the breech

Line of sight: The imaginary line from the sights of a firearm to a target

Long gun: A firearm designed to be supported by the shoulder

Magazine: The internal or detachable box that contains a supply of ammunition that is fed into the chamber of a firearm

Magazine follower: A ramp-like device that cartridges rest upon and that allow the cartridges to be raised by a spring to be fed into the chamber

Magazine safety: A mechanism that prevents a firearm from discharging without the presence of a magazine

Muzzle: The open end of the barrel

Muzzle blast: The explosive shockwave at the muzzle as the result of combustion of propellants after discharge

Muzzle imprint: An abrasion in the skin resembling the muzzle of a firearm following a close or near contact shot

Muzzle velocity: The speed of a bullet at the moment of exiting the barrel

Near contact shot: A shot fired from a firearm where the muzzle of the firearm is not firmly pressed against the target, but exhibits a small gap between the muzzle and the target

Pellet: small round shot used in shotgun shells

Penetration: A bullet that enters a target, but remains within the last substrate it impacted

Perforation: A bullet that remains within the last substrate it impacts

Pinch-point: The first impact point of a ricochet

Powder stippling: Powder particles resulting from the discharge of a cartridge that impact the skin, causing small abrasions that are imbedded into the skin (also known as tattooing)

Primer: A cup containing a shock-sensitive propellant containing lead, antimony, and barium, that is seated in the base of a cartridge when struck produces the ignition process of the cartridge propellant

Propellant: The combustible unit of a cartridge or shotgun shell

Radial fracture: Fracture lines in glass that radiate outward from a bullet impact site

Revolver: A firearm that uses a rotating cylinder to hold and fire cartridges

Ricochet: A bullet that has altered its original trajectory by skipping, bouncing, or deflecting off of a surface but maintains its integrity

Ricochet crease: An indentation or furrow in a surface caused by a bullet striking a surface but being deflected without penetration of perforation
Rifling: Spiral grooves cut into the interior of a barrel consisting of lands and grooves that provide spin for the bullet as it travels the length of the barrel
Rifling twist: The direction of the rotation of rifling (right or left) in which the grooves are cut
Safety glass: Invented in 1903 by French scientist Edouard Benedictus, safety glass uses layers of transparent coatings to prevent glass from shattering into shards with sharp edges
Semi-automatic: A firearm that automatically fires, ejects, and loads cartridges in its chamber after every shot fired and with each pulling of a trigger
Shell casing: A suitable term for a cartridge casing
Shot accountability: The determination of the known number of cartridges available in a shooting incident and the potential for bullet strikes (necessary in officer-involved shootings)
Shotgun shell: A rimmed, cylindrical (straight-walled) cartridge used in shotguns
Slug: A single projectile loaded into a shotgun shell
Sodium rhodizonate: A presumptive test used to detect the lead compound in gunshot residue
Soot: A carbon-based residue resulting from the combustion of a propellant
Spin stabilization: The left or right rotation of a bullet produced by the rifling in a barrel of a firearm
Tempered glass: A type of safety glass produced by controlled thermal or chemical treatments to increase its strength and is commonly used in vehicles
Trajectory: The flight path of a bullet or shot after leaving the barrel
Trajectory rod: A plastic, metal, wood, or fiberglass rod inserted into a bullet defect presenting two points of reference and used to determine the vertical and horizontal angles of impact
Zero-edge protractor: A protractor with a flat edge that crime scene investigators use to determine the horizontal, and vertical, angle of impact
Zone of possibility: In shooting scene reconstruction, the zone of possibility is the determination of the likely position of a shooter or shooters based on bullet defect analysis, trajectory analysis, shell casing ejection pattern analysis, and the understanding a firearm may not be in a fixed position

Calculation of the Distance and Angle of Impact from Elevated Positions

Math and I are not friends in any way; however, since most jails and prisons have policies for the minimum and maximum distances officers can shoot the various weapons at their discretion, it is very important that distance and angle of impact are determined as best as possible following the discharge of a firearm, and it might take a bit of trigonometry and geometry. I will say there is always a challenge in determining the actual distance and angle of impact simply because movement is always involved. Rare are the cases when a tower officer discharges their firearm and then remains in the exact position they were in when they fired the shot. Also, jails and prisons tend to select long guns that are incredibly accurate, but fire bullets that are very small and tend to fragment upon striking anything hard, making it hard to find the bullet impact site. Unless you are fortunate enough to have an officer fire through a gun port that might give you something resembling a fixed position, just keep in mind that your efforts will be approximations at best. Also, remember to take your measurements from where the muzzle of the firearm was at the time of discharge, and not just the position where the officer was standing.

Warning shots fired into soft dirt or grass must also be documented, if only for the sake of the officer who fired the shot to determine they fired within the guidelines of departmental policy. It is generally easy to determine the trajectory and distance provided the impact site of the bullet can be located. Once located, however, a trajectory rod can be placed within the shot cavity and will easily point the investigator in the direction from whence the shot was fired. After that, it is just a matter of stringing the trajectory back to the position where the officer likely fired, collecting the vertical and horizontal angle of impact data using an angel-finder and zero-edge protractor and measuring the length of the string. In some cases, this is possible in lethal and non-lethal use of force when the impact site is on soft ground, provided there was not a significant deflection of the bullet once it encountered its target.

An angle finder (Fig. 7.3) is a device that provides the ability to determine the vertical rise or fall of a trajectory. It is best used by placing it onto a trajectory rod and recording the needle reading. There are many angle finders on the market and my shooting reconstruction kit has at least three of various manufacturers including the one depicted below.

Vertical trajectory should always be documented as upward (down to up) or downward (up to down) with the angle measured plus or minus of a flat trajectory.

Figure 7.3 Angle finder.

The zero-edge protractor (Fig. 7.4) is used to determine the horizontal angle of impact, that is, from left or right on a horizontal plane.

For those of you who are not keen on measuring 45′ of string, you can use a fiberglass measuring tape or laser tape measure (Fig. 7.5A and B). Just remember to allow for the slack that might occur with a fiberglass measuring tape, and hope it is not a windy day.

And now the bit with the math. Thanks to a Greek fellow named Pythagoras, if we know two of the measurements of our imaginary triangle, we can easily figure out the third, well, sort of easy. If we look at Fig. 7.6, we have determined the muzzle of the officer's firearm was 34′ 9″ from the ground (Leg "A") on a vertical axis, and the impact site is 31′ 9″ from the base on a horizontal axis (Leg "B"). The unknown measurement becomes the hypotenuse ("C"). The first thing we should do is convert the feet into inches. Thus, leg "A" becomes 417″ and leg "B" becomes 381″. The formula to figure

Custodial CSI in Escapes, Use of Force, and Shooting Incidents 93

Figure 7.4 The zero-edge protractor.

Figure 7.5 A and B Any brand will do but be certain to verify the measurement accuracy.

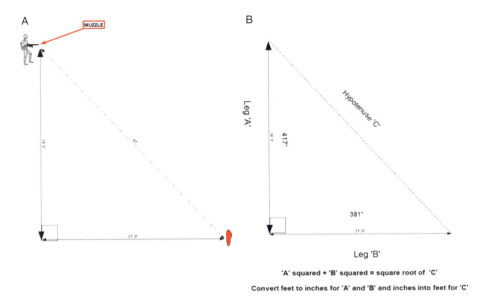

Figure 7.6 Pythagorean theorem. Thank you, Pythagoras.

out the hypotenuse is leg "A" squared added to leg "B" squared equals the square root of "C". Therefore 173,889 + 145,161 = 319,050. The square root of 319,050 is 564.84″ or 47′.

Documenting Bullet or Pellet Defects

When presented with a bullet defect, it is essential that the crime scene investigator properly documents the appearance of the defect before any alteration occurs, especially if the defect itself will be destroyed while recovering the bullet. My preferred method of documentation is to "frame" the defect with photographic scales indicating the number or alphabetical designation of the defect and the measurements in millimeters (you will have to do math a bit later; therefore, it is easier to document the defect in metrics and then do the conversion to inches later). I also add a small round pricing sticker (I call them "Dog dots") to ensure that I am photographing the defect with the camera parallel and perpendicular to the plane (the horizontal and vertical measurements of the "dot" will be in agreement). In this regard, I can collect my measurements of the defect using the photograph as there will be minimal distortions (Figs. 7.7A–C). Always remember to include within your report that you identified each defect in the order of discovery and not in the order of deposition.

Custodial CSI in Escapes, Use of Force, and Shooting Incidents

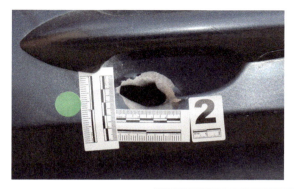

Figure 7.7 (A) Bullet defect in the car door. (B) Bullet defects in the rear window. (C) Bullet defect in front windshield.

Penetration Vs. Perforation

A bullet penetration occurs when a bullet impacts an object and then remains within the last object it hits. A bullet perforation occurs when a bullet passes completely through an object that it hits, leaving entry and exit defects. It is possible for a bullet to perforate an object and then penetrate an opposing object.

Unintentional Vs. Accidental Discharge

This is one of the subjects that make me cringe when the wrong term is used to categorize a discharge of a firearm, especially when it is done by someone who is in forensics or law enforcement. An accidental discharge of a firearm occurs when the weapon discharges because of wear, improper design, mechanical fault or defect, or alteration without the process of actually pulling the trigger. An unintentional discharge of a firearm occurs when interaction between a human and the process of pulling a trigger when it was not intended to be fired.

Figure 7.8 Bullet defect in car door glass.

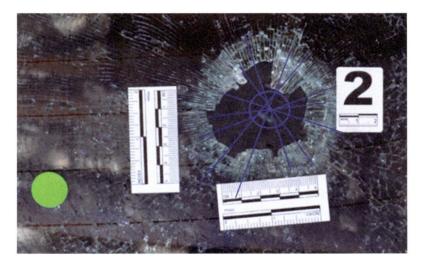

Figure 7.9 Determining the area of convergence.

Determining the Area of Convergence

Owing to the nature of safety glass and the application of window tint material, it is possible to determine the approximate impact site of a bullet within a defect in the glass. By connecting the fracture lines of the surrounding glass, it is possible to establish an area of convergence (a common area of intersection). This can be done either at the scene using string or later using the photograph provided the photograph was captured without distortion (Figs. 7.8 and 7.9).

Remember this determination is only an approximation.

Custodial CSI in Escapes, Use of Force, and Shooting Incidents

Determining the Angle of Impact Using a Trajectory Rod

As described earlier, if the bullet defect provides sufficient depth, or if two points of reference are present, the insertion of a trajectory rod can be quite useful for determining the flight path of a bullet (Fig. 7.10). Once the rod is adequately positioned (let the rod tell you where it wants to point), it is important to photograph the rod from every angle possible, including the direction to where it is pointing should the defect remain in the crime scene.

You can then utilize a zero-edge protractor to determine the horizontal angle of impact from right or left, and either a plumb-bob or angle-finder to determine the upward or downward angle of impact by degree (Fig. 7.11A and /B).

If a trajectory must be determined that spans a distance greater than the available trajectory rods, a laser shown through the center of corresponding defects can provide a visual representation. The best way to photograph a laser is in low light using a laser fog or hairspray (Fig. 7.12). Be certain that you have collected DNA specimen swabs and have conducted latent print development techniques before applying the spray.

As a case example, let us look at fatal defect #83 below. Utilizing the trajectory rod, it is possible to determine the bullet that perforated the left rear

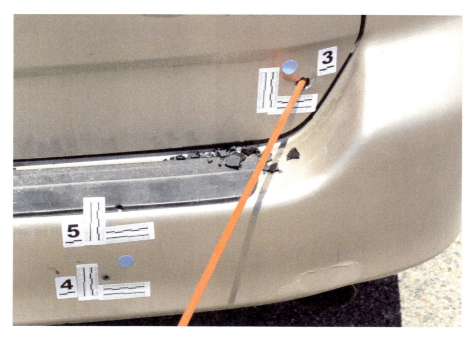

Figure 7.10 Determining the horizontal angle of impact using a trajectory rod.

98　Crime Scene Processing in Correctional Facilities and Prisons

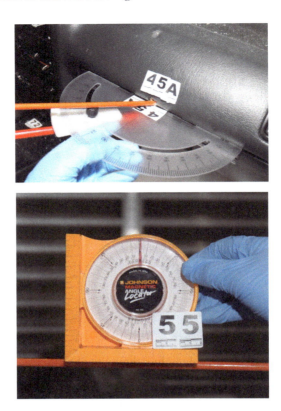

Figure 7.11 **A and B** Determining the horizontal and vertical angle of impact.

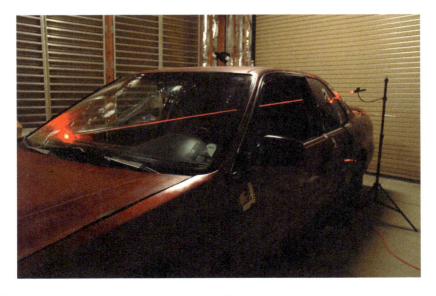

Figure 7.12 Using lasers to visualize bullet trajectory.

Custodial CSI in Escapes, Use of Force, and Shooting Incidents 99

Figure 7.13 The fatal bullet.

passenger window at defect #61 perforated the rear driver's seat and penetrated the driver, killing him instantly (Fig. 7.13).

The horizontal path of the bullet was from left to right at 47 degrees and the vertical path of the bullet was downward at 25 degrees (Figs. 7.14A–D).

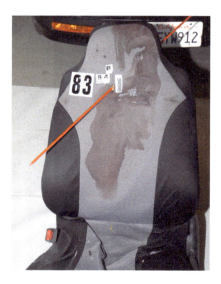

Figure 7.14 (A) The horizontal path of the bullet. (B) Using a zero-edge protractor. (C). Using an angle finder. (D) "X" and "Y" axis. (*Continued*)

Figure 7.14 (*Continued*)

The bullet exited the seat back 8.25″ on the "X" axis and 21.25″ on the "Y" axis. The defect itself measured approximately 8mm in width and 10 mm in length, although this is not an accurate measurement owing to the self-compressing nature of the material. My documentation would look something like that shown in Table 14.1.

Table 14.1 Example Defect Measurement

Defect #	X-axis"	Y-axis"	Width (mm)	Length (mm)	Horizontal	Vertical	W/L	Angle
83	8.25"	21.25"	8	10	47 L>R	25 U>D	0.8	53.1301

Determining the Angle of Impact by Measuring the Defect

At times you will be presented with a bullet defect, but the inability to use a trajectory rod to determine the angle of impact. In these cases, you may still be able to determine at least the horizontal angle of impact by collecting accurate measurements of the bullet defect. Measure the interior walls of the bullet defect by width and by length (the length will always be the larger of the two numbers). By dividing the width by the length, you will have the sine impact angle, but not the actual angle. To obtain the actual angle, you will need to be either brilliant in math or will need the assistance of a scientific calculator to find the inverse or arc sine of the sine angle. The easiest way to do the calculation is to use the second function mode of a scientific calculator and press the Sin-1 button. This will give you the value of the impact angle. For example, let us look at the following defect (Fig. 7.15A and B):

Custodial CSI in Escapes, Use of Force, and Shooting Incidents

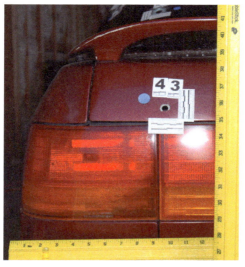

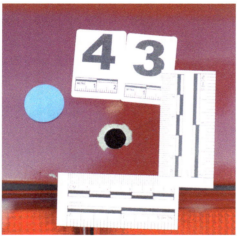

Figure 7.15 (A) Defect in the trunk lid. (B) Close-up.

The width of the defect is 9mm. The length is 10mm. Dividing the width by the length gives us a sine angle of .90. Using the second function and the Sin-1 button, we can determine the actual angle of impact to be 64 degrees. For the math wizards (or those like me who rely heavily on the ability to manipulate Excel into doing all of my math work for me), the equation is as follows: W/L=ASIN*180/pi (Fig. 7.16).

There is only one problem with this mathematical angle of impact: the true angle of that particular defect when determined by the trajectory rod was 84 degrees. Therein lies the problem, because of the flight of the bullet and its characteristics upon hitting a hard surface, the mathematical angle of impact

Figure 7.16 Scientific calculator.

determination is quite often wrong, especially when the defect is on a metal surface. When documenting the mathematical angle of impact of a bullet, I always include a caveat that the measurement is an approximation at best.

Determining Direction and Angle of Impact of Ricochets

A ricochet occurs when a bullet has altered its original trajectory by skipping, bouncing, or deflecting off a surface but maintains its integrity. As the bullet does so, it may produce a ricochet crease, which is an indentation or furrow in a surface caused by a bullet striking a surface but being deflected without penetration of perforation. Quite often a careful examination of this crease will provide the crime scene investigator with the direction of travel of the bullet, especially when the ricochet is on a metal surface (Fig. 7.17).

Figure 7.17 Ricochet on car trunk lid.

Custodial CSI in Escapes, Use of Force, and Shooting Incidents

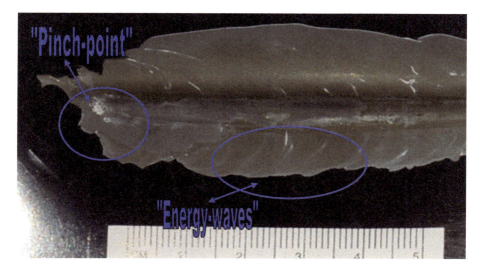

Figure 7.18 Pinch-point and energy waves.

An examination of the above photograph with a magnifying glass will reflect a pinch-point on the far left of the crease. This is a good indication that the bullet first impacted the surface at this point (Fig. 7.18). The second clue is the energy-wave effect rippled into the metal (especially observable in metallic paints). If you think of the wake produced by a boat as it travels through water, you can imagine the same for a bullet moving across the surface.

Therefore, the direction of travel of the bullet for the above ricochet is from left to right.

Collecting Fired and Unfired Cartridge Casings and Bullets as Evidence

Obviously, whenever there is a shooting, the most common evidence in the scene will be cartridge casings, fired cartridge casings, and bullets. Generally, in a jail or prison, the identity of the shooter is known, and hopefully, the shooting was within departmental policy and protocols. However, there may be occasions when the identity of a shooter is not known, such as an attempted escape or any other occurrence where an unidentified person is firing upon a jail or prison, the employees, or the inmates. Fortunately, these incidents are rare, but it is best to have policies in place just in case. In this regard, the unfired cartridge casings fired cartridge casings, and bullets may provide valuable information that may link the crime to a weapon or person.

Ballistic examinations of the fired and unfired cartridge casings and recovered bullets may match those collected at the scene to weapons either subsequently seized or in a database. Some latent fingerprint development techniques, like Vacuum Metal Deposition or cyanoacrylate ester fuming, may develop usable ridge-print impressions on fired and unfired cartridge casings; however, advancements in touch-DNA extraction suitable for typing are becoming the best forensic application for this type of evidence. With this advancement in technology, we must have increased awareness of contamination when handling this evidence at a crime scene. The following guidelines must be observed when collecting bullets, unfired and fired casings at a crime scene:

- Extreme caution must be made to mitigate the possibility of contamination while handling spent shell casings
- PPE should be utilized with an emphasis on covering the hands and face of the technician
- Collection of the casings should be done in a way to limit cross-contamination by other items of evidence
- Recommend handling cases with sterile tweezers near the mouth of the casing or near the base
- Plastic evidence containers should be avoided. It is recommended to wrap the casing in a gauze pad and to place it carefully into a small Kraft paper cardboard boxes
- The larger, the better – Rifle, shotgun, and handgun shell casings larger than .32acp are best for the recovery of DNA (.22short/LR, .25acp, and .32acp tend not to have a sufficient surface area for the recovery of DNA)
- Aluminum casings are better than brass casings for the recovery of DNA
- It is imperative to submit shell casings to the ATF laboratory prior to IBIS/NIBIN analysis (IBIS/NIBIN will clean the casings as their first step prior to analysis)
- Cyanoacrylate fuming does not interfere with the ability of the ATF to recover DNA
- Long-term storage of spent shell casings *must be* in a dry and humidity-free environment
- DO NOT place evidence markers directly against spent shell casings or cartridges
- Wear latex gloves, arm coverings, face mask, and glasses/goggles when handling spent shell casings
- Utilize sterile tweezers or rubber-tipped tweezers that are cleaned between each casing collected

Custodial CSI in Escapes, Use of Force, and Shooting Incidents

- Utilize small Kraft paper cardboard boxes and gauze pads to prevent the shell casing from coming in prolonged contact with porous packaging material
- Subsequent laboratory examination of the spent shell casings (headstamp, latent print development, etc.) should be done with attention to contamination mitigation

Crime Scene

I created crime scene kits that were specifically used for collecting shooting scene evidence. These kits included latex gloves, an N-94 mask, two sets of tweezers, and alcohol pads. It is imperative that anyone who collects casings at a crime scene must don latex gloves and a face mask, cover bare arms, wear head coverings, and be considerate of potential contamination from incidental contact with any object that is not sterilized. Follow these steps:

- Prepare evidence boxes before handling the shell casing
- Have handy sterile gauze packets
- Don PPEs
- Open alcohol prep pad packet
- Clean the tips of the tweezers with the alcohol pads
- Carefully collect the spent shell casing with the cleaned tweezer tips by carefully grasping the opening of the casing
- Make a visual inspection of the headstamp for manufacture and caliber information
- Open the gauze pad packet
- Carefully drop the shell casing into the packet with the gauze
- Fold the gauze packet and place it within the evidence box*
  - *If the gauze packet is too large for the box, gently wrap the shell casing in the gauze strip and place that in the box. Discard the gauze packaging
- Place the lid on the evidence box and refrain from opening it again

Although ideal, it may be impractical to don fresh gloves between each item collected. However, if great care is taken not to contact the shell casing with the gloved hand (i.e., sterile or clean tweezer usage), frequent glove changes may not be required. One does run the risk of incidental contact, however.

Discussions should be had with investigators regarding subsequent cartridge casing analysis. Submission of fired cartridge casings to IBIS (NIBIN) would preclude any additional forensic examination as the cases are

Figure 7.19 Jewelry boxes for fired and unfired cartridges.

thoroughly cleaned before imaging. The history of casings from cold-case investigations must be either known or deduced prior to submission to soak and sonicate laboratories, since the process is expensive and laborious.

I prefer using jewelry boxes for long-term evidence storage of fired and unfired cartridge casings and recovered bullets, as they are less expensive than small evidence boxes available from forensic supply vendors, and they have cotton batting that provides a cushion (Fig. 7.19). The object is to keep the items from rolling around within the box; therefore, each box should contain only one item. Furthermore, I find it best to use 2″ × 2″ sterile gauze pads by wrapping the evidence item in the gauze pad, replacing it in the sterile envelope from which the pad was removed, folding it in a manner to keep the item from falling out (perhaps even a small piece of tape to secure the open end of the envelope), and placing it within the jewelry box.

Recovering Fired Cartridge Casings and Bullets

Not only for evidentiary purpose but also for the security of the jail or prison, it is very important that every effort is made to recover fired cartridge casings and bullets from shooting scenes, even if the shooting scene was just a warning shot fired. Not only are these items essential evidence from the shooting scene, but brass or aluminum-fired cartridge casings can be rolled out into a flat, sharp blade for a stabbing weapon, and bullets make excellent projectiles for inmate-manufactured slingshots. I also had a nice collection of inmate-manufactured zip guns at the prison where I worked.

Just as an aside, I have a confession to make. I am likely the only officer in history who thoroughly enjoyed Fog Watch. Fog Watch occurred when the fog was so dense the perimeter and yard towers could not see each other. When announced, an officer was selected (usually by inverse seniority) to walk the distance between the towers along the fence line on foot carrying a Remington Model 870 pump shotgun loaded with three 00 buck shotgun shells, and two at hand for combat reloading. I would assume the duties of a sentry, with absolute conviction with my trusty shotgun either at port arms or right shoulder with only the sound of the fog and a keen ear trained on the galvanized steel barrier separating the inner sanctuary of the prison with the freedom that lay beyond. With extreme concentration and military precision, I marched back and forth between the towers. It was not until years later when I uncovered a plot by an inmate to escape utilizing the cover of dense fog that I realized how essential Fog Watch was to maintain the safety and security of the institution.

Forensic Pathology in the Correctional Setting 8

It is not necessary to have a medical degree or for that matter to be a forensic pathologist to be proficient at documenting injuries that occur in the correctional setting. However, it is absolutely essential that the crime scene investigator understands, at the very least, the definitions relating to bludgeoning, slashing, and stabbing injuries and how to appropriately use the terms properly in report writing. The reason for this is that certain injuries are produced by certain weapons or certain types of force. You will find that the word "laceration" means something completely different than what most people, and most medical department personnel, use it to represent; and this could have a disastrous effect on your testimony on the stand. Consider that you have observed a "cut" on an inmate's head and caught another inmate holding a razor-type weapon. You recorded the cut in your report as a laceration, a shearing, or crushing injury caused by blunt force trauma, when in fact it was an incised wound caused by a sharp instrument. Well, you can see where the defense attorney would point out the discrepancy as you have certainly exonerated his client. Another thing to consider is that people who work in the medical profession tend to use terms like laceration and incision interchangeably with other injuries. Medical examiners or forensic pathologists, on the other hand, use words that are very specific to describe injuries, and those words are generally accepted by their industry. For this reason, your author recommends the book *Forensic Pathology,* by Dominick and Vincent DiMaio. It has been around for a long time, but it is still generally accepted by the profession.

Abrasions and Contusions

An abrasion occurs when there is a removal of the epidermis layer of skin by scraping due to friction against a surface such as gravel, dirt, concrete, sand, grass, or wood. We see abrasions all the time in the correctional setting as inmates will often get abrasions by the simple act of complying with staff instructions to quickly assume a prone position. These injuries most often appear on palms, elbows, and knees. Although some abrasions

Forensic Pathology in the Correctional Setting

can be quite deep, they are hardly life-threatening. A contusion, on the other hand, is a bruise that occurs when blood vessels rupture and seep into the skin tissue thus producing a discoloration in the skin caused by the collection of this blood. Contusions can appear not only in the skin but also in the major organs of the body and can be exemplary of serious internal hematoma. Patterned contusions occur when the bruise takes the shape of the object that produced the injury. In the correctional setting, this can oftentimes be attributed to staff efforts to restore peace and order, such as with the use of the 40mm eXact iMpact projectile or the baton (Figs. 8.1–8.6A and B).

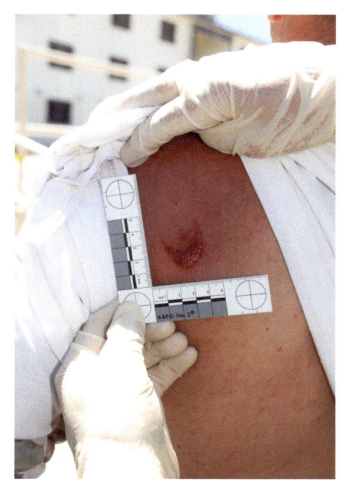

Figure 8.1 A contused abrasion caused by the sliding impact of a 40mm eXact iMpact projectile.

110 Crime Scene Processing in Correctional Facilities and Prisons

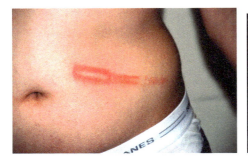 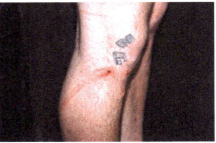

Figures 8.2 and 8.3 A contusion caused by the impact of a Monodnock expandable baton.

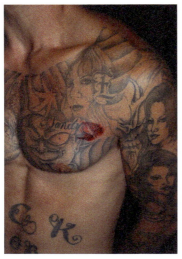

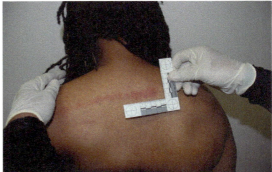

Figure 8.5 A contusion caused by the impact of a Monodnock expandable baton.

Figure 8.4 A contusion caused by the direct impact of a 40mm eXact iMpact projectile.

Forensic Pathology in the Correctional Setting 111

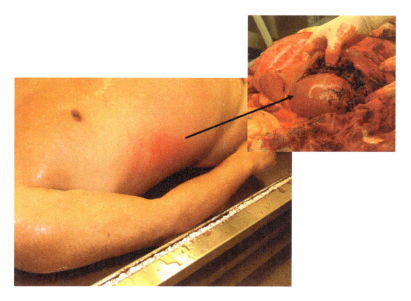

Figure 8.6 A contusion caused by a kick that bursts the liver.

Contusions should not be confused with lividity (livor mortis), which is the pooling of the blood in the dependent areas of the body post-mortem, resulting in a pink to reddish-purple discoloration in the skin. You can tell the difference between lividity and contusions by firmly pressing the area with your gloved fingers. The discoloration produced by lividity will blanch, whereas the discoloration caused by contusion will remain the same color (Fig. 8.7).

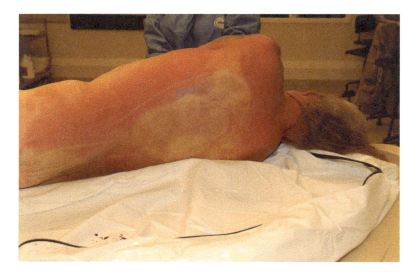

Figure 8.7 Livor mortis in dependent areas.

Lacerations

As previously mentioned, a laceration is a blunt-force injury produced by a shearing or crushing force, such as caused by a fist, a lock-in-a-sock, a broom handle, or an impact-type weapon. Lacerations are characterized by their jagged, uneven, or irregular shape with abraded (worn away) contusions and often have areas where the skin "bridges" the opening where it did not separate completely (Fig. 8.8A–C).

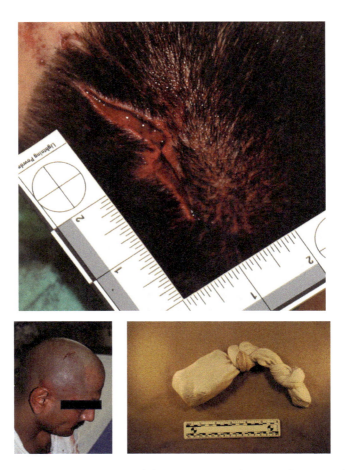

Figure 8.8 (A) Laceration caused by contact with a car bumper. (B and C) Laceration caused by a batteries-in-a-sock weapon.

Forensic Pathology in the Correctional Setting

An avulsive laceration is an injury where the impacting force strikes the skin at an angle causing the skin to slip or rip (Figs. 8.9 and 8.10).

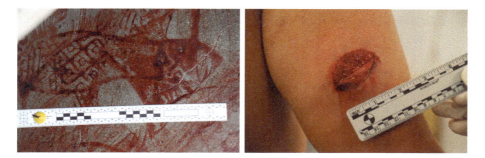

Figure 8.9 An avulsive laceration caused by a fall against a metal table.

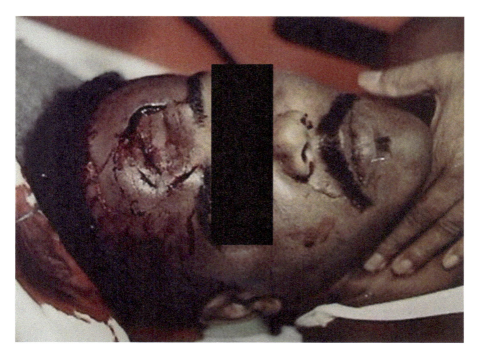

Figure 8.10 Avulsive laceration caused by a 45lb. dumbbell dropped from a distance of about five feet – Author's collection

Stab Wounds

Stab wounds are produced by weapons that have a point. The edges of the wound caused by a sharp weapon are well-defined and are without abrasion or contusion (except in the case where a pointed weapon is inserted with such force that it causes bruising from either the strike of the hilt or the hand of the assailant). The edges of a wound caused by a dull weapon may be irregular and jagged or abraded. The depth of the wound in the body may or may not exceed the width of the wound on the skin. Unlike lacerations, where the shape of the wound does not reflect the shape of the object causing the injury, a stab wound will generally indicate the type of pointed weapon that was used. A double-edged weapon will have ends that are "V" shaped (Figs. 8.11–8.13). A single-edged weapon will have one end that is "V" shaped and the other that is flat. An ice-pick type weapon will be round, oftentimes resembling a bullet wound (Figs. 8.14–8.16). Unfortunately, inmate-manufactured weapons sometimes have shapes that are not defined by single or double-edged, and the resultant wounds are therefore open to interpretation. Langer's lines, the connective tissue layer that lies beneath the skin covering the muscles throughout the entire body, can also affect the appearance of the wound. In other words, a stab wound that follows parallel to a Langer's line may appear narrow whereas one that is perpendicular might be broad or irregular. Under no circumstances should you allow medical personnel to remove the weapon from the crime scene to compare it to the victim's wound. I cannot tell you how many times I have had to prevent this very issue from happening. Provide them instead with a well-scaled photograph.

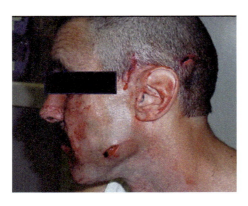
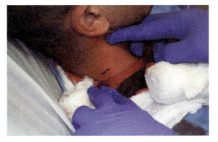

Figures 8.11, 8.12, and 8.13 Both inmates were stab wounds with the same crudely made double-edged yet effective stabbing weapon.

Forensic Pathology in the Correctional Setting   115

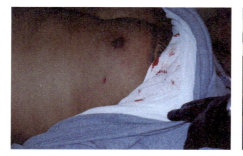 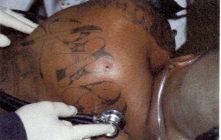

Figure 8.14 Stab wound to the chest with an ice-pick type weapon

Figure 8.15 Stab wound to the back with an ice-pick type weapon

Figure 8.16 The ice-pick type weapon

This near-fatal stabbing was the result of an assault with an ice-pick type weapon. The blade penetrated far enough into the chest cavity to pierce the heart. It was the on-scene CSI who noticed the inmate was bleeding internally and convinced medical staff to call for an air ambulance.

Incised Wounds

Incised wounds are caused by the extremely sharp, razor-like edges of hand-held weapons. These are the most common injuries encountered by correctional personnel. These are also the most common injuries inflicted upon correctional personnel owing to the diminutive size of the weapons that produce them and their ease of concealment. Fortunately, the injuries are generally not fatal but meant to send a message and to leave a permanent mark on the victim. Characteristically, incised wounds have sharp, defined, and clean-cut edges. In the correctional setting, these types of injuries are most often called "slashing-type" wounds. The proper terminology, however, is an incised wound (Figs. 8.17 and 8.18A–C).

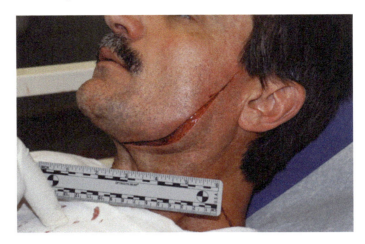

Figure 8.17 This incised wound is a classic prison "debt" mark. The victim owed a sizeable sum for the purchase of drugs that he could not pay.

Figure 8.18 **A–C** Various "slashing" type weapons. Incised injury weapons.

Forensic Pathology in the Correctional Setting 117

The most dangerous weapons in a correctional setting, these razor blade weapons can be made by an inmate in a matter of minutes from items found in any cell. They are easily concealed and can cause severe, disfiguring incised injuries to inmates and staff.

Some wounds caused by inmate-manufactured stabbing and slashing weapons are hard to define owing to the irregular shape of the weapons used. In this case, it is up to the investigator's experience to determine how to categorize the injury (Figs. 8.19A and B, 8.20A and B, 8.21A and B, and 8.22).

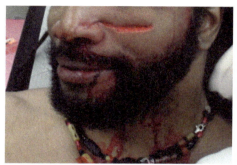 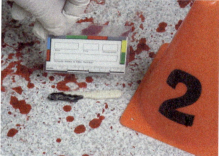

Figure 8.19 **A and B** A deep cut made by a heat-tempered "slashing" type weapon and the weapon that produced the injury.

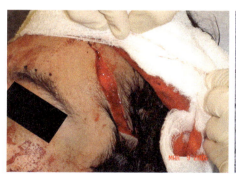 

Figure 8.20 **A/B** A cut that resembles a laceration made by a sharpened metal "slashing -stabbing" type weapon and the weapon that produced the injury.

In the above photographs, the irregular shape of the weapon left a wound that appeared to be a chopping-type injury, when in fact it was a slashing-type injury. In the second photographed injury, the movement of the victim caused the assailant to use the double-edged stabbing weapon in the accompanied photograph as a slashing-type weapon.

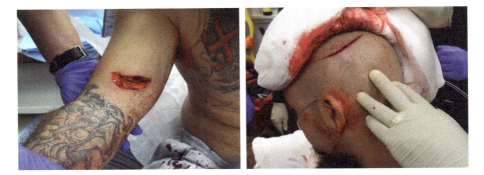

Figure 8.21 A and B Although I was unable to convince the medical personnel at the scene, I believe the two injuries above were caused by the same razor-blade weapon. I maintain that when an arm receives an incised wound while the bicep is flexed, the resulting injury will appear quite different when the arm is extended. I might be wrong, but only one weapon was located at the scene and staff witnessed only one assailant.

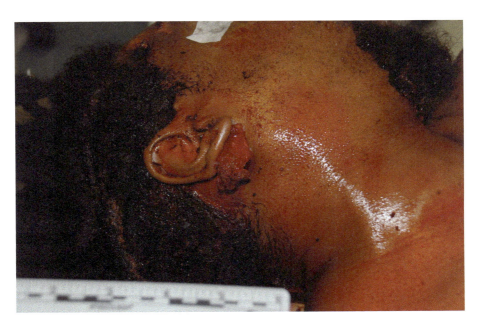

Figure 8.22 This near-fatal injury was caused by a sharpened piece of glass. The tip of the glass pierced the earlobe and entered the area just behind the ear, severing the jugular-minor vein causing the victim to suffer severe internal bleeding. He died twice en route to the hospital but was revived by air ambulance medical personnel. He was stabbed for stealing an old television. He survived the attack. The suspect eventually confessed and pleaded guilty to a 12-year sentence for attempted homicide.

Forensic Pathology in the Correctional Setting 119

A closing note about inmate-manufactured improvised weapons. It is my experience that inmates confined in jails and prisons are capable of manufacturing hand-held improvised stabbing/slashing/puncturing weapons from harmless objects that are commonly found in cells, housing units, and worksites and discarded by the careless actions of staff. A plastic toothbrush can be fashioned into a sharpened weapon, as can an ink pen, by the application of heat to pull, twist, and temper the plastic into a surface that is harder than its original manufacture. The weapon can then be sharpened on a concrete cell floor, concrete pathway, roughened metal, or a stone found in the exercise yard. It is this process of tempering the plastic that converts a benign plastic object into a useful weapon. Binder clips used to hold paperwork together can be vigorously bent until the thin metal loses its temper and breaks forming a small hacksaw device that can be used to cut metal strips from any metal surface normally found in a cell, the culinary, dining rooms, or worksites. These metal strips can be sharpened into a blade in the same manner as a plastic weapon. These are only a few examples of weapon manufacturing techniques. Common to all weapon manufacturing techniques is the use of tape, cloth, twine, dental floss, or other soft material to form a handle for grip and retention. These weapons have blades that are irregular in shape as they are not milled, forged, or stamped with any precision like a commercially manufactured knife, blade, or tool. Therefore, these improvised weapons produce injuries that are dissimilar to precision-made weapons. However, the injuries they produce can be just as lethal.

Head Injuries

Whether it is an aluminum baseball bat, a few "C" cell batteries in a sock, or the one-punch knock-out, your author has seen a lot of head injuries while working at the prison (Fig. 8.23). Quite often, what one may consider a minor knock to the head might indeed turn out to be a life-threatening event. These head injuries can be produced either by a forceful impact to the head or by a rapid acceleration or deceleration force of the head.

Obviously, an impact injury is caused by either an object striking the head or the head striking an object. This reminds me of the line in the *Adventures of Don Quixote de la Mancha* (p.466), by Miguel de Cervantes Saavedra that reads, "Whether the stone hits the pitcher, or the pitcher hits the stone, it is bound to be bad for the pitcher." Externally, impact injuries typically produce lacerations, abrasions, and contusions of the face and scalp. Internally, however, what may be unnoticed are contusions of the brain, epidural hematomas (an accumulation of blood between the scull and the dura mater membrane that covers the brain), or intracerebral hemorrhages (bleeding into the brain tissue). Heads are incredibly hard, but when they come in contact with

Figure 8.23 A bit of swelling resulting from an impact injury (padlock in a sock).

an equally hard, unyielding object, fractures of the skull may occur. Skull fractures may be a good indication that something more serious is going on internally, but that is not always the case. The DiMaio brothers stress that there is no *absolute* correlation between the presence of a linear skull fracture and brain injury, and vice versa. Regardless, it does not take a lot of force to fracture a skull. The DiMaio brothers suggest that a fracture produced by an impact force of 33.3 to 75 foot pounds of energy will create a fracture identical to that requiring 268 to 581-foot pounds of energy; therefore only a force of 33.3 to 75 foot pounds of energy is required to create a fracture.

Acceleration/deceleration injuries typically result in either subdural hematoma (a collection of blood between the covering and surface of the brain) or diffuse axonal injury (the tearing of the connecting nerve fibers of the brain due to acceleration/deceleration force within the skull). Subdural hematoma is an injury related to head trauma that is the most commonly fatal because of the brain damage that is associated with the injury. Diffuse axonal injury occurs when there is a violent front-to-back, back-to-front, or side-to-side motion applied to the head. These injuries are associated with coup and contrecoup injuries of the brain wherein an external force causes violent, rapid movement of the head. In a coup injury, the head moves rapidly forward. The brain, which is not solidly fixed within the cranial cavity (it floats in a cerebrospinal fluid), slams against the interior front of the skull.

Forensic Pathology in the Correctional Setting

In a contrecoup injury, the brain impacts the side of the interior of the skull opposite of the impacting force. The DiMaio brothers suggest that side-to-side (coronal) head motion injuries can be more severe than front-to-back or back-to-front (sagittal) head motion injuries, but either way immediate medical (if not surgical) attention must be a priority.

Traumatic brain swelling (edema) may occur following a severe head injury as the result of an excessive buildup of fluids in the cranial cavity. Your skull does a good job of protecting your brain, but it is incapable of expanding to accommodate severe swelling of the brain. This may result in death should the swelling not be reduced, or the skull enlarged. In the latter, surgical procedures called a craniectomy or craniotomy are performed wherein a portion of the skull is removed to allow room for the swelling to occur. In a craniectomy, a portion of the skull is removed. In a craniotomy, the portion of the skull is removed but later replaced (Fig. 8.24).

Even a mild traumatic head injury can result in a concussion. Although it is a less-severe form of brain injury, it can still no doubt cause major concern for the well-being of the recipient of the injury. Your author has had more than a few occasions working as a housing unit officer when an inmate had fallen from the upper bunk to the floor, only later to discover that the inmate had received a concussion while playing sports in the yard, but either did not tell anyone or was told to "walk it off" by the other inmates. Any place where

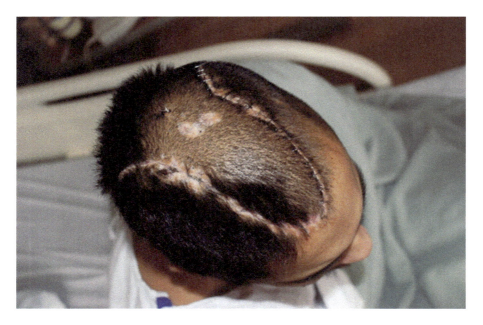

Figure 8.24 A one-punch knock-out resulting in cerebral edema requiring a craniotomy.

intramural sports are allowed should have concussion protocols in effect, and that includes jails and prisons.

Of course, this is an overly simplified explanation of traumatic head injuries that can be the product of physical assaults, falls, or debilitating medical episodes. Head injuries cannot be ignored in a jail or prison setting, and consideration must be given to the potential for the loss of life that may come with undiagnosed or untreated trauma to the brain.

Fractures

Although the terms fracture and broken bone are often used interchangeably in the medical profession, the term most commonly used in forensic pathology is fracture. When it comes to fractures, your author has noticed two things: Some non-medical personnel do not know the difference between a simple fracture and a compound fracture; and "boxer's" or "brawler's" fractures of the hands are commonly overlooked in reports.

Rather than provide a lengthy dissertation on the numerous forms of fractures, and what may have caused them, I will instead focus on the types of fractures generally associated with a jail or prison setting. Therefore, I will highlight the following: Compound fractures, comminuted fractures, focal fractures, facial fractures, and "boxer's" or "brawler's" fractures.

A compound or open fracture occurs when a bone is broken, and a portion of that bone punctures the skin and is exposed to the exterior of the body. Compound fractures typically are accompanied by a goodly amount of bleeding. Nerve damage may also be a consideration, as is the potential for infection. Conversely, a bone break that does not puncture the skin is called a simple or closed fracture. Compound fractures in the jail or prison environment are generally the result of a fall and accidents at maintenance area assignments or vocational trades programs. The culinary is also a good contributor to compound fractures with the ever-present slippery floors and metal appliances and tables.

Comminuted fractures occur most commonly in the forearm or lower leg and have a bone that is broken in more than one place. Although normally associated with car accidents or a crushing force, your author has witnessed comminuted fractures that resulted from gunshot wounds inflicted by rifle bullets such as the .223 Remington cartridge (Fig. 8.25).

Focal fractures occur when a force is applied to a small area such as the wrist, forearm, elbow, knee, ulna, or fibula. Of course, the first thing to come to mind is the strike of the power tip of an expandable baton being delivered to a concentrated target. These may also be defensive injuries incurred while fending off a broken broom or mop handle. An example of

Forensic Pathology in the Correctional Setting

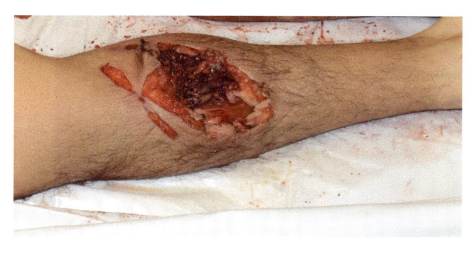

Figure 8.25 The tibia of the right leg was shattered in four places by the impact of a .223 Remington bullet. Note the grazed wound above. Also, this is not a compound fracture as the break in the skin was caused by the bullet and not a protruding bone.

a focal fracture is a transverse fracture where the bone is broken at a right angle to its axis (Fig. 8.26).

Facial fractures of the face are very common in the jail or prison setting and are typically not from walking into doors. But, as a 73-year-old Watch Commander at my facility would say, "Boys will be boys." The most common facial fractures of the skull and face are those found on the nasal bone,

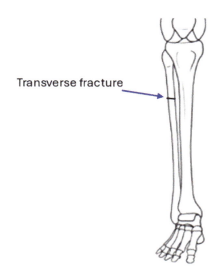

Figure 8.26 An artist's rendition of a transverse fracture of the right fibula.

124   Crime Scene Processing in Correctional Facilities and Prisons

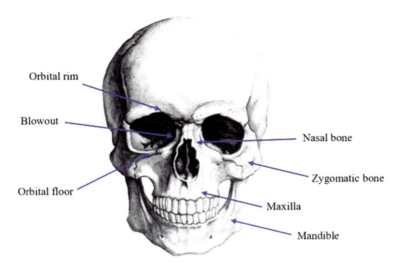

Figure 8.27 Anatomical drawing with common facial fractures. It should be noted that the orbital rim is a very thick bone that requires a good amount of force to break.

Zygomatic bone (cheek and part of the eye socket), the maxilla, mandible, and orbital bones surrounding the eye socket (blowout fracture, orbital rim fracture, and orbital floor fracture). Albeit discomforting, fractures of the face are rarely fatal (Figs. 8.27 and 8.28).

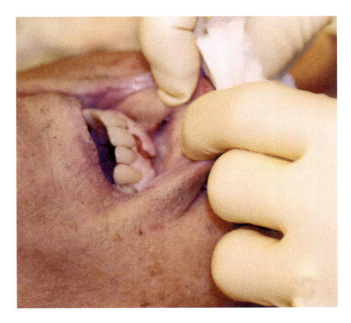

Figure 8.28 Fracture of the Maxilla.

Forensic Pathology in the Correctional Setting   125

Fractures of the hand and wrist are a staple of fist fights and other places of incarceration disturbances. They are also most common in preemptive disabling assaults that are the precursor to fatal in-cell stabbing assaults. I have conducted post-incident analysis on several gang-related in-cell stabbings that resulted in the death of one of the cell's occupants by multiple sharp-force stabbing injuries. Based on my analysis, it was determined the victims in these assaults had been surprised by, and incapacitated by, a rapid series of punches to the face, which incapacitated the victim and therefore making the chore of delivering dozens of stab wounds relatively an easy task. While reviewing photographs of a few of the suspects, I noticed that they had very swollen dominant hands. As the corresponding victims exhibited facial fractures, it was an easy assumption to connect the two events. This conclusion, however, explained why in both cases the stab wounds were delivered by the non-dominant hand of the assailants, which, in turn, explained the bloodstain patterns in the cell and the complete lack of defensive injuries on the decedents. Interestingly, in both cases, the presence of the swollen hands was overlooked by the attending medical personnel who, I am certain, were more concerned with the well-punctured cellmates. Fortunately, the suspects were photographed by the investigative staff in a timely manner (Figs. 8.29 and 8.30).

Wrist fractures are cracks or breaks in one or many of the eight bones in the wrist, called the carpals, and are most commonly associated with falls when people extend their hands as impromptu shock absorbers, which is

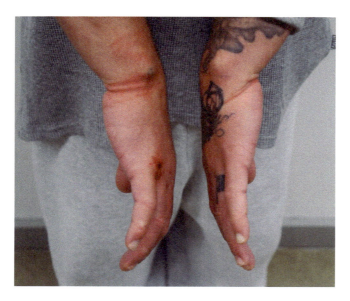

Figure 8.29 Fracture of the 2nd and 3rd metacarpal bones of the left hand.

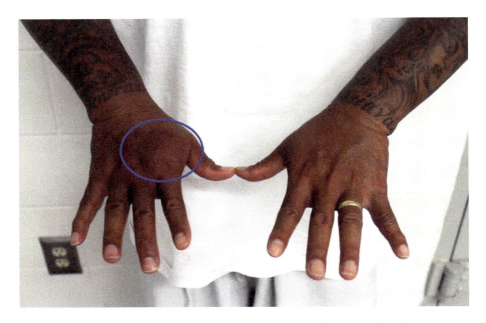

Figure 8.30 A fracture of the 2nd metacarpal bone of the right hand.

generally either a bad idea or preferable to losing a few teeth. Fractures oftentimes caused by punching a hard object are primarily to the metacarpals, the breaks are called boxer's or brawler's fractures, or the metacarpophalangeal joint, the structures around the first knuckle of a finger, a break also known as a boxer's knuckle. Fractures to the phalanges are less likely to occur in a closed-fist punch, unless a finger is out of position during the punch, but your author has known them to occur during open-hand slaps or chops, and by getting rings caught on the slightest of protruding objects.

Chop Wounds

Although rare, chop wounds every now and then are found in the correctional setting. These wounds are caused by heavy weapons, generally with a cutting edge, that are being swung with momentum. These weapons include hatchets, axes, maintenance tools, and meat cleavers. These injuries may exhibit an incised wound of the skin with underlying multiple fractures or a deep groove in the bone. Weapons with dull edges may exhibit both incised and lacerated characteristics. Furthermore, if the weapon embeds itself in the bone, the effort needed to extract the weapon, especially if a twisting action is required, would result in the fracturing of adjacent bones (Fig. 8.31).

Forensic Pathology in the Correctional Setting

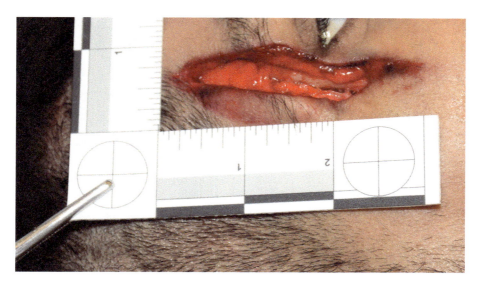

Figure 8.31 A chop wound to the zygomatic arch caused by a dull ax-type weapon. Note the deep groove in the bone.

Bloodstain Pattern Evidence in Jails and Prisons

9

The topic of bloodstain pattern analysis is best left to the many competent training programs available on the forensic training market and to textbooks dedicated to bloodstain pattern analysis such as Tom Bevel and Ross Gardner's *Bloodstain Pattern Analysis,* 3rd edition, CRC Press or Toby Wolson's *Handbook or Bloodstain Pattern Analysis*, 1st edition, CRC Press. However, your author does believe that the crime scene investigator in jails or prisons must have the ability to recognize bloodstain patterns within the crime scene and to understand the potential significance of bloodstain patterns to the successful investigation of a violent blood-letting event or crime. Therefore, the purpose of this chapter is to familiarize the reader with an understanding of the proper discovery, recognition, preservation, documentation, and collection of specimens, the result of a blood-letting event, but not necessarily the ability to perform bloodstain pattern interpretation or analysis. For contemporary bloodstain pattern terminology, please refer to the American Academy of Forensic Science Standards Board Technical Report 033, June 2017 (www.aafs.org/sites/default/files/media/documents/033_TR_e1_2017.pdf).

For an inexpensive and excellent visual guide to bloodstain patterns, I recommend Jeffrey Gentry's *A Visual Guide to Bloodstain Analysis,* available, as they say, where books are sold, or by contacting him at JeffreyGentry.BPA@gmail.com. Jeff also provides free videos on bloodstain pattern analysis on YouTube at/Jeffrey Gentry BPA Bloodstain Pattern Analyst and offers a 4.5-hour online bloodstain pattern analysis training course at hhttp://www.ditacademyonline.org/courses/blood-pattern-analysis. For those investigators who have caught the bloodstain pattern analysis bug, I highly recommend joining the International Association of Bloodstain Pattern Analysts and seeking certification through the International Association for Identification.

Although it may not be necessary to have a bloodstain pattern analyst on staff at a jail or prison, it is absolutely essential that serious blood-letting events must be properly mapped, diagrammed, and photographed. Contrary to the beliefs of some defense attorneys, a bloodstain pattern analyst can effectively analyze a blood-letting event using photographs taken at the scene, provided the photographs include overall measurements, the predominant stains are represented with a scale, and that a means to determine that the camera was perpendicular and parallel to the target is present. Documenting the crime scene for bloodstains is time-consuming and requires the technician to develop

Bloodstain Pattern Evidence in Jails and Prisons

a "mapping" plan and to be meticulous about documenting and measuring the stains. Thus, the technician will need to have at least a rudimentary understanding of the characteristics of blood in flight. For that, it is important for the technician to understand that blood is a non-Newtonian viscoelastic fluid. Unlike water, which is held together by surface tension, blood is cohesive, and is therefore held together by viscosity and internal cohesion. Therefore, blood is harder to break apart when energy is applied. Because of this, blood maintains a spherical shape in flight (Fig. 9.1A and B). It is because of this round shape that we can make an analytical examination of the resultant stains once the blood has impacted a surface. We can apply the laws of physics and mathematics to the observable characteristics of these patterns to determine the nature of the force that produced the patterns, the number of blows struck, the type of force applied, the sequence of events, the angle of impact and origin of the blood-letting source, and the position of the participants. The technician

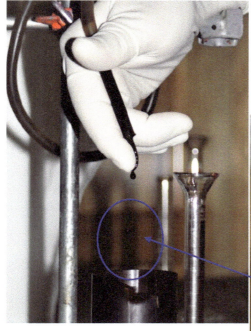
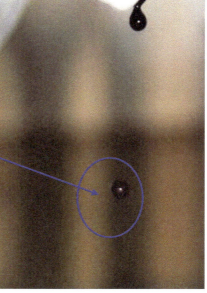

Figure 9.1 A and B A falling drop of blood and the same drop enlarged. Note the spherical shape. It is because of this shape that bloodstain pattern analysis is possible.

must also understand that a distribution of bloodstains on a target is called *spatter* patterns. This is of emphatical insistence with bloodstain pattern analysts and is beyond debate. The word "splatter" is a portmanteau word (a word created by blending the sounds of two words that have a similar meaning) created by combining the words "splash" and "spatter." Although our terminology includes a splash bloodstain pattern, which is produced when a large volume of blood spills onto a surface, the majority of bloodstain patterns are not the result of a splash. Therefore, it would be incorrect to generalize all bloodstain patterns with a word that includes "splash."

The technician will need a camera mounted on a tripod and must be cognizant of the need to augment or control lighting. The photographs need to be sharp and in focus. It is also essential that the analyst know that the stains being photographed are indeed bloodstains. Therefore, the technician must conduct presumptive testing of the predominant stains using a product like phenolphthalein or leuco-crystal malachite, and ideally, the Hexagon OBTI Immunochromatographic Rapid Test™ to determine species, as well as collect specimen and control swabs for DNA analysis. The surface upon which the blood has landed is referred to as the target.

The technician should assess the crime scene and assign each target, the area where the blood impacted, with an individual alphabetical or numeric designation. Each pattern within the designated target will then be given a sub-designation. Therefore, if the technician assigns one target area, such as the north wall in a cell, with the capital letter "A" then the patterns within that area will have a numeric sub-designation, such as pattern 1, and a predominant stain can be selected from this pattern and documented. If the technician decides to document more than one stain in the pattern, each of the individual stains is then represented by a small letter. Therefore, a cast-off impression on the north wall will be designated as target "A," pattern 1, and stain "a" (A1a), "b" (A1b), and so forth (Fig. 9.2A and B).

 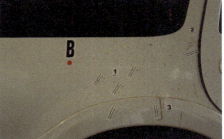

Figure 9.2 A and B Impact pattern bloodstains on the exterior of a vehicle. Note the use of the orange dot underneath the capital letter to indicate the plane of the camera.

Bloodstain Pattern Evidence in Jails and Prisons

It is important to note that one stain does not a pattern make. It is necessary to include full-length measuring tapes vertically and horizontally in the mapping photographs. Although I do have a few 48″ yellow construction bubble sticks that work great in the cells, there is nothing that beats Evident Crime Scene Products' 48″ SuperSticks™ for bloodstain mapping and Sirchie's SEARCH™ or Pocket Rod ™ tape measure used with the metal base that allows the tape to stand by itself (Figs. 9.3–9.5). Both products are reasonably priced and an essential tool in the crime scene kit. Larger areas may require the use of fiberglass tape measures for horizontal measurements. Your author keeps a drawer full of disposable soft sewing tape measures. They are reasonably inexpensive and can be discarded after use to prevent contamination. Be certain to have strong adhesive tape on hand to keep the tape measures on the wall for the photographs.

The technician will also need alphabetic and numeric adhesive-backed stickers, adhesive-backed scales, and adhesive-backed circles. Although many of these products are available at all the forensic supply retailers, I find mine at craft and hardware stores.

Figure 9.3 A large area with multiple blood-letting events recorded. Note the discarded latex gloves carelessly contributed to the crime scene by responding medical personnel.

Figure 9.4 "Mapped" bloodstain patterns on a cell door. It is always a good idea to put something behind the door so that it does not open as you are taking the photograph.

Some important bloodstain patterns to document are impact spatter, cast-off and cessation cast-off, transfer and transfer impressions, voids, drip trails, flow, pooled, and projected blood. Of course, these are only a few of the bloodstain patterns the technician will need to understand.

Bloodstain Pattern Evidence in Jails and Prisons

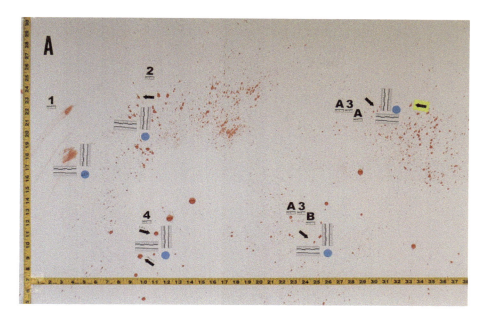

Figure 9.5 Examples of different mapping techniques.

Impact Spatter

When force is applied to a blood-letting source, blood will take flight primarily out and away from the source causing impact spatter. The faster (higher) the force (energy) applied, the smaller the blood droplets. When a high-velocity force such as a gunshot is applied, the resulting impact spatter will be mist-like, whereas a blunt or sharp force blow may produce an impact spatter that is much larger. Remember, in order for a mist-like pattern to be associated with impact spatter resulting from a gunshot wound, there must be an exit wound and a corresponding bullet defect on the target. The direction of the force can be determined by the angle the blood impacts the surface. Forward spatter is the blood that takes flight in the direction of the force of energy. Back spatter is the blood that takes flight back toward the force of energy. Round stains indicate the blood impacted the surface at or near 90 degrees. Elliptical stains indicate an impact of less than 90 degrees. The more elliptical the stain, the lower the angle of impact. The direction of the stain can be determined by noting the "tail" of the stain known as the wave cast-off (Figs. 9.6–9.9). The impact angle is determined using the same

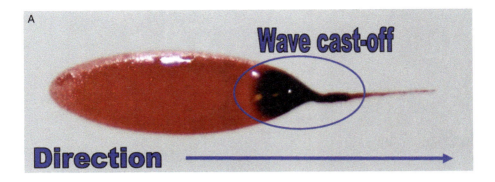

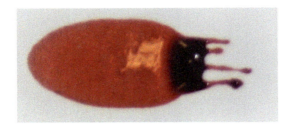

Figures 9.6 and 9.7 The above stains impacted the surface at 40 (top) and 60 (bottom) degrees, respectively. The direction of the energy was from right to left.

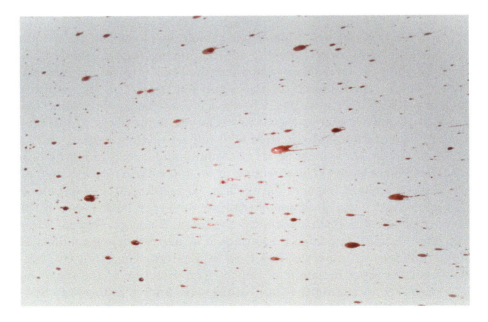

Figure 9.8 Impact spatter caused by a bat striking a blood source. Note the force of energy was from left to right.

Bloodstain Pattern Evidence in Jails and Prisons

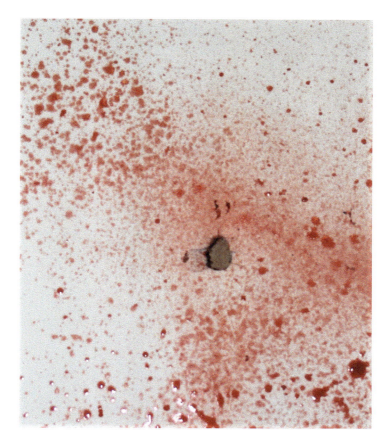

Figure 9.9 Forward mist-like impact spatter created by the perforation of a high-velocity bullet. Note the bullet defect in the center of the pattern.

mathematical principles used to measure bullet defects. It is essential the bloodstains must have a scale, preferably in metric, to facilitate the calculations.

Void Patterns

A void pattern will result when an object intervenes with the distribution of blood. The resulting pattern is the absence of blood from an otherwise continuous stain. These voids can provide valuable information to the crime scene analyst and criminal investigator regarding weapons that might have been removed from the scene or the positions of victims, witnesses, or suspects (Figs. 9.10A and B and 9.11).

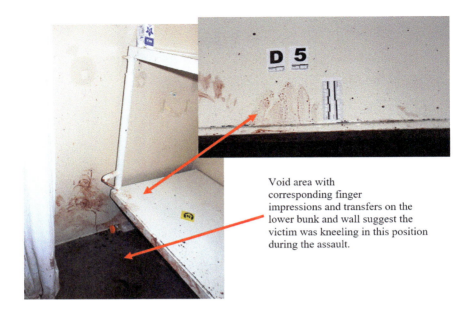

Figure 9.10 A and B Note the points of interest pointed out, particularly the void area, finger impressions, and transfers.

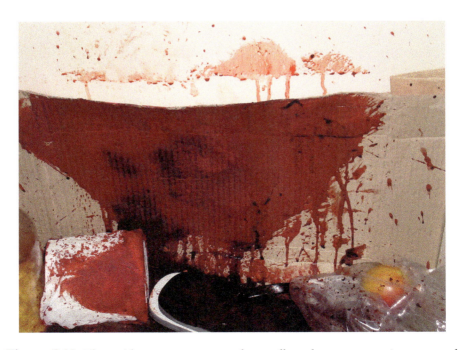

Figure 9.11 The void pattern suggests the cardboard was at one time pressed against the wall during the blood-letting event.

Cast-off and Cessation Cast-off

Spatter resulting from blood being flung or "cast-off" from an object can also provide valuable information to the investigation. Case in point, an inmate was found at the base of a stairwell, deceased with a severe head wound. His cellmate was found kneeling by the decedent saying, "Don't die, buddy. Stay with me." When asked, the cellmate stated that the victim, who uses a cane for mobility, had fallen down the stairs. The tier officer called for a medical response and assumed the fall was accidental. The cane remained at the top of the stairs.

An investigative officer heard the radio call for medical assistance and responded out of curiosity. He asked the cellmate about the circumstances and received the same response as that given to the tier officer. The investigator noticed blood on the cellmate's gray sweatpants and T-shirt. Without giving any indication of doubt about the statement of the cellmate but being concerned for the duress exhibited by the inmate, the investigator said, "I notice you have blood on your clothes. Let's go to your cell and get you some clean clothes to wear." The cellmate stated that he likely got the blood while caring for the victim. Clean clothes were procured for the cellmate and the investigator maintained possession of the bloodstained clothing.

A subsequent inspection of the clothing in the laboratory revealed small spatters on the front and rear left leg (Fig. 9.12A and B). White reinforcement tabs were placed over the spatter to improve visualization, and phenolphthalein and Hexagon OBTI tests were positive for suspected blood and species. An inspection of the T-shirt revealed a transfer pattern that also tested positive for suspected blood and species. A swab taken from the cane also produced a positive result for suspected blood, even though blood was not readily visible upon the cane itself. With this information, the investigator placed the cellmate in the Administrative-Segregation Unit where it was revealed during a subsequent interview that the decedent had shoved the cellmate at the top of the stairs in an argument over a gambling debt.

The cellmate grabbed the decedent's cane and struck him several times on the head. The blows sent the decedent tumbling down the stairs. As the cellmate beat the victim with the cane, blood cast-off the cane striking the front left leg of the cellmate's sweatpants. As he brought the cane back for another swing, the cessation of the action caused the blood to cast-off the cane striking the back left leg of the sweatpants. The cellmate then wiped the blood from the cane onto his T-shirt and placed it to look like the victim had dropped it in his fall. Oddly, cast-off spatter was not detected on the walls or ceiling above the stairwell. As you can see, what would have ordinarily

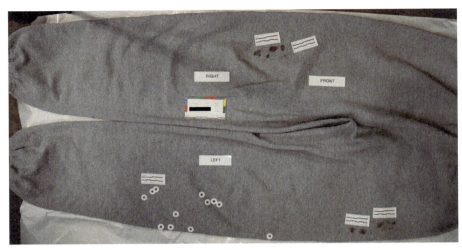

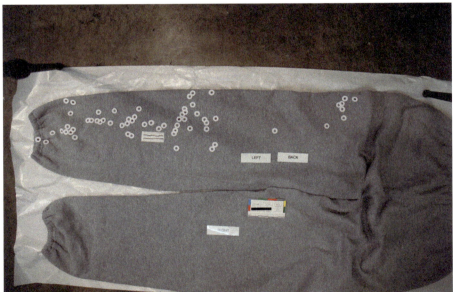

Figure 9.12 A and B The suspect's gray sweatpants with cast-off patterns on the front and cessation cast-off on the rear left leg.

been classified as an accidental fall resulting in death was, in fact, a homicide. Although the actual details of this case have been modified for this chapter, the gist of the investigation remains the same.

As mentioned before, when looking for cast-off spatter, the investigator should inspect the ceiling and walls of the crime scene (Fig. 9.13). Cessation cast-off is likely to be found low on walls and on the floor.

Bloodstain Pattern Evidence in Jails and Prisons 139

Figure 9.13 Cast-off spatter being flung from a broken mop handle during an assault.

Transfer and Transfer Impressions

A transfer occurs when a bloodstained object presses against another surface thus transferring the blood from one surface to another. A bloodstain transfer impression occurs when a bloodstained object presses against another surface, leaving behind an image of the bloodstained object (Figs. 9.14 and 9.15).

Figure 9.14 There is no doubt what created this transfer impression.

Figure 9.15 Blood drops transferred to the bottom of a shoe heel.

Drip Trail

Drip trails occur as the result of the movement of a blood source between two points. This can be passive blood-letting, falling from a victim who is ambulatory, being carried or removed from the scene on a gurney, or blood falling from an object like a knife or blood-soaked garment. This is often the first clue to determining the direction of travel. Dripped bloodstains that are close together can represent a blood source that is slowly moving through the crime scene. Dripped bloodstains that are further apart may indicate the blood source was moving quickly through the scene (Fig. 9.16).

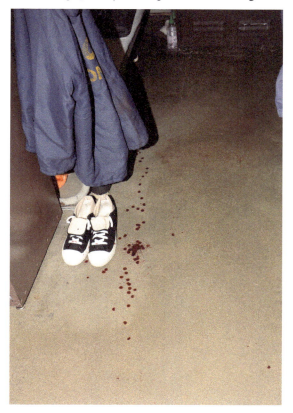

Figure 9.16 The blood drip-trail of a stabbing victim.

Flow

Blood flow occurs as the result of the movement of a volume of blood on a surface due to the pull of gravity or the movement of the surface upon which it was deposited, and before the blood had dried. Flow patterns can be an indicator that a victim has been moved after death (Fig. 9.17).

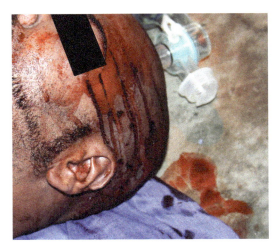

Figure 9.17 The inmate in this photograph was discovered in the supine position, but the flow patterns on the left side of his head indicate he was in the prone position during the blood-letting event.

Pooled Blood

Pooled blood occurs when a blood-letting source remains stationary in one area for a period of time sufficient resulting in the passive accumulation of blood. Pooled blood is often found in the final resting area of a victim of a blood-letting event (Fig. 9.18).

Figure 9.18 Pooled blood from the final position of a gunshot victim. Note the emergency medical services left something behind.

Bloodstain Pattern Evidence in Jails and Prisons 143

Figure 9.19 Blood projected through an open wound by a breach in a tributary vein of the jugular.

Projected Bloodstains

Projected blood stains occur when blood is forced out of an opening under pressure by the breach of an artery or large vein. Because this pattern is produced by the pumping action of the heart, the technician can deduce the victim was alive at the time of the blood-letting event (Figs. 9.19 and 9.20).

Figure 9.20 Blood projected from the nose following a bullet wound to the head.

Collecting Specimen

The one thing that is often neglected while processing the blood-letting event crime scene is the proper collection of specimen swabs for presumptive testing and laboratory analysis. Obviously, there will come a time either during analysis or when testifying in court that the question of who bled where will need to be resolved. Because of this, it is imperative that bloodstains must be swabbed and sampled. This is actually a very easy process, but it must be done properly. Step one is to don PPE including an N-95 mask and gloves. Your author uses sterile 100% cotton-tipped wood applicator swabs that are in sterile packaging, like those found in a medical office. Prior to opening the swab envelope, your author uses a soft-tipped pen to write the important case information on the exterior of the envelope. I then carefully open the envelope at the stick end (not the cotton end). I carefully push both applicators out of the envelope just far enough to slide an applicator collar on the end of each applicator. I push the collars up to the middle of the envelope and then draw both applicators out of the envelope together, being very careful not to touch anything as I remove them from the envelope. Retain the envelope because you are going to use it again. If the blood being collected is dry, you will need to apply sterile water to the applicator tip. Be sure to use a sterile water ampoule, and never touch the tip of the cotton swab with the tip of the ampoule. Instead, drop the water from a height of about one inch. If the blood is wet, you may disregard the need for sterile water. Dab the applicator tip into the blood, being sure not to collect from the periphery of the stain, or the clotted center (Fig. 9.21A–C).

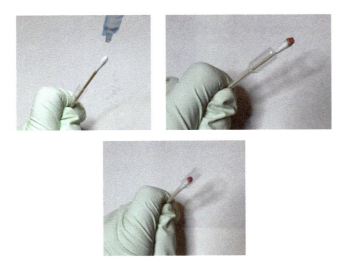

Figure 9.21 A–C Presumptive testing: be careful not to touch the tip of the vial to the swab.

Bloodstain Pattern Evidence in Jails and Prisons 145

Slide the collar up over the cotton tip, break off about one-third of the remaining stick from the bottom, and carefully place the swabs back into the sterile envelope with the collar and cotton tip near the opening (stick end first). Be sure to air-dry the swabs before sealing the envelope with evidence tape. It is very important for the swabs to be dry before sealing the envelope for long-term evidence storage. If the blood specimen has dried to the point of flaking, you can use the above wet method, or scrape the flaked blood into a coin envelope. Be sure to wear safety goggles whenever handling flaked blood as blood-borne pathogens may become airborne.

Note that it is not necessary to use the plastic collars when collecting blood swabs for presumptive testing, as you will likely sacrifice the swab during the testing process. Personally, I use swab collars that are open on both ends (one small opening and one large opening), such as the Sirchie brand applicator shield (stock number AS24), or something similar. The open-ended collar allows for faster drying, in my opinion. Furthermore, it is imperative that you swab one stain at a time. This will prevent placing the wrong swab in the wrong envelope.

Finally, it is important to examine the suspect, and suspect clothing, of a blood-letting crime for signs of blood spatter. Document the discovery with photography and swab the stains in the manner explained above (Fig. 9.22).

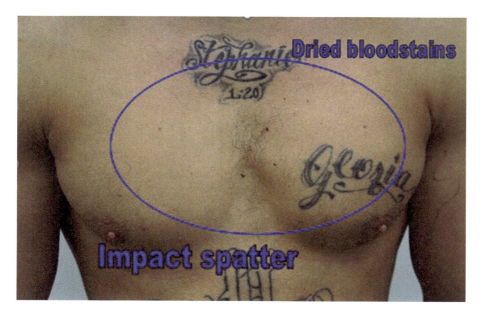

Figure 9.22 Spatter on the chest of the suspect of a brutal stabbing incident. Fortunately, the eagle-eyed investigators noticed it when the suspect had not.

Bloodstain Scenario

One of my favorite bloodstain stories occurred while assisting the prosecutor's office with an attempted homicide in a neighboring city. County jail officials overheard a telephone conversation between a recent in-custody inmate charged with the crime and his mother. During the telephone conversation, the inmate told his mother to be certain to "clean" the garage thoroughly, and she may need to "use bleach." The prosecutor's office petitioned a search warrant and asked if I was available to process the garage to see if bleach had been used to clean up a blood-letting event. I used the trademarked blood reagent BLUESTAR, which produces a vibrant deep blue chemiluminescence (420–440 nm range) when in contact with latent blood. Fortunately, the mother had missed two 90 degrees dripped bloodstains, which later matched the DNA of the victim, but she also neglected to bleach the doorknob leading into the house.

Figure 9.23 Blood evidence on the doorknob visualized with BLUESTAR™.

Suicide Investigations in Jails and Prisons 10

Suicide Investigations

It goes without saying that suicides do occur in jails and prisons. Your author is not, however, convinced that they occur at a greater rate than in the public setting. The prison where I worked generally experienced two or three successful suicides a year, with about a half-dozen attempted suicides. I maintain the diligence of a good housing unit officer to the welfare of the inmates can do much to prevent needless loss of life associated with the natural depression of the prison or jail setting. Holidays, family deaths, failed relationships, parole denials, and the grim environment for first-term inmates can contribute to suicidal ideations. A tier officer who is keen to observe subtle changes in the behavior of a particular inmate can do much to prevent suicide. The best prevention is compassionate and empathetic conversation. In my opinion, the best counselor for these situations is the officer who can understand the daily stresses and conditions that the inmate is experiencing. Religious or lay counselors may not fully appreciate the unique environment associated with prison life. The officer, however, must have sufficient life experience themselves to be able to know what to say and when. Useless is the officer who maintains the "Oh, well, just another inmate" mentality. Also in my opinion, "Suicide Watch" where an inmate expressing ideations of self-harm is given a padded gown, placed into a concrete cell sans mattress, blanket, or any form of audio or visual stimulation, and constantly observed by an officer sitting silently in a chair, does little to ameliorate the situation. In fact, I was convinced if an inmate was not suicidal prior to entering a Suicide Watch cell, they will be by the time they come out. Another important role to play in suicide prevention is annual training provided by investigators who are subject matter experts in suicide investigations to provide vital information regarding the devices or techniques most commonly used by inmates to commit suicide so that officers are more capable of identifying these items during cell searches and inspections. Items such as torn bedsheets braided into a length of cord, single-edged razor blades, stockpiled prescription medications, lengths of shoestring tied together, or caustic chemicals should be considered as devices of suicide. Officers tasked with reading outgoing correspondence should pay close attention to hints of suicide. I recall many years ago reading an outgoing letter written by an inmate serving a life sentence who wrote to his mother informing her that he would "see dad soon." I checked the visiting records of the inmate and discovered that his father was not an approved visitor. While checking the approved list of visitors, I noticed that his mother was in her 80s. I checked the next of kin form on file for the inmate and I noticed that his father was originally listed, but the form had been changed to a sibling approximately five years prior to the date on the letter. A further review of the prison records for the inmate revealed a filing for a temporary compassionate release to attend the funeral of his father. With my investigation concluded, I brought the inmate to my office, and we had a long, genuine discussion regarding life and the loss of loved ones.

In the old days, as we old prison investigators are keen to remember, "hot shots" were the preferred method of suicide; wherein an inmate would take a purposeful dosage of heroin sufficient to produce an overdose and subsequent death. This method was considered a noble death in the heroin-abuser community, like the old Webley service revolver to the compromised English gentleman. With the introduction of Narcan (Naloxone) to the medical personnel toolbox, this method has fallen out of favor as the overdose is quickly reversed, so these days the preferred method is either death by strangulation or self-incised wounds. In my career, I have known of only one instance where an inmate committed suicide by scaling a perimeter fence in a successful attempt to be shot and killed by an armed tower officer, and that incident did not occur at the prison where I worked.

Strangulation by Hanging

It takes only a matter of minutes for an inmate to attach a ligature to a cell ventilation grate or bunk rail, place it around the neck, and apply the pressure necessary to prevent the blood and oxygen from reaching the brain. Once the inmate loses consciousness, gravity will take care of the rest resulting in asphyxia death. Therefore, even if security checks are shortened to 15 minutes on the hour, which is unreasonable given the responsibilities of today's correctional personnel, suicides by strangulation are still going to happen with the greatest chance of death. Also, regardless of the focus of the correctional personnel to prevent suicides through effective communication, watchfulness, and intervention, sometimes an inmate will commit the act without any previous warning or signs of despondency.

When referencing death by strangulation, it is important to note the differences in terminology. Asphyxia caused by hanging results when a noose or other constrictive device (ligature) is tightened firmly around the neck by the weight of the body and the pull of gravity.

Manual strangulation is the act of compressing the neck by use of the hands, forearm, or legs. I cannot imagine a person committing suicide by manual strangulation since the moment they passed out they would simply let go and the pressure necessary to prevent the blood vessels from carrying oxygenated blood to the brain would be gone. Therefore, manual strangulation, if not accidental in nature, will also be categorized as homicide.

Ligature strangulation occurs when a constrictive device is applied to the neck and tightened by a means other than the weight of the body, such as in the case of a suspect tightening a shoestring with his hands around the neck of a victim. In some jurisdictions, the device used in ligature strangulation is still referred to as a garrote. Except for the rare occasion when someone's neck gets in the way of a falling object and its tether, ligature strangulation will almost certainly be categorized as a homicide. Choking occurs when an object is swallowed and obstructs a person's ability to breathe. Choking does not occur when an inmate has his hands around the neck of his cellmate in a constricting manner. That would be manual strangulation.

Ligatures can be fashioned from dental floss, shoelaces, a belt, bedsheets torn into strips, a T-shirt, a towel, or even the elastic band from underwear. The inmate will be found either in complete suspension with his feet completely off the floor, or incomplete suspension wherein the feet, knees, thigh, or buttocks are partially or completely in contact with the floor. If rigor mortis is present when the inmate is discovered by the first responder and no life-saving efforts are employed, it is imperative that the body remain where and as it was found. The position of the ligature should be documented, indicating the placement of the knot (right lateral, left lateral, center posterior, center anterior, or any degree in-between) and the point of suspension. It should be noted if the ligature slants upward toward the point of suspension in a "V" notch or if it encircles or tends to encircle the neck. Although a furrow that completely encircles the neck is most common with ligature strangulation, it is not of itself solely indicative of the application of a garrote-type device; just as the absence of a visible point of suspension does not eliminate strangulation by hanging. Once this documentation has been accomplished, the ligature should be carefully cut in a manner that preserves the knot and processed into evidence.

If more than one strand is used to fashion the ligature, I place tape on each of the cut end and label the tape with corresponding letters to indicate which end matches the other. An examination should be made of the ligature mark or furrow that is present on the neck of the victim (Figs. 10.1 and 10.2). In short, it should match the ligature in width and construction. If it does not, you may want to consider that the inmate is the victim of a homicide who was killed either by manual or ligature strangulation and then staged to appear as if death was caused by suicide. This should be considered especially in circumstances where the inmate was not the sole occupant of a cell or when the body was discovered in an unconfined area. It is strongly recommended that the ligature be present at the time of the autopsy, but great care should be taken not to contaminate the item when it is viewed by the medical examiner or pathologist.

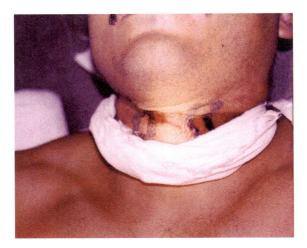 

Figure 10.1 Ligature mark or furrow caused by a bedsheet.

Figure 10.2 Bedsheet tied to cell vent.

I recommend viewing the ligature on clean butcher paper in a room other than the autopsy suite. Conjunctivae petechiae or facial petechiae may or may not be present, the lack of which may indicate that death occurred rapidly. Purpura or bruising may be present at or proximal to the ligature furrow (Fig. 10.3A and B).

It is not uncommon that a suicide note is not found in the cell or among the inmate's possessions and the absence of a note does not necessarily indicate that the death is suspicious. I can think of only a handful of cases where a note was recovered; and in the missive, blame was placed on the department or family members for "not caring" about the general welfare of the inmate. It is also advisable to check the outgoing mail immediately following the

 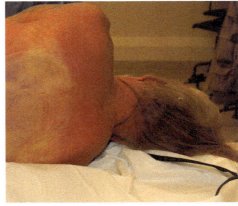

Figure 10.3 A and B Ligature strangulation: "V" notch ligature mark. Note the purpura proximal to the furrow. Also, note that the ligature mark slants upward toward the point of suspension.

discovery of the decedent to see if a farewell letter had been written, placed on the tier, and had already been collected by staff or if it was placed in the housing unit mailbox earlier by the inmate. I have noticed that when a suicide occurs in the Administrative Segregation Unit, I will almost always find something written on a cell wall; oftentimes the writing will be very small and written in an obscure place.

Of critical importance to the investigation is that the cell of an inmate discovered hanging must be "dead-lined" and sealed until after the autopsy and, at the least, the preliminary findings of the medical examiner or pathologist are known. Although it has not occurred at the institution where I worked, I do know of an incident at a nearby institution wherein the cellmate was allowed to return to the cell on the same night of the incident, only to find out two days later at autopsy that his cellmate was the victim of a homicide. The consequences are imaginable.

Self-Inflicted Incised Wounds

Fatal self-inflicted incised wounds are less common in housing units where supervision is either constant or routine, such as a dormitory or observation cell, than it is in a cell block where observation might be done randomly or on an hourly basis, because of the time required for the body to lose a sufficient amount of blood to cause exsanguinations, shock, and death. However, individuals determined to end their lives have found ways to conceal the activity from observation. Your author has known inmates to sit on a toilet or wrap the cut limb in plastic and lay underneath the covers of their bunk or to sever major veins or arteries that speed the blood loss process. The preferred method of self-inflicting a fatal incised wound is to cut either the radial artery in the wrist or arm, the femoral artery in the leg, or the carotid artery or jugular veins in the neck. Hesitation marks may be present in suicide victims. Often an individual will make superficial "test" cuts to determine pain levels or to establish the force necessary to make the cut. Although inmates who have cellmates present most often do not employ this method of suicide, it has happened at my facility wherein an inmate in the top bunk waited for his cellmate to fall asleep and then he made several deep cuts in his wrist. The cellmate was awakened by the dropping of blood on his forehead from the upper bunk and he alerted staff of the incident. The victim survived the attempt and confirmed the story. One can imagine the attempt would have been successful if the sleeping arrangements had been reversed. However, if an inmate is discovered with incised wounds in a cell with a cellmate, it would be best to isolate the cellmate until such time as the matter can be investigated.

A self-inflicted incised wound of the radial artery will be on the anterior forearm or wrist of the non-dominant arm. In other words, a right-handed person will cut the left arm or wrist, and vice versa. Defensive incised wounds tend to be on the posterior surface of arms and hands or the palms of hands as the victim attempts to ward off the attack. Flailing and struggling victims of slashing assaults tend to incur injuries that are not precisely placed unless the assault is exceptionally fast and deliberately targets a victim who is incapacitated or caught otherwise unaware. However, slashing assaults can be extremely fast, with exceptionally sharp instruments, and the victim is quite often caught completely unaware. Unfortunately, self-inflicted incised wounds to the neck tend to resemble incised wounds from a slashing assault where the suspect attacked the victim from behind. In other words, the wound will start higher toward the back of the neck and then angle downward slightly toward the terminal stroke, starting shallow at first and getting deep as the blade is drawn across the neck, perhaps even becoming shallow again at the terminating stroke.

Furthermore, self-inflicted incised wounds do not always have the classic "sliced" appearance as inmates may cut themselves with whatever sharp object is at hand. Years ago, I remember an inmate who sliced his neck with the folded-over lid of a tuna fish can. The cut resembled that of a serrated bread knife blade. Another inmate cut and dug at his jugular vein with a pair of tweezers and the nail file from fingernail clippers.

In one of the most persistent self-inflicted incised wound suicides that your author experienced occurred when an inmate waited until his cellmate had left the cell for his job assignment and watched the tier officer finish his routine security check of the tiers when he produced a single-edged razor blade from its hiding place and made an incision to his left wrist. As the injury was not producing a sufficient flow of blood, he continued to cut his wrist until the left hand was almost all the way removed (Fig. 10.4A and B).

 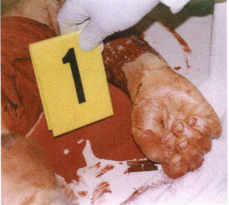

Figure 10.4 A and B The decedent as he was found in his cell. The T-shirt he was wearing was originally white. Interestingly the razor blade found at the scene was old. The decedent had a new, sharper blade in the locker containing his property.

Suicide Investigations in Jails and Prisons

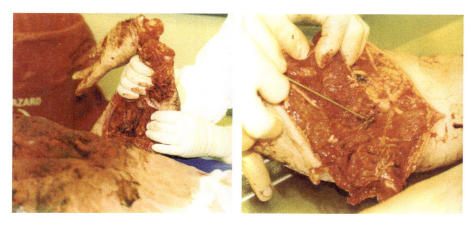

Figure 10.5 A and B The wrist was almost completely severed, with the forearm opened exposing the radial artery.

This still did not produce the desired blood loss, so he explored his forearm looking for the radial artery, which he eventually found (Fig. 10.5A and B). This produced the desired blood flow. Just before losing consciousness, he made three incised wounds on his left thigh (Fig. 10.6A and B). Interestingly, these wounds produced very little blood loss. The inmate died within the 35 minutes it took for the officer to make his next security check of the tier.

Upon responding to the cell, my partner and I strongly suspected a homicide until such time as I located the razor blade and noted a notch in the distal phalanx of the right index finger that corresponded to a notch in the distal phalanx of the right thumb. The notch was the size and shape of the corner

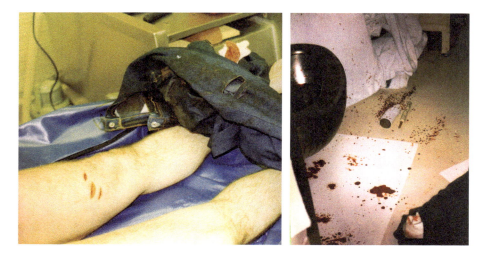

Figure 10.6 A and B Three deep cuts to the thigh produced a limited blood loss. The toilet used by the decedent to collect the blood flow.

of the razor blade. The inmate had applied so much pressure to the blade that it left an impression on these digits. It was determined following toxicology analysis that the inmate had no intoxicants in his system. No note was left, but inmates who knew the decedent stated that he would often say, "If I take myself out, it's going to be like I did my [victims*]." A review of his criminal history indicated that he had killed his victims (girlfriends), dismembered their body parts, and placed the body parts in plastic barrels.

*It is alleged that the inmate used a more derogatory term when referring to his girlfriends.

Although in the above incident, the blade used was the kind normally found in a box knife, very small pieces of metal can be used to great effect by the sheer determination of the user (Figs. 10.7A and B and 10.8).

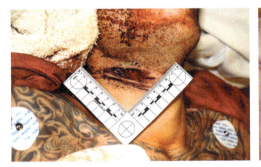 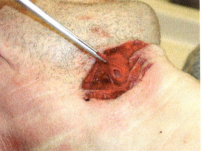

Figure 10.7 **A and B** The incised wound is on the neck between the Laryngeal prominence and the Sternocleidomastoid muscle with a small hesitation cut near the jugular vein.

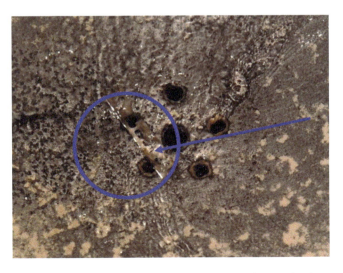

Figure 10.8 The razor blade used in the above incident, which was removed from a safety razor.

Footwear Evidence in Jails and Prisons

11

Footwear impressions are the first type of evidence to be overlooked at the crime scene and usually the first to be inadvertently destroyed by responding staff. Yet, footwear impressions can lead you directly to your suspect, or an eyewitness, and can be a critical aspect of your investigation. It is imperative that first responders are trained in the detection and preservation of footwear impressions that are relevant to the crime scene. Several years ago, I responded to an alarm raised at one of our housing units. An inmate had been brutally beaten by two other inmates. The first officer on the scene noticed a bloodstained footwear impression next to the unconscious victim. He noticed that the pattern did not match that of the shoes worn by the victim, so he immediately grabbed an empty cardboard box that was lying nearby and placed it over the impression. He then positioned himself between the overturned box and responding officers to protect his treasured find.

In an error of judgment, the first supervisor on the scene locked up the inmates who were on the tier at the time of the incident before documenting their identities or positions relative to the crime scene. Upon my arrival, the officer who discovered the footwear impression promptly and proudly showed me his finding. I took a photograph of the impression with the digital camera and showed it to the officers who had been assembled to conduct cell-to-cell skin searches. The suspect was found in his cell, washing his hands and upper body in the cell sink. He was still wearing the shoes that made the impression and had made a second impression on a towel upon which he had been standing in front of the sink. Had the footwear impression been overlooked or accidentally destroyed, we would not have had that essential evidence linking the suspect to the crime. I can think of three other crimes that were solved, in part, because of an impression of the suspect's shoes left at the crime scene.

Footwear impressions are not difficult to document and collect, provided you follow a systematic method. The equipment that you will need to document the impression will include a camera, a flash that can be operated off the camera (either wireless or slaved), a shutter release cable, a tripod that will allow the camera to be suspended upside-down, a level, and an L-scale. Your author uses the standard vinyl reversible macrophotography L-scale (300mm × 150mm), but I glue a golf-ball marker to the face of the scale to assist the analyst in determining the direction of artificial and natural light. Using the flash to add light between near-oblique and 45 degrees can add contrast and depth to the furrows left by footwear that are molded (such as those left in mud, sand, or soft dirt), thereby providing an image that has more definition and detail. However, the analyst may need to know if the detail is an individual characteristic made by the shoe or a shadow caused by the addition of the electronic flash. The shadow cast by the golf ball marker allows the analyst to make this determination (Fig. 11.1).

Figure 11.1 Note that the scale has a small circle embossed on its face. This circle is useful to the analyst in determining if the photograph was taken with the film plane parallel and perpendicular to the object. Any deviation would result in an oblong image. That is also why it is important to use a level to make the final adjustments to your camera prior to taking the photographs.

Footwear Evidence in Jails and Prisons 157

The first step is to set your camera on the tripod with the center post inverted (Fig. 11.2). Many agencies utilize tripods with extended booms or multi-position center posts that project over the image being photographed. These tripods are terrific and extremely useful in the crime scene but beware of balance issues; a slight bump of the tripod might send your camera head-first into your evidence.

Note that it is best not to put the flash on the camera until it has been properly focused and leveled. Also, it is best to use the flash on an off-camera cord as there is nothing worse than having it fall into the impression while making the final adjustments to the camera or tripod. I recommend attaching the off-camera shutter release wire before attaching the camera

Figure 11.2 A tripod with the center post inverted and camera mounted.

to the tripod; I generally use a clamp to hold that device from falling into the impression as well. Remote off-camera shutter releases or flash devices are excellent for this application provided you do not have to configure their operation after each photograph. The less you must physically touch the camera, the less the chance of knocking it out of level. Of course, pulling on the wires or cables attaching non-remote devices can also pull the camera slightly off level. So, the best policy is to handle everything with diligent care.

Check the level of the camera with the impression once before focusing the camera and again after the addition of the flash (Fig. 11.3).

The step that is often forgotten when teaching this technique is to furrow a trench in an L-shape far enough away from the impression so as not to

Figure 11.3 Adjusting the level of the camera with that of the impression.

Footwear Evidence in Jails and Prisons

Figure 11.4 **A and B** Furrowing a trench to the depth of the impression will reduce distortion and ensure that the scale is on the same plane as the impression.

damage it or any physical evidence that might be present, yet close enough that the scale will be captured in the frame (Fig. 11.4A and B).

The reason for this trench is to allow the scale to be photographed at the same plane as the impression. This accomplishes two purposes: it ensures that the scale and the impression will both be in focus, and it corrects distortions caused by the scale not being on the same plane as the object (parallax error).

While holding the flash between oblique and 45-degree angles, take photographs of the impression, firing the flash between the openings of the legs on each side of the tripod (Fig. 11.5A–H). Once you have accomplished this, take a photograph without the flash, if ambient lighting

Figure 11.5 **A–H** Photographing footwear impressions: Here, the investigative officer takes a photograph of the footwear impression with the use of a flash, and one final photograph without the use of the flash. (*Continued*)

Figure 11.5 (*Continued*)

Footwear Evidence in Jails and Prisons

permits (or if you can make manual adjustments to the camera such as increasing the film speed).

Once the photographs have been taken, a casting of the impression can be made using one of the casting materials commonly available from the forensic supply companies (such as Sirchie's Shake-N-Cast™, Lynn Peavey's Copy Cast™, or Arrowhead Forensics' Arrowstone™, among others). The process of casting the impression is simple, just follow the instructions provided with the casting medium, mix the compound to the consistency of pancake batter, gently pour it into the impression, and allow it to dry. You may also use an alternate method whereby you pour water into the impression and then sift in the casting compound until it thickens if there are concerns that pouring in the mixture will alter the impression. You may have to use or construct a frame that will hold the compound until it dries. Your author takes evidentiary photographs of the casting in the laboratory once it is dry enough to package as evidence. The best method of packaging the casting into evidence is to place the casting on a piece of cardboard that will fit the dimensions of a box the size of a shoe box. I then use electrician's plastic wire ties to firmly affix the casting to the cardboard, placing gauze between the plastic wire ties and the casting, and then gently lowering it into the box.

Molded impressions are not as common to the interior correctional setting as are bloodstained or dust impressions left on concrete (Fig. 11.6A and B). Bloodstained impressions are documented using the same equipment as the molded impressions, only without using the flash to introduce oblique lighting as the flash may cause a "hot spot" or "burned" area that might obscure the details. Dust impressions may require the application of a clean white light at an oblique angle to aid in visualization. This application is best

Figure 11.6 A and B Bloodstain impressions deposited on concrete and photographed in the crime scenes. Note the hot spot in the photograph on the right. This was caused by the light fixture in the shower area, but it does not interfere with the image or scale.

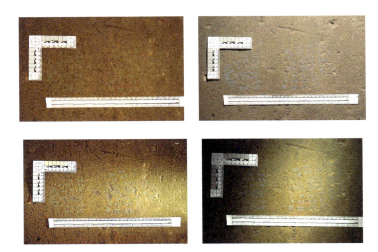

Figure 11.7 A–D Clockwise from top to bottom: This was a difficult dust print to document. It was deposited directly on top of the only part of the concrete floor that had been stained by an unknown dark substance. The dust medium was a type of talcum powder. (A) Photograph was taken using just ambient light. (B) Photograph was taken using an off-camera flash. (C and D) Photographs were taken using oblique lighting from a soft white light (Lynn Peavey's Battle Lite™). I am most partial to the bottom right photograph. Note that I used an adhesive scale and an ABFO scale. The adhesive scale allowed me to photograph the scale nearer to the same plane as the impression while the ABFO scale provided the round circles to ensure the camera was level.

done with a soft white light as opposed to a flash (Fig. 11.7A–D). The technique for capturing the image of a dust impression still requires the use of a tripod.

The above impression can be lifted and preserved using either a gel-lifter, which is my preferred method or by using an electrostatic dust lifter such as Evident Crime Scene Product's PathFinder™ or Sirchie's Electrostatic Dust Print Lifter™.

Dark prints left in dust or dried bloodstained footwear impressions can be lifted using casting material. It is important to make a frame around the impression using duct tape and then pour the casting material directly over the impression, making sure that the casting material is of the consistency of pancake batter. Allow the casting to dry thoroughly and use a putty knife to gently pry the duct tape away from the surface, lifting the entire casting like a hinge. Remember that the recovered impression will be a mirrored image of the original. Also, keep in mind that these castings are extremely thin and fragile. It is best to photograph them as quickly as possible and to firmly mount them in a covered box as described earlier (Fig. 11.8A–C).

Footwear Evidence in Jails and Prisons

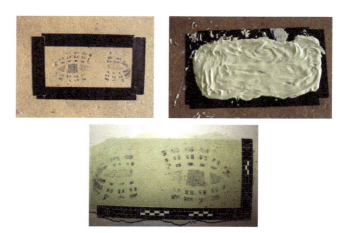

Figure 11.8 **A–C** Dust impressions lifted using casting materials. The application of duct tape provides a frame for the thinly applied mixture. It also allows the technician to lift the impression like a giant hinge by freeing only three sides of the tape from the concrete. Once the casting has been flipped over, the tape can be cut away using a utility knife blade.

Footwear impressions deposited on carpeting may also be challenging for the investigator to document and collect and may take some creative solutions by creating a sample impression on a nearby piece of carpeting and the trial-and-error success of lifting the sample impression (Fig. 11.9A–C).

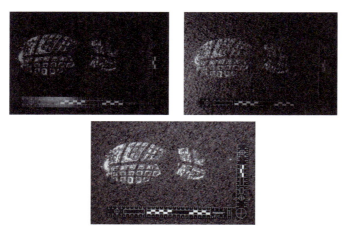

Figure 11.9 **A–C** Clockwise from top to bottom: This impression was deposited on a dark gray carpet in a classroom. The medium appeared to be chalk dust. I attempted to illuminate the print using oblique lighting; however, the fibers of the carpeting prevented the light from falling evenly onto the impression (A). I then attempted to capture the image using diffused flash with the camera set at f/22 (B). Setting the camera at f/13, while bouncing the flash off a nearby white wall, provided the best image (C). Lifting this impression proved equally difficult, with the best result coming from the PathFinder™ electrostatic dust lifter.

Figure 11.10 **A and B** Bloodstained shoe print lifted with a gel lifter and treated with Hungarian Red, photographed with alternate light source at 540nm with a red barrier filter.

Exemplar footwear impressions should be collected from first responders, medical and fire personnel, and the investigative staff on the scene. Fortunately, there is no need to actually collect the shoes or even photograph them as there are several inkless shoe print documentation kits available on the market, such as Lynn Peavey's Inkless Shoe Print™ kit, which produce quality impressions that can be stored for extended periods of time. It is an easy process that requires the wearer to simply step up on the invisible inking pad and then place their foot on the special paper for the impressions.

Bloodstained footwear worn by the suspect or victim should be documented and collected immediately in order to prevent contamination or destruction through wear or movement (Fig. 11.10A–C). All footwear and garments should be collected prior to decontamination procedures being implemented. There is nothing more frustrating to a crime scene analyst than to approach a scene only to see valuable evidence being washed down a drain as the running water is poured over the suspect's head to relieve the effects of the chemical agents (Figs. 11.11A–C and 11.12).

Figure 11.11 **(A–C)** Quick thinking by responding officers prevented the destruction of the blood evidence on the shoes of one suspect.

Footwear Evidence in Jails and Prisons

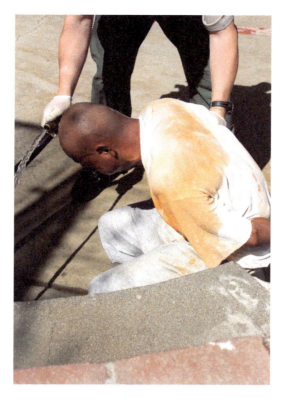

Figure 11.12 Regrettably, the bloodstained footwear was not collected prior to the decontamination process in this incident.

Your author cannot stress enough the importance of collecting the footwear of the victim and suspect at the scene. I had a homicide investigation resulting from an inmate being kicked to death by his cellmate, a former professional Cambodian kickboxer, inside a cell. When I responded to the scene, I discovered that the victim had been removed to the Infirmary and the suspect had been taken to a holding cell. In order to take the suspect to the holding cell, the escorting officers had to walk him up a corridor that was approximately 60 yards from the housing unit. As I was processing the scene, a supervisor informed me that he had photographed the bloodstained socks of the suspect and wanted to know if he should collect them into evidence (Fig. 11.13A and B). This was the first time I had heard of the existence of this important evidence. "Of course," was my answer, "Where are they now?" "Still on the suspect," was the reply. Indeed, in this case, it was still imperative to collect the socks as having tremendous evidentiary value, but you can imagine that the significance of the DNA evidence was somewhat diminished owing to the fact that the inmate was walked up a corridor that had been trafficked by thousands of inmates, including the victim countless times before his death, every day.

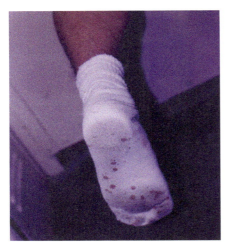 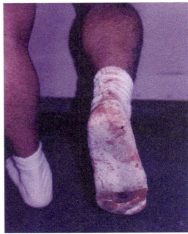

Figure 11.13 A and B Bloodstain evidence on the socks of the suspect in the alleged kicking death of his cellmate. The socks should have been collected prior to the suspect having been escorted to a holding cell.

Had the socks of the suspect been collected at the scene prior to his being removed from the area, the obvious contamination of the evidence would have been greatly reduced.

Footwear that is collected at the crime scene should be stored as evidence in a box of a size consistent with the original shoe box in which they were purchased. Never place shoes in an evidence box with the soles facing or touching each other. Your author generally wraps bloodstained shoes loosely in butcher paper and places them individually into boxes. I prefer not to store shoes in paper bags. Socks may be stored in paper bags but be certain to record the foot from which the sock was removed. I have seen more than one officer wish they had done just that when being questioned on the stand. Our protocols prohibit an officer or CSI from writing anything on the sock, especially if the sock is to be submitted for DNA analysis. If it is necessary to mark the sock for identification in court, I recommend that the officer complete an evidence tag and then use a piece of clean string to tie the tag to the sock, then fold the sock into butcher paper, and place the tag on the outside of the butcher paper wrapper. Finally, place the butcher paper-wrapped sock into an evidence bag.

Footwear Scenario

Narrative: Your author provided a mutual aid response to the report of the stabbing of a male victim in the north-east bedroom of a residence in a neighboring city. On scene, emergency medical assistance was terminated, and the victim was declared deceased. A suspect had been located several blocks

Footwear Evidence in Jails and Prisons 167

from the residence and was taken into custody. His clothing and shoes were collected immediately and processed into evidence.

Observations: The crime scene was located within a single-family, single-story, two-bedroom, one-bath house, green in color, with a north-east exposure. The front door of the residence was open. All rooms were well-lit, with sufficient electric lighting available for scene inspection and processing. Photographic documentation was conducted using an electronic flash for supplemental lighting. The ambient temperature was approximately 70°F. The kitchen door, the only other ingress/egress door, was closed and locked. The television set in the living room was on. An armchair was askew, pushed against a sofa. A floor lamp had been upset near the front door. Four bloodstained footwear impressions from a right Nike brand Air Jordan tennis shoe were apparent on the living room floor. Each impression was spaced by approximately three and a half feet apart, indicating the contributor was running (Figs. 11.14 and 11.15).

Figure 11.14 Bloodstained footwear impressions on the tile floor, spaced to suggest the suspect was running.

Figure 11.15 The width of the impression (at its widest point) is 110mm and the length exceeds 280mm.

Observations of the north bedroom: The north bedroom measured approximately 11′6″ in width and 12′10″ in length. The room was well-lit by electric lighting. The window was open, but the screen was intact and did not display evidence of tampering or removal. The decedent was lying in the supine position in a south-east orientation, between two twin beds. His right arm was extended, partially underneath the north-east bed. His chest was bare, and he was clad in blue and white checkered boxer shorts and bloodstained white socks. A red, white, and blue checkered long-sleeve shirt and white long-sleeve undershirt were on the floor partially underneath the decedent's left shoulder. A pair of blood-saturated denim pants, which had been cut from the decedent, were beneath his legs. A tourniquet was fastened to his right thigh, along with gauze bandaging. A compression bandage was placed on the left side of his chest. Artifacts from life-saving measures, including a resuscitator "Ambubag," were strewn across the bedroom and living room. Significant blood pooling was noted on the floor, with the largest concentration of pooling underneath and at the head of the north-east bed. A nightstand was in close proximity to the decedent's legs. Officers on scene informed me the decedent was originally on top of the north-east bed and was placed on the floor for support during chest-compressions. They also pulled the nightstand away from the wall in order to use it to elevate the right leg of the decedent.

Blood transfers on the nightstand, and objects atop the nightstand, were created by the placement of the leg on top of the nightstand. Blood transfer was present on the torso, arms, and legs of the decedent. Contusions were noted on the left upper cheek and brow ridge of the decedent.

Impact blood spatter was noted on the lower wall in proximity to the headboard of the north-east bed, and the spines of surface effect spatter, consistent with a heavy object contacting pooled blood, was noted on the floor in proximity to the head of the north-east bed (Figs. 11.16 and 11.17).

Transfer and pooled blood patterns were present on both bed coverings. Your author designated the bed coverings of the north-west bed as target "B" for testing and sampling purposes. Footwear impressions from first responders, fire, or medical personnel were also located within the bedroom. These impressions were documented and compared to responding personnel.

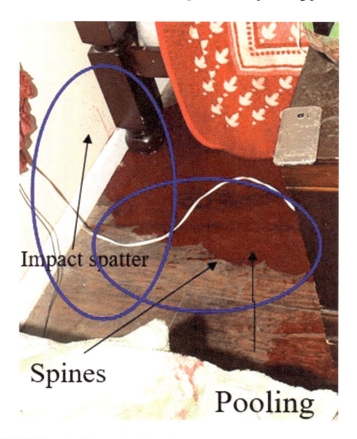

Figure 11.16 Blood evidence in the crime scene.

170   Crime Scene Processing in Correctional Facilities and Prisons

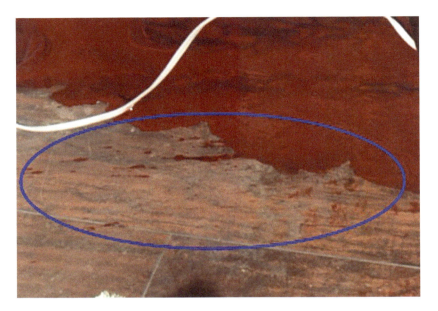

Figure 11.17 Spines indicate a heavy object struck the pooled blood.

Processing the scene: Your author documented the scene in its entirety by digital photography and collected measurements for diagramming prior to any alterations of the scene. Following this, your author removed trauma bags left by first responders to better assess the scene. Your author documented the living room floor as target "A," and the four bloodstained Nike brand tennis shoe impressions in the living room as items A-1 through A-4, beginning at the threshold of the north-west bedroom, and ending at the front door (Fig. 11.18A–D).

Figure 11.18 A–D The four bloodstained footwear transfer impressions in the crime scene. Note the impressions are getting lighter as the supply of blood is diminishing. Also, note that all four impressions are of the right shoe. (*Continued*)

Footwear Evidence in Jails and Prisons 171

Figure 11.18 (*Continued*)

Figure 11.19 The right shoe recovered from the suspect.

Your author collected sacrificial swabs from stain A-1, stain B-1, and the right foreleg of the decedent. Your author conducted presumptive testing of these swabs using the phenolphthalein (Kastle–Meyer) test method. This test method produced positive results for suspected blood. I conducted presumptive species testing of the remaining swabs using the Hexagon OBTI Immunochromatographic Rapid Test method. This test method produced positive results for suspected blood with the species consistent with humans. Gel-lift specimens of the footwear impressions were collected from the scene following documentation.

Forensic analysis: Your author prepared a sterile work surface and utilized a photographic copy stand to document the exterior of the shoe with digital photography (Fig. 11.19). Your author noted the shoe to be a men's size 10.

Your author determined the width of the shoe sole to be consistent with the bloodstained footwear impressions deposited at the crime scene at 110mm (at the widest point), and the length of the shoe sole also to be consistent with the bloodstained footwear impressions left at the scene. To determine the length of the shoe, your author measured the distance from the edge of the heel (impression A-2) to the distal circle of the ball pivot and documented the distance at 227mm in both the right tennis shoe and impression A-2 (Figs. 11.20 and 11.21).

Your author collected sacrificial swabs from the outer concentric circle of the right shoe sole. Your author conducted presumptive testing of one swab

Footwear Evidence in Jails and Prisons

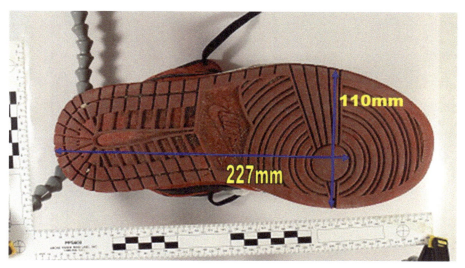

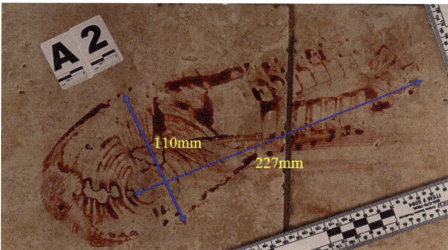

Figures 11.20 and 11.21 Determining the size of the shoe with the bloodstain transfer impressions.

using the phenolphthalein (Kastle–Meyer) test method. This test method produced positive results for suspected blood. Your author conducted presumptive species testing of the second swab using the Hexagon OBTI Immunochromatographic Rapid Test method. This test method produced positive results for suspected blood with the species consistent with humans. Your author collected two blood specimen swabs from the surrounding area and processed them collectively into evidence (Fig. 11.22).

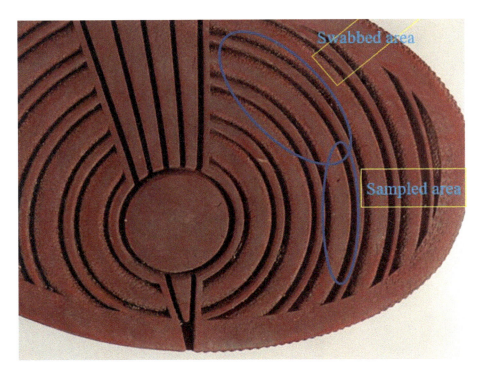

Figure 11.22 Collecting swabs for analysis from the outsole.

Bloodstains were also noted on the right and left side outsole of the right shoe, as indicated by the photographic scales in Fig. 11.23A and B.

DNA analysis of the blood specimen swabs collected from the crime scene matched the DNA of the decedent. DNA analysis of the blood specimen collected from the shoe matched the DNA of the victim. DNA analysis of the specimen collected from the inner sole, as well as the analysis of the inner

Figure 11.23 **A and B** Blood evidence recovered from both shoes. (*Continued*)

Footwear Evidence in Jails and Prisons 175

Figure 11.23 (*Continued*)

sole itself, matched the DNA of the suspect. It was determined the suspect was the only wearer of the shoe.

The inner soles were forensically analyzed following a claim by the suspect that the shoes belonged to a friend, and he had only just borrowed them before he was arrested. As noted, DNA swabs collected from the interior of the shoe, along with the analysis of the inner sole with a casting of the suspect's foot, reflected the suspect was the sole wearer of the shoe.

Fingerprint Evidence in Jails and Prison

12

When it comes down to it, the fingerprint development technician in a prison or jail will be quite busy with fingerprint impressions deposited on either porous surfaces where the impressions are absorbed into the surface of an object, such as the ubiquitous anonymous note or death threat, or non-porous surfaces, like inmate manufactured weapons or the odd pilfered cabinet or culinary cart, where the impressions remain on top of the surface of the object. Therefore, it really is not necessary to have a fingerprint laboratory stocked with anything more than ninhydrin, powders, cyanoacrylate, sticky-side tape formula, Doje's Skin Print Black™ for the occasional throttling, and perhaps a few bottles of small particle reagent (SPR) stashed away for the odd early morning escape.

Powders are the old faithful partner of the fingerprint technician. Let's face it, sometimes it is just the easiest solution to throw some powder. I have only two colors of powder in my lab, black and silver. I do not use white powder as I find it almost impossible to lift prints developed with white powders. I also prefer an ostrich feather brush with a light, twirling touch, and a camel hair (or squirrel hair) brush for finishing. Whatever technique or brush the technician finds that works best is fine, but practice, practice, practice. Be sure not to mix your brushes and to have one brush designated for each type of powder. I try to hold the item being printed at oblique angles, sometimes using a small flashlight, to look for inherently luminescent, glistening ridge prints before I apply the powders. If I see a good impression that I am confident that I can develop, lift, and identify, I proceed with my dusting. If it looks like it is a good, but faint impression, or just a partial ridge impression without sufficient detail for identification, I either swab the print for DNA typing or use a sterile brush and sterile powders so that whatever develops, if not identifiable, can be submitted for DNA typing. Magnetic brushes and powders work great for non-metallic items of evidence. It is also very easy to sterilize a magnetic brush or to use a sterile plastic cover for your favorite magnetic brush. I also have a host of fluorescent powders that I use with my alternate light source (ALS). Be forewarned, a little fluorescent powder goes a long way. Fluorescent green tends to be my preferred powder and I dip my brush maybe once every three or four dustings, relying on what remains in the brush from the previous use to do the job (Fig. 12.1). Photography with a scale is always recommended before attempting your lift. Even the

Fingerprint Evidence in Jails and Prisons

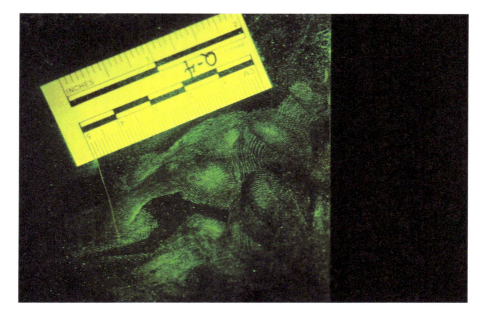

Figure 12.1 A print developed on a computer screen using fluorescent powders.

most experienced technician has lost a print during the lift. In the past, it has always been best to take the Julia Child approach, when she dropped the turkey on the floor and announced, "Sometimes it is always best to be the only person in the kitchen." However, with digital cameras, there is no reason why you should not photograph the print before attempting the lift. I preserve the lift either on a fingerprint record/backing card or on a hinge-lifter. As for keeping your negative lifts, I will leave that to the protocols of your agency. Most of my negative lists are completely consumed by swabbing.

Ninhydrin

Ninhydrin is a chemical reagent used to visualize latent prints on porous items, such as paper, through a reaction with the amino acids present in sweat secretions, which turn the prints a violet color called Ruhemann's purple (Fig. 12.2). The technician will either spray the ninhydrin on a surface using a pre-mixed solution, available from any forensic supply company, in a spray bottle, or apply it by brushing or dipping the item with the solution in a pan that contains the solution, which is the preferred method by your author, and then hang the item to dry. The best results can be achieved using a fuming cabinet heated to 175°F with an attached humidifier. Using this method,

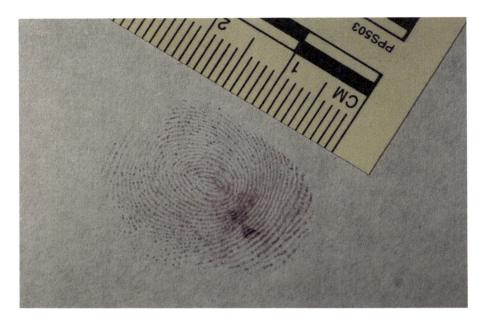

Figure 12.2 Right thumbprint developed using the ninhydrin process.

prints will begin to develop in 5–10 minutes. Without the chamber, prints will begin to develop in about an hour. The chamber is invaluable to the technician, who is constantly harried by administrators who are anxious to know if a print was developed on a death threat to staff, as the reaction time is greatly reduced. I allow the item to hang dry for up to 24 hours to allow faint prints to fully develop. I do not recommend using ninhydrin sold in aerosol cans unless the laboratory is equipped with a good breathing apparatus and a well-ventilated fuming chamber. Even with these precautions, the technician will still have some exposure to the invasive fumes. It is imperative that the technician wears several layers of latex gloves and a respirator when working with ninhydrin and that the laboratory is well-ventilated to an area that will not inconvenience people passing by.

Remember that any uncovered part of the technician's skin will stain purple when it comes in contact with the chemical, and it might remain that way for a few hours regardless of washing. So, if you do not want to have purple streaks on your cheeks and forehead, do not scratch until you have discarded your gloves and washed your hands. Be careful when using premixed ninhydrin that also contains acetone, as this chemical may obliterate some soluble inks. The same can be said for some fixatives. It is always best to experiment before processing the actual item of evidence. I also will always photograph the document before processing and again immediately after. Using a green-colored filter will help correct the purple color if you find it difficult to analyze. You may also use the ALS at 535nm without a barrier filter or 485nm (450nm for Manila envelopes) with an orange filter to visualize.

I will admit that I have had great success with ninhydrin over the years and have even developed prints on a document that had not been touched in 10 years. I also pulled a thumbprint off an untreated piece of wood that had been fashioned into a handle for an inmate-manufactured stabbing weapon. With some experience, the technician will also become an expert at determining which prints belong to the writer of the note and which belong to staff members who have handled the document with their bare hands. Staff members tend to leave partial prints on the extreme corners of the document or thumbprints on the margins about one-third of the way up from the bottom of the page, with corresponding index finger impressions opposing. Should an inmate wear latex gloves while drafting their machinations, they will seldom wear them while carrying the note to the mailbox. Therefore, do not forget to treat the envelope that housed the offensive document. Special formulations are available for developing prints on thermal paper. Bear in mind that papers that have been coated in wax, like milk cartons, do not lend themselves to ninhydrin processing. For this type of evidence, it is best to use powders, cyano-acrylate fuming, or Sudan Black.

Another great thing about ninhydrin is that even if you only develop partials or smudged impressions, the ninhydrin process does not interfere with DNA typing.

Cyanoacrylate Ester

Cyanoacrylate ester fuming has replaced powders as the workhorse of the fingerprint laboratory. With the advent of easy-to-use fuming kits, the ever-popular and inexpensive cotton-ball method, and fuming wands there is no reason for any jail or prison laboratory not to be equipped with a fuming chamber or to bring cyanoacrylate to the crime scene. The technician will place the item of evidence in the fuming chamber and place either the super glue on a foil tray on top of a heating plate with a humidity source or will introduce a fuming kit, such as Sirchie's Cyano-Shot™ or Lynn Peavey's Hot Shot™, by placing the activator canister into the jar containing the activator solution and emptying the glue vial on top of the activator canister. It is best to have a fan in the chamber for the circulation of the fumes evenly onto the items being fumed. Cyanoacrylate esters react with the amino acids, fatty acids, and proteins in the latent fingerprint to create a visible print that is white along the ridge lines and absent on the furrows. Cyanoacrylate also will not degrade DNA, so if you only get partials, you can still submit the item for DNA typing. Fuming chambers can be made from any cabinet or fish tank or can be commercially purchased. Your author's fuming chamber at the prison was made from a 1950s pharmacy cabinet, and it had served faithfully for over 20 years. My current fuming chamber was made

180   Crime Scene Processing in Correctional Facilities and Prisons

from a large stainless-steel medical cabinet with a glass door. The technician should keep a constant eye on the fuming process to make sure that the items of evidence are not over-fumed. To reduce the chance of over-fuming, your author places a black print card with a nice greasy nose-oil thumbprint prominently in the center on a string in the chamber where a keen eye can be kept. As soon as I see that print develop, I stop the fuming process. The best method for documenting the visualized print is with digital photography using a format that is acceptable to the agency that administers the automated fingerprint database. Do not forget to add a metric scale to the frame. The California Department of Justice recommends either JPEG-Fine or TIFF. The experienced fingerprint comparison analyst usually has no difficulty matching the white ridges on the developed print to the black ridges of the inked exemplar. However, when making exhibits for the jury I always color-reverse the image, with an explanation of the steps I took and a reason for the enhancement, so that the jury will not be confused by the color contradiction (Fig. 12.3A–C).

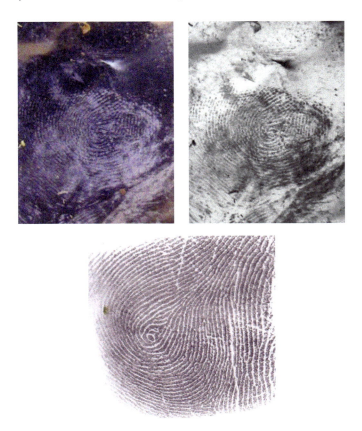

Figure 12.3 **A–C** Cyanoacrylate: A fingerprint impression on a plastic bag developed using cyanoacrylate ester fuming next to the same print that was color-reversed for use as a court exhibit. Below is the exemplar print.

Fingerprint Evidence in Jails and Prisons

So, what happens if the surface upon which you want to develop the print is of a white color? There's a dye for that. Treat the item as normal and examine it under magnification. If you detect only partials or fragments, submit the item for DNA typing, should the investigation warrant. If you detect good impressions under magnification, you can treat the item with Ardrox, Basic Yellow, Basic Red, or Rhodamine 6G. If your laboratory does not have dyes on hand, you can try using a fluorescent medium and an ALS. SPR can also be used to dye the ridges black; providing the surface is washable.

Sticky-Side Tape

The sticky-side (or adhesive-side) tape formula method is another staple of the fingerprint technician in the jail or prison setting owing to the abundance of inmate-manufactured weapons with tape-wrapped handles. There are several formulations on the market including Forensics Source Sticky-Side Powder Kit, Wet Wop, and Evident's Wet Powder that are extremely easy to use. The technician merely paints the adhesive side of the tape with the formula using a brush, waits a few minutes, gently rinses the tape using tap water or a Nalgene wash bottle, and allows the tape to dry. The resulting developed prints will appear on the tape (Fig. 12.4A–D). The trickiest part of using the sticky-side tape formula is pulling the tape apart from itself and the object. Pulling the

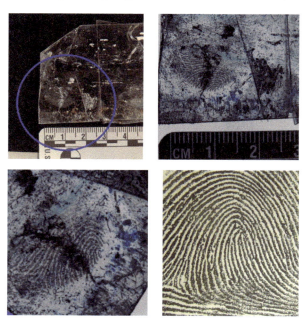

Figure 12.4 **A–D** Above is a fingerprint impression developed on tape using the sticky-side tape method, along with the enhanced image and the exemplar.

tape steadily and slowly is the best method. The other tricky part is holding the tape down while you apply the formula. I use a pair of forceps and an old ridge pick. Sticky-side tape formula will also recover lip impressions if the tape is used to cover a victim's mouth. Think how great it would be to have the suspect's fingerprints and the victim's lip print on the same item of evidence.

Skin Print Black

Doje's Skin Print Black™ is a product that I keep in my lab for those "just in case" events. It is a magnetic powder that is formulated to have less ink than normal magnetic powders. The technician inserts a small dowel into a roll of clean cotton cash register tape (do not use thermal paper) and rolls it, with some pressure, on the skin of a victim as a means to transfer the impressions to the paper. The technician then dusts the paper with the powder. This product is great if you can get to the victim before they wash or rub the area that was grasped. Thus, if an inmate is strangled by their cellmate or grabbed hard upon the arm, this method may well recover either fingerprint impressions or other sweat transfers like those produced by the assailant's inner arm. Even if the technician develops an impression on the paper that does not yield significant ridge detail for identification purposes, the technician will still be able to see where the victim was grabbed or strangled and therefore, they can vigorously swab that particular area for a DNA specimen. This is the least obtrusive examination of a decedent person, with the least amount of contamination, an investigator can make while awaiting personnel from the coroner's office to arrive.

Small Particle Reagent

SPR is a chemical reagent that is extremely useful in developing fingerprint impressions on difficult surfaces like vehicles that are wet with dew, cold soda cans, surfaces that are covered in oils or dirt, and glass (Fig. 12.5). SPR is easy to use and inexpensive. The technician can either use a pre-mixed solution, available from all of the forensic supply companies or can purchase the individual vials (containing molybdenum disulfide) and mix them with water, shaking vigorously. The solution is then sprayed on the surface with a gentle misting spray. Wait a few minutes and then spray the area again with clean water from another spray bottle. The prints will appear as the excess SPR washes away. The process can be repeated for faint impressions. Once the surface has dried completely, the impressions can be photographed and lifted using common lifting methods. One thing to remember is to be sure that the technician has black and white reagent on hand as there is nothing worse

Fingerprint Evidence in Jails and Prisons

Figure 12.5 Fingerprint impression developed on a soda can directly from a vending machine using SPR.

than being called out to a vehicle crime scene with a dark-colored car and all that the technician has brought is black SPR. A quick look at some of the forensic supply sources reflect a fluorescent SPR is now also available.

Enhancing Ridge Print Impressions in Blood

On occasion, the investigator will come across a faint impression deposited on a surface in blood, whether ridge print or footwear impression, and the hope is that the impression can be enhanced in a manner in which it can be visualized and documented using photography. Coomassie blue is an enhancement chemical used to dye blood-contaminated fingerprints on porous or non-porous surfaces, which produce bright blue visible prints. Amido black is commonly used for the same purpose and will produce a dark blue stained impression. Amido black is sprayed onto the area of interest and then rinsed with a destaining product. Acid fuchsin, also known as Hungarian red, is an aqueous solution used to enhance fingerprint deposits in blood but must be used with an ALS with a wavelength between 520 and 560nm. Your author prefers Leucocrystal Violet (LCV) because of its ease of use, safety, versatility, and ability to find impressions in large scenes that were previously unseen. LCV, also known as Aqueous LCV, is a reduced form of gentian violet; it is a highly sensitive formula to visually enhance blood prints and the reaction to blood will produce a vibrant violet result (Fig. 12.6).

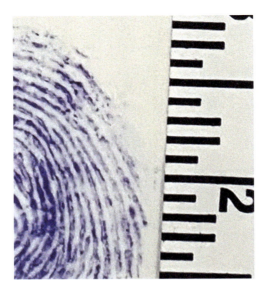

Figure 12.6 Blood print developed with LCV.

Of course, all the above-listed latent print development techniques are all for naught if the items being processed were not collected in a manner that preserved the fragile deposited evidence. The technician should tirelessly impress upon first responders, crime scene investigators, and civilian employees that fingerprints are delicate and easily obliterated. The technician should instruct all personnel that wearing latex gloves while handling evidence is essential; however, they are not sufficient to prevent the destruction of latent fingerprints, which are composed, depending on the source, from 20% to 90% water. Items of evidence must be handled in a way to preserve the latent print impressions. In other words, you do not pick up a knife by the handle and expect the prints on the handle to be intact. You must pick up the item in a manner that is not instinctive, such as by the end, hilt, or the very edges of the blade near the handle. Once the item is in an evidence envelope or paper bag, hold the bag or envelope so that you are not pressing the inside against the object. In other words, hold it by the top or the bottom, but not with your hand grasping the item as the impression may be absorbed into the paper or smudged beyond individualization. Be sure to get that evidence into the lab as soon as possible. I find the fresher the evidence, the better chance of recovering prints.

The Mini-Forensic Laboratory

Your author is a big proponent of each prison or jail having an on-site mini-forensic laboratory and a trained crime scene analyst who can operate the laboratory. The mini-laboratory need not occupy too much space, perhaps

Fingerprint Evidence in Jails and Prisons

one large 14′ × 14′ room or two smaller attached rooms. The most important item of equipment for any mini-laboratory is a downdraft workstation, preferably one with a short-wave ultraviolet light system for sterilization and a HEPA filter. Of equal importance is a good ALS system or forensic light for the forensic analysis of clothing and items of evidence developed with fluorescent powders or dyes. The next important items to the technician will be a ninhydrin chamber with a humidifier and a cyanoacrylate fuming chamber. The technician will need one area with a countertop solely for the purpose of processing items for fingerprint impressions using powders. This area should be on the opposite side of the room from any other examination areas owing to the distribution of powder particulates in the air. I have an ash vacuum nozzle placed over the area where I dust for fingerprints, and it does a great job of collecting most of the powder that finds its way into the air.

This countertop should have a supply of butcher paper handy to spread a new sheet of paper prior to the countertop being used for the examination of evidence (Fig. 12.7). Only one item of evidence from any one case should be analyzed at a time.

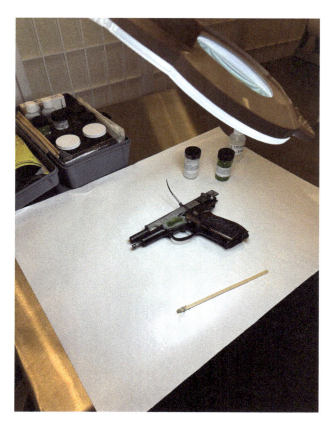

Figure 12.7 Serial number recovery on a clean sheet of butcher paper.

In another part of the room, the technician will need an area with a table or wide countertop solely for the processing of clothing for biological or serological evidence. This work area should also have a butcher paper dispenser with a cutting blade and should be in close proximity to the downdraft workstation. Evidence being prepared or processed for DNA analysis should only be processed in the sterilized downdraft workstation.

Copy stands are an essential component of the mini-laboratory. A copy stand does not require a lot of space, but it should be placed as far away from the fingerprint dusting area as possible, if for no other reason than to protect your valuable camera from damage. A good copy stand with plenty of clamps and holders is a must for taking quality evidentiary photographs (Fig. 12.8).

Figure 12.8 Copy stand with camera, lights, and "soldering third hand."

Fingerprint Evidence in Jails and Prisons

Proper ventilation is essential to the function of the mini-laboratory, with positive airflow venting to an outside area. The laboratory also needs a water source and basin, as well as a locker for the storage of evidence while it is in the laboratory, an evidence inventory and logging computer system, and a workstation with a microscope for the analysis of processed evidence. The technician should have access to laboratory coats, cotton and latex gloves, shoe and head covers, and N-95 filter masks.

Although getting a bit long in the tooth, one of the best purchases I made was a laminar-flow PCR downdraft chamber equipped with short-wave ultra-violet light for sterilization (Fig. 12.9). Over the years, your author has recovered DNA specimens in that cabinet that have led to many successful prosecutions.

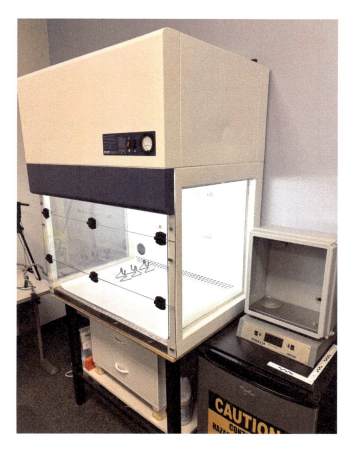

Figure 12.9 My faithful laminar-flow PCR downdraft chamber.

Cleanliness is critical to the mini-forensic laboratory and the technician should sterilize all work areas using a 10% bleach solution before processing any evidence. The technician should maintain a logbook to record routine cleaning and a binder containing the material storage data sheets. The laboratory should also have an area with a photographic copy stand with lights and other photographic accessories such as a small photographic tent or additional lighting. A hazardous materials locker should be maintained, with appropriate safety data sheets, in proximity to the laboratory for the storage of powders, dyes, and other chemicals used in forensic analysis.

Fingerprint Scenario

One of my favorite fingerprint development stories involved mutual aid to a neighboring city. The local police were experiencing a repeated crime involving a young man who was on State parole, wherein the parolee would stand on a corner near his residence and point a handgun at the motorists while shouting gang slogans. Upon hearing the sirens of responding police cars, the parolee would sprint back to his house and hide. After three days of this cat-and-mouse game, the local police formulated a plan to catch the culprit. They stationed marked and unmarked police vehicles strategically around the block. They also had officers on foot hiding nearby. When the parolee repeated his daily shenanigans, the officers were in quick pursuit. Unfortunately, the parolee was fleet-footed and ducked behind an abandoned vehicle parked in the driveway of his house. Officers arrived just as he locked and closed the door to the vehicle. The Deputy Chief of the agency arrived on the scene, looked through the dirty front passenger door window, and saw what he believed to be the butt of a handgun protruding from under the driver's seat. Therefore, the vehicle was seized as evidence, towed to the station, and a search warrant petitioned. Once the warrant was approved, the Deputy Chief called to see if I was available to process the vehicle for the suspected handgun. Upon my arrival, I photographed the vehicle in its entirety and worked my magic to unlock the locked door. I then went to my vehicle to prepare for the task of recovering the suspected handgun and collecting DNA evidence. As I did this, I noticed that four of the police officers, along with one sergeant, had gathered in the parking lot. Not to my surprise, sadly, I observed the sergeant don a pair of gloves and advanced one step toward the suspect vehicle. I knew that I would have to stop them from contaminating the evidence, but before I had a chance to move, the Deputy Chief appeared and scolded them most harshly. "But D.C., we just want to see if the gun is stolen." Knowing this, I cut a sheet of clean butcher paper and laid it on the front footwell of the vehicle. I carefully moved the gun onto the shiny side of the paper and photographed the serial number, which I provided to

Fingerprint Evidence in Jails and Prisons

the gathered curious personnel. Vindicated that the gun was indeed stolen, they retreated into the station, and I was left to finish processing the gun. Carefully, I swabbed the gun for touch-DNA, and then gently removed the stainless-steel magazine. It was then that I observed the glistening inherent luminescence of a left thumbprint, in fact, the suspect's left thumbprint (Fig. 12.10). No development was needed, as the print was patent. I am confident, had the sergeant manipulated the handgun to "render it safe" or to copy the serial number, the thumb print may not have survived. As it was, the print was enough to send the parolee back to prison for three additional years.

Figure 12.10 One patent left thumb print.

Dealing with the Evidence   13

Although the crime scene you inherit in the correctional setting may come to you previously contaminated, the biological, physical, transfer, and trace evidence need not to be. The target upon which the blood is sitting may have been trampled upon by hundreds, if not thousands, of inmates, but that does not mean the blood, if properly collected and preserved, is without evidentiary merit. The clothing worn by the suspect and the victim is not compromised if properly collected. The trace and transfer evidence on the weapon found in the crime scene still has integrity. The fecal matter or urine thrown on the custodial officer still supports the elements of the criminal charge and may contain at least minimal amounts of DNA of the inmate who, if not thrown it, certainly contributed to its construction. The biological evidence left on the rape victim or the victim or suspect's clothing will still provide the courts with the evidence needed for a conviction.

Collecting Biological Evidence

Most crime laboratories have the ability to conduct DNA typing on blood and other human biological samples to determine genetic markers. DNA testing does not require a large sample of material; however, the samples must be collected in a manner to prevent contamination or degradation, which can render DNA testing useless.

Types of Biological Evidence Suitable for DNA Testing Include:

- Bloodstains/liquid blood
- Semen
- Vaginal fluid
- Hairs
- Saliva
- Mucus
- Bones, nails, teeth
- Fecal samples – large, harder samples will have a greater likelihood of cells on them than softer or loose samples
- Perspiration stains

Urine is not the best source of DNA owing to the low concentration of nucleated cells present in human urine. DNA also deteriorates quickly in urine if it is present. Mucus can be a good source of DNA, especially if there is bloody discharge with the mucus, but it may degrade if not processed within a month. Vomit is a poor source of DNA, but that does not mean it cannot be attempted. It is best to check with your laboratory before submitting urine or vomit for analysis.

The techniques used for collecting the specimen will depend on the stain itself and the surface upon which it was deposited. The absolute best method for collecting the specimen is to collect the item upon which the stain is found, like a shirt or pair of pants. Unfortunately, the specimen is usually found on a cell wall, door, bunk rail, locker, or floor. When this happens, you have no alternative but to collect the specimen *in situ*. It is important to document the specimen's location and relative position to the crime scene and other items of evidence with notes and photography prior to collection. The investigator must use universal precautions before handling any biological evidence to prevent contamination or the contribution of their own DNA to the specimen. Wearing proper personal protective equipment, especially an N95 mask and gloves, can also minimize exposure to possible infectious diseases and hazardous materials.

Gloves

Sweat from the collector's bare hands will very likely contaminate evidence. Latex gloves provide a simple barrier against contamination for the evidence collector. The investigator should change their gloves each time a new piece of evidence is handled to prevent cross-contamination of the evidence. I highly recommend to "double glove," which is wearing one pair of latex gloves over another. This keeps the investigator's hands covered at all times, even when changing gloves. I also recommend wearing cotton gloves underneath the first layer of latex gloves. This helps to collect perspiration and makes changing gloves much easier. The investigator should avoid wiping their forehead, scratching their noses, or wiping their eyes while handling items of evidence. Fight the urge to handle a cellular telephone or adjust glasses. Any time gloves have come in contact with such items, it is essential to change them before proceeding to handle items of evidence in the scene. Another thing to consider with latex gloves is the manner in which they are removed from the box. Obviously reaching into the box of gloves with bare hands has the potential to transfer the investigator's DNA onto the very gloves that they hope will prevent contamination. The same applies to that pair of gloves you shoved in your trouser pockets at the beginning of your shift. The proper method of extracting a latex glove from the box is to look for the cuff, lift it with a hooked little finger, remove the glove from the box by the cuff, and carefully don the glove. Then lift the second glove with the gloved hand in the same manner. For gloves that you have prepared and placed in a pouch at the beginning of the shift, your author dons gloves in the manner prescribed, rolls out a clean sheet of butcher's paper, and removes two gloves from the box. I place the gloves on the paper, roll them into a ball, and turn the ball inside out. This will keep the outer surface protected until used.

Masks

Excessive talking, sneezing, or coughing in the vicinity of the evidence may cause small, but detectable amounts of the DNA of the crime scene team members to be inadvertently transferred to the evidence. It is essential for all persons entering the crime scene to don a good mask, such as the N-95, in order to reduce the potential for contamination. Most of the contamination in a crime scene likely comes from the mouth or nose of the technician.

Collection Devices

Disposable tweezers, scalpels, and scissors are the best instruments to use while collecting human biological evidence. I use a 10% bleach solution with a distilled water rinse to sterilize the instruments. I then place them in my down-draft workstation and subject them to three minutes of short-wave ultra-violet light, before placing them in a clear plastic zip-lock bag.

Touch DNA

Touch DNA is a "touchy subject" for crime laboratories as many law enforcement agencies now submit hundreds of items of evidence for processing in cases ranging from petty theft to murder. Unfortunately, the laboratories are already overwhelmed with submissions, and testing every possible item that a suspect may have touched or may not have touched is adding to an already burdensome backlog. I try not to submit evidence unless I am certain that the item was handled by the suspect. For example, prior to processing an item for latent prints that was likely touched by the suspect I first inspect the item for the inherent luminescence or glistening of the undeveloped print. A clean white light used at an oblique angle can assist you in this examination. If it appears to be a partial print or smudge, I swab the area for touch DNA typing instead of developing it further for fingerprint impressions. In major cases, I will use sterile powders and brushes to dust an area for potential latent prints. Smudges and partials that are developed can be collected for touch DNA typing. Cyanoacrylate fuming will develop prints that can later be typed for DNA. Unfortunately, most of our cyanoacrylate fuming chambers are not cleaned and sterilized between uses and

Dealing with the Evidence

there may be the potential for cross-contamination. I have shortwave UV light lamps that I can place in my chamber prior to use. Cloth handles used on inmate-manufactured weapons have the potential for the recovery of DNA. However, great care must be taken when processing these items of evidence to prevent contamination.

Bloodstain Collection

Swabbing a suspected bloodstain is the easiest way to collect samples from large or immobile objects. If the stain is still wet, the swab can be dabbed into the stain until the blood is absorbed into the tip of the swab. I avoid swabbing all the way to the target, instead focusing on collecting just the blood and not a potentially contaminated surface. Remember, you only need a small amount of blood for DNA testing. Wet blood should never be frozen; it is always best to place it in refrigerated evidence storage. Never store blood, whether wet or dry, in a plastic evidence container. Always use a paper bag or paper evidence envelope. If the stain is dry, moisten a sterile cotton swab with distilled water from an ampoule. Do not touch the ampoule to the swab, or the stain. Instead, drop the water onto the swab or stain from a distance of about ½ of an inch. Touching the ampoule could cause contamination of both the swab and the ampoule. With the moistened swab, dab the stain until the swab contains blood. Remember to collect the blood specimen from the area between the center, which is clotted blood, and the edge, which may be serum. When collecting dried blood, you may have to scrub down to the target. It is unfortunately unavoidable. It is important not to place more than one sample into an evidence envelope and never collect multiple stains on the same swab. If you collected several swabs from the same stain, be sure to label each swab as coming from the same stain. Take a control sample in the same manner as the specimen from the area surrounding the stain without actually collecting blood or DNA evidence should your agency protocols require the collection of control samples. If sufficient sample remains, collect a dry-swab specimen as well. This swab is collected in the same manner as the specimen without using distilled water to moisten the swab. This specimen is generally retained for use by the defense.

Dried Flaked Blood

Blood that is dried and flaky can still have DNA value. The best method for collecting dried blood is to scrape it into a pharmaceutical fold or coin envelope using a sterile razor blade, or by picking up large flakes with sterilized tweezers. Be absolutely certain to wear safety glasses and a mask whenever manipulating dried blood as the last thing you want to do is flick a flake into your eye or mouth.

Processing Wet Bloodstained Items

Many an old-time prison investigator will remember processing wet bloodstained garments in open 'drying cages' overnight before carefully folding them up and placing them in paper bags the next day. That was in the days before DNA typing. Today, it is absolutely essential that your prison or jail have contamination-free drying cabinets that use filters to purify circulating air. These cabinets must be lockable and have the means to clean and sterilize between uses and a logbook must be maintained to document the cleaning and sterilization process. These cabinets can be very expensive but are well worth the cost and are one of the most important acquisitions that your facility can make.

An item of evidence that is thoroughly wet with blood or other human biological evidence can be transported from the crime scene to the evidence processing area in plastic bags. It is best to put only one item of evidence in each bag. The items should only remain in the bag from the time that they have been collected to the time that they arrive at the processing area. The item should then be immediately transferred to the drying cabinet. The plastic bags and any paper placed underneath the item as it was drying also need to be dried and processed as they may contain trace evidence that may have fallen off the original item. Once the item has been dried, it needs to be properly packaged and processed in an evidence locker.

Items that are only slightly wet may not need to be cabinet-dried and may complete the drying process while in an appropriate non-plastic evidence container. Should this be the case, it is best to follow the package instructions listed below.

Bloodied Evidence Not at the Scene

Bloodstained items of evidence oftentimes do not remain at the crime scene. They are instead transported to holding cells, infirmaries, or outside hospitals while the victims or suspects are still wearing them. Although every effort should be made to collect these items before they leave the crime scene, sometimes it is an unavoidable consequence of necessity. It is critical that these items are collected as soon as possible and that a proper chain of custody is maintained by those individuals who did the collection. During a recent homicide investigation, I needed a crucial piece of evidence: the shoes worn by the victim. After three days of searching, I finally found them in a cabinet at the outside hospital where the victim was taken and pronounced dead. As you can imagine, there was no chain of custody for the shoes. Regardless, I collected them and processed them into evidence.

As mentioned, you must never process wet, bloodied items in plastic. This can cause mold to grow that will degrade the DNA. Plastic should only be used to transport items to prevent cross-contamination.

Remember that the best short- and long-term storage for liquid blood (such as that collected from a suspect or victim in a vial) is refrigeration. Never freeze liquid blood. Dried human biological evidence is best stored in a temperature-controlled storage area; however, room temperature is acceptable for short-term storage. The same applies to buccal swab samples.

Other Important Information

Collecting and preserving trace evidence can be a challenge. There is little worse than finding that fiber or hair on evidence from the crime scene that definitely associates a suspect with a crime, and then, when it is most needed, not being able to find it for analysis or court because it was loosely placed in a coin envelope. The best method for collecting and preserving trace evidence such as hairs, fibers, epithelial cells, etc., are best collected, and subsequently preserved, by tape-lifting or forensic vacuuming. Tape lifts should be placed in sterile glass jars. Forensic vacuums collect the evidence in their own sterile collection containers. Questioned documents can be placed in paper evidence envelopes but take care to sandwich the document between thin sheets of stock paper or cardboard and be certain to fill out the information on the outside of the envelope before inserting the evidence. Indentations are fundamental to handwriting comparison. It is therefore best to not contribute additional indentations while filling out the documentation on the exterior of the envelope.

Soil samples should be collected in clean glass jars. Materials from suspicious fires should be placed in metal paint cans leaving approximately one-third of the can empty for gases to collect in that space. Keep in mind that fire material that is wet from firefighting efforts may ultimately rust the bottom of the can. Therefore, the material should be sent off for analysis as quickly as possible. Used condoms can present the investigator with a challenge. If semen is noted within the condom, collect it immediately using either a sterile cotton or foam-tipped swab, or by pouring the semen onto a sterile gauze pad. The condom should then be allowed to dry. I clip a sterilized binder clip to the top of the condom to allow it to be manipulated without touching the condom itself. Once it is dried, the condom can be wrapped in clean butcher paper.

Items of clothing evidence should be packaged wrapped separately in butcher paper and placed loosely in paper bags. This allows for the analysts to open the evidence, make their examination, and then return the item in its original packaging, thus preserving the original chain of custody.

Suitable Wrapping Technique

Hopefully, the practice of initialing items of evidence, especially garments, that may be tested for DNA evidence has been discontinued. Placing initials on the garment may either contaminate the sample or provide a contamination challenge in court. Instead, garments that are of evidentiary importance to a criminal investigation should be processed in the following manner (Figs. 13.1A–I):

- Lay the garment out flat on a clean sheet of butcher paper (shiny side up).
- Be sure to use sufficient sheets of butcher paper to cover the entire garment.
- Place a sheet of butcher paper on top of the garment (shiny side down) under each arm.
- Fold the paper in a manner as shown in Fig. 13.1.

Figure 13.1 **A–I** Packaging clothing: The proper way to package clothing as evidence. (*Continued*)

Dealing with the Evidence

Figure 13.1 *(Continued)*

- Fold the butcher paper small enough to fit into an evidence bag.
- Print and sign your name, with the date along with the suspect information and date on one side of the outside of the folded butcher paper (or use a gummed evidence label) and affix a chain of custody sticker to the other side.
- If it is necessary to identify an area of the garment that you wish to be sampled for DNA evidence, draw a picture of the garment on the outside of the butcher paper and mark the picture with a circle and an "x" where you want the sample taken (Fig. 13.2).

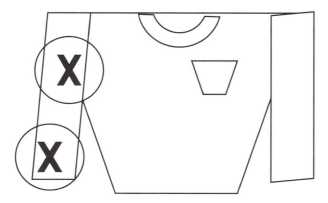

Figure 13.2 Draw the item of evidence on the outside of the packaging and indicate the areas where stains appear.

Should an agency require the officer's initials to identify the item of evidence, they can tie an evidence tag to a buttonhole and then the tag is either placed outside of the folded package or tucked between two sheets of paper inside of the package. Try to limit the potential for contamination by not writing directly on the garment.

Testing for Blood

In some cases, testing to determine if the stain contains blood may be necessary prior to collection. Testing can help to rule out stains that are not blood, saving time and effort in the collection process. The test used for this process is the phenolphthalein color test or other suitable color test methods such as leucocrystal malachite. Hexagon OBTI Immunochromatographic Rapid Test™ can be used to determine if the blood is of human origin. Presumptive testing of blood should only be done by qualified personnel.

Biological Evidence from Victim and Suspects

Buccal Swabs

Buccal cells are located on the inner cheeks of the mouth and can be collected for DNA typing. Buccal swabs are usually used in place of obtaining blood.

- Only one sterile swab is needed for a mouth.
- Swab the inside of both cheeks by scrubbing the cheek walls on both sides with a sterile cotton swab.
- Place a shield over the applicator and return it to the sterile packaging. Seal the packaging and process it into evidence as normal. If the specimen is wet, it is best to place it in a refrigerated evidence locker. If the specimen is dry, it is acceptable to store it in temperature-controlled dry storage.

Fingernail Scrapings

Fingernail scrapings may contain trace evidence including blood, tissue, hairs, fibers, or other foreign material that may have collected under the nails of the suspect or victim during a struggle or violent interaction. Moisten a sterile cotton swab in the manner described above and vigorously scrub under each nail to the nail bed. Use a separate swab for each finger and process the swabs individually. It is best to use an applicator shield to cover the cotton tip. Place a shield over the applicator and return it to the sterile packaging. Seal the packaging and process it into evidence as normal. If the specimen is wet, it is best to place it in a refrigerated evidence locker. If the specimen is dry, it is acceptable to store it in temperature-controlled dry storage.

Bite Marks

Bite mark impressions may be found on victims of an assault and can be compared with the teeth of the suspect. Photograph the bite marks with and without a scale and color chart. When using a scale, it is preferable to use a small L-shaped ruler, such as an ABFO #5 ruler, that is designed for bite marks. Also document the bite mark, including measurements. Slightly moisten a sterile cotton swab or sterile gauze pad with sterile water and rub around the bite mark area. Swab a second time around the area using a dry swab. Place the swab bag in its original sterile packaging and process it into evidence after allowing it to air dry in an area free of contamination.

Observations

Before handling an item of evidence, consider how a person would hold the item and avoid grasping it in the same place. Inspect these areas for human biological evidence and consider collecting a specimen swab as soon as possible. Consider your options before using any forensic process that will destroy, alter, or contaminate potential DNA evidence. Make every effort possible not to contribute your own DNA to the crime scene or upon items of evidence found within that crime scene. Never discard your used latex gloves into the crime scene and prevent others from doing the same. I still cringe every time I think of the time one of our nurses pulled off her latex gloves and tossed them into the scene of a homicide, or the time I entrusted a suspicious death crime scene into the capable hands of a housing unit officer to protect until I returned with my CSI equipment. Upon my return, I was shocked to see the officer enjoying a bag of sunflower seeds and the entire time I was gone he was spitting the shells onto the floor next to the body of the deceased inmate.

Presumptive Drugs Testing

I have done a lot of presumptive drugs testing at the facility where I worked. When I was first assigned to the Investigative Services Unit, our drugs' testing kit was a box with numerous pharmaceutical glass bottles containing the various chemicals used to test each suspected controlled substance or narcotic. The kit was provided to us by the California Department of Justice, and we each had to be certified by that same agency to conduct the testing. I was always concerned that we had a very large bottle of chloroform in the evidence refrigerator, and I never fell for the "smell this" trick played by my partner.

Of course, these bottles were replaced by very convenient microcrystalline test packets. No more mixing chemicals with a dropper in a spot well. Happily, I tested suspected drugs every day using these kits, and as they were color tests, I never had to be an actual chemist to understand just how they worked. That was until one day testifying in a preliminary hearing on a drug smuggling case. While on the stand, I was asked by the public defender, "How do these tests work?" I explained the process of putting a small amount of the substance in the bottom of the pouch, crushing each ampoule, and observing the color change. The follow-up question was, "Yes, but how do they work? What makes the chemicals change colors?" I was stumped and had no answer other than, "they just do." Well, believe me when I say that I was ready for him when it came time for the jury trial, very much to his surprise. This chapter will help you avoid that same embarrassment. The first thing to understand is that any test conducted at the jail or prison is a presumptive test only. This test will allow the investigator to say it is or is not a suspected drug. The confirmatory test must be done by a qualified laboratory.

Microcrystalline Test Kits

Microcrystalline test kits are small collection pouches that contain various ampoules with reagents that cause a chemical color reaction when a drug is introduced. Each reagent will react differently and will produce a color change that is specific to that drug. They are easy to use, are cost-effective, and use a very small amount of the drug to conduct the test, which is very important in the custodial setting. It is important to understand that the results of most of these tests are empirical in nature only. This means that although you can repeat the experiment and results consistently, even scientists do not truly understand why they produce the results they do. According to Richard Saferstein, "When tests are properly chosen and are used in proper combination, their results constitute an analytical scheme that is characteristic for one and only one drug." This section of the chapter will focus primarily on the drugs most often found inside jails and prisons, such as heroin, methamphetamine, cocaine, and marijuana. A quick look at the forensic supply vendor catalogs, like Lynn Peavey or Sirchie, will produce a myriad of microcrystalline test kits for every known controlled substance or narcotic.

Marquis Reagent

The Marquis Reagent is a general-purpose presumptive testing method used to suspect if a substance is a drug, such as heroin (opiate), methamphetamine, 3,4-Methylenedioxymethamphetamine (MDMA or ecstasy), LSD (lysergic acid diethylamide), methadone, mescaline, oxycodone, aspirin, or sugar.

Dealing with the Evidence

The reagent is 2% formaldehyde in a sulfuric acid base. Upon contact with the substance, the test will produce the following results:

- Opiates = deep purple with wispy appendages
- Methamphetamine = dark orange to brown
- MDMA = dark purple to black
- LSD = olive green to black
- Methadone = light yellowish pink
- Mescaline = vibrant orange
- Oxycodone = pale violet
- Aspirin = deep red
- Sugar = dark brown

If you are not sure what substance you have to test, start with the Marquis Reagent since it tests for most substances.

Mecke Reagent

Mecke reagent, or the heroin test, is a standard test for opiates. It is a mixture of 95% selenious acid and 1 g of concentrated sulfuric acid. The test can also be used for LSD.

- Opiates = bluish green
- LSD = greenish black
- Oxycodone = moderate olive
- Sugar = brilliant greenish yellow

I generally do not use the Mecke reagent for black-tar heroin because it is too easy to mistake color leaching from the drug as a positive test. However, the Mecke reagent works quite well for powdered forms of opiate.

Scott's Reagent

Scott's reagent was developed by chemist and former DEA Special Agent L. J. Scott to test for cocaine and cocaine base (crack). The reagent is composed of cobalt (II) thiocyanate plus acetic acid plus glycerin plus concentrated hydrochloric acid and chloroform. The reaction will be speckles of blue over a pink background.

Duqenois–Levine

The Duqenois–Levine color test method is used to test marijuana and for the presence of delta-nine-tetrahydrocannabinol (D-9-THC), the psychoactive ingredient in marijuana. The Duqenois–Levine test is a three-step process;

four, if you count the first part of the test, which is the signature smell of marijuana. Step one of the chemical tests is to snip a very small portion of a marijuana leaf (about ¼″ is all that is needed) and place it in a test tube or test kit pouch. Introduce the 2% vanillin plus acetaldehyde in an ethyl alcohol solution and agitate gently for about 30 seconds. The solution may turn a pale green. Then introduce the concentrated hydrochloride solution, which should turn a deep purple color. The final step will determine if D-9-THC is present. Add chloroform to the step two result. If D-9-THC is present, a pink "eyeball" will appear at the bottom of the test tube or test pouch. A supplemental test is available as well, but it would take a bit of magnification provided by a scanning electron microscope. On the underside of the marijuana leaf are tiny "hairs" called cystoliths. Cystoliths are used by the laboratories to support positive confirmatory results for marijuana.

Confirmatory Drugs Testing

Confirmatory testing of drugs is done by laboratories equipped with the gas chromatograph (GC) mass spectrometry analytical techniques. GC is used to separate and detect the chemical components of a controlled substance or narcotic to determine the presence (or absence), and quantities, of specific molecules or gases. The results are plotted on a graph reflecting the recorder response (vertical axis) versus time (horizontal axis). However, this alone does not allow a forensic chemist to confirm a substance. For this, the chemist will use the mass spectrometer. The material first exits the gas chromatograph and enters a high-vacuum chamber where a beam of high-energy electrons is aimed at the sample molecules. The electrons collide and cause them to lose one electron and gain one positive electron (ion). The ions form unstable smaller fragments that pass through an electronic or magnetic field, where they are separated according to their masses. According to Richard Saferstein, "The unique feature of mass spectrometry is that under carefully controlled conditions, no two substances produce the same fragmentation pattern." That, in a nutshell, is about as confirmatory as you can get.

Chain of Custody

Your author will close this chapter with a few words regarding the chain of custody. As you may know, chain of custody is the chronological documentation of the movement and possession of an item of evidence from the time it was discovered and collected to the time it is presented in court. In other words, it documents who had possession of the item of evidence, for how long, and for what purpose. Quite often, the "for what purpose" gets overlooked, and a "break" in the chain occurs which might have a significant impact on the subsequent investigation or courtroom proceedings.

For example, a housing unit officer finds an inmate-manufactured stabbing weapon during a cell search. The proper chain of custody for the weapon would be as such: The officer who found the weapon maintains sole possession of the weapon and processes it into evidence and thus begins the chain of custody. The investigator or analyst requests the weapon from the evidence custodian in a process that documents the request and release of the weapon. The investigator conducts an analysis of the weapon, which might include photographic documentation for disciplinary or courtroom purposes, swabbing the item for DNA typing, and fingerprint development. The investigator then returns the item to documented evidence storage and writes a detailed report. Developed or collected specimen from the weapon is documented and sent off to a laboratory for subsequent analysis, comparison, or typing. The weapon itself is retained by the evidence custodian until it is presented in disciplinary or court proceedings. For this example, let us assume that a DNA profile is developed from the collected specimen swab, but the profile did not match the inmates assigned to the cell and was not found in the DNA database. This would present a sizeable concern for the prosecution. Let us then imagine another series of events that was never documented in the chain of custody. The housing unit officer discovered the weapon and contacted the Watch Commander, Captain, or other administrator on duty. That administrator sends another officer to the housing unit to "borrow" the weapon and bring it to the administrator's office for inspection. The weapon is retrieved and brought before the administrator who examines it and instructs the clerk to put it on the photocopier so that an image of the weapon can be attached to a routine report sent to the Superintendent or Warden of the facility. The weapon was then returned to the original officer with the instructions to process it into evidence. All of this was done without documentation, and the original officer's report reflected only that he had "retained possession of the weapon." Sadly, this story is not fictitious.

Fire Investigations 14

Although fires in a jail or prison are less common than in the public, they do happen with enough regularity that it is advisable to have an investigator who is knowledgeable about fire and arson investigations on staff. It is true that the concrete and metal construction of the jail or prison will limit the available fuel for a conflagration, but the things that are inside those buildings do burn quite well. In general, most jail or prison fires are the product of the miscreant inmate who sets fire to some paper in a cell or worksite, or as a larger demonstration of discontent such as a riot, or as a diversion for an escape attempt. Fires can also be the result of the careless mishandling or alteration of an electrical appliance or the product of vocational training that did not go quite as intended. Fires in jails and prisons can lead to deaths, perchance even mass casualty events. The United States Fire Administration estimated that smoke inhalation during a fire may amount to 60%–80% of fire-related deaths. Often forgotten are the toxic or asphyxiant chemicals that are being produced during a fire, which may include hydrogen sulfides, ammonia, hydrochloric acids, methyl bromides, fluorine, and, of course, carbon monoxide. A staple of every jail or prison cell is the gray wool blanket. Wool blankets when burning produce hydrogen cyanide, a particularly deadly gas, especially when it is your laundry facility that is on fire.

A major fire incident at a jail or prison will require a greater degree of attention than that of a house fire in the public. Your author has responded to both categories of fires in progress. At a house fire, the role of the responder is to ensure that the residence is abandoned, and all residents are accounted for, including the pets, and to provide cursory medical attention if needed. Following this, the responder will evacuate any nearby houses that may be in danger from the fire spreading by winds or embers. Once this is accomplished, the responder will provide traffic control for the firefighters. Bear in mind that the police or sheriff responder will generally arrive before the fire apparatus arrives on the scene. Therefore, initial observations by the officers are of tremendous value to the fire investigator. A major fire incident in a jail or prison may require the orderly evacuation of hundreds or thousands of inmates from housing units or dormitories to the safety of an exercise yard. Additional staff may be required to be posted in elevated gun positions above the exercise yard to prevent assaults, and on foot on the outer perimeter fence line to prevent escape. All personnel must be accounted for, and their locations known. Firefighting efforts by custodial staff should be minimal owing to the lack of fire extinguishing equipment and proper breathing apparatus. Sallyport officers must be given authorization to allow mutual aid firefighters and equipment into the secured areas of the facility. Elevated gun positions that are in direct line with the smoke generated by the fire may need to be evacuated in a safe manner. Areas of the prison that cannot be immediately evacuated, such as Control Rooms and Administrative Segregation wings, will need to be ventilated by large exhaust fans until such time as a safe evacuation plan can be implemented. Administrative officials with oversight of the facilities must be notified, as well as requests for mutual aid from nearby outside agencies and nearby correctional facilities, and a call-out to off-duty personnel to return to duty. Preparations must be made for the assembly of a triage area, press staging area, and landing zones for firefighting and medical helicopters, and call-outs to transportation and hospital guarding teams. Structural engineers will need to be staged to determine the integrity of the buildings following firefighting efforts, or if alternate plans will need to be made for the feeding and housing of hundreds, if not thousands, of displaced inmates. All of this must be done with the goal of maintaining the safety and security of the institution, the inmates, the staff, and the public. Finally, crime scene and fire scene investigators should be requested.

As with Chapter 9, the purpose of this chapter is not to provide the reader with everything needed to be a competent fire investigator. Rather, the purpose of this chapter is to provide you with a fundamental understanding of the behavior of fire in a fire incident, determining its origin, and its eventual spread. It is my hope that this chapter will spark an interest in the reader in furthering their understanding of fire investigation through proper training. The International Association of Arson Investigators (www.firearson.com) offers quality training programs for its members and offers valuable resources on its website. They administer the Fire Investigator certification program, and they also publish the *Fire & Arson Investigator Journal* quarterly magazine, which truly is a treasure. Furthermore, they publish the *Fire Investigator Health and Safety Best Practices, Third Edition*. Fire scenes present tremendous hazards to the investigator, which will be discussed later in this chapter. Two publications that are mandatory for the fire and arson investigator to study are the *National Fire Protection Association's NFPA 921 Guide to Fire and Bomb Investigations* and *NFPA 1321 Standards for Fire Investigation Units*. Your author also highly recommends *Scientific Protocols for Fire Investigation*, 3rd edition, CRC Press, by John J. Lentini.

There is a difference between a fire investigator and an arson investigator. A fire investigator uses a scientific methodology to determine the cause, origin, and dynamic behavior of the fire. An arson investigator will attempt to identify the individual who is responsible for setting the fire. Both fire and arson investigators examine the physical characteristics of a fire scene and identify, document, preserve, and collect physical evidence from the scene.

In order for there to be fire, there must be fuel for consumption, oxygen to support the chemical process, an ignition source to begin the process, and heat to supply the energy necessary to maintain the temperature of the fuel to a point where sufficient gases are emitted for ignition to occur and to be sustained. There must be an uninhibited reaction between these components. Fuel is simply all the things in the structure that will burn. The flash point of the fuel is the minimal temperature that is required to which the fuel must be heated before it produces sufficient vapors that will ignite when in contact with a flame or other ignitable source. Fire consists of carbon dioxide, vaporized water, oxygen, and nitrogen, producing heat, light, and various combustion byproducts such as embers, smoke, and gases. What remains after the fire are condensed soot, char, ash, metal oxides, sulfur dioxide, volatile organic chemicals, polycyclic organic matter, inorganic solids, and other chemical compounds depending on the fuel being consumed.

Fire scenes can be the most problematic scenes for the fire and arson investigator. Fire and firefighting efforts may leave the structure soggy, toxically gaseous, dark, and unstable. If aqueous film-forming foam (AFFF) is used, it may take many hours for the foam to dissipate sufficiently to see what the foam might be hiding on the lower surfaces of the structure. Fire and arson investigators tend to spend a lot of their time in a structure looking up, therefore tripping over debris is always an option, and it is best to have someone else nearby who can give a trip hazard advisory. Your author, being a clumsy fellow anyway, has learned this lesson the hard way. In this regard, do not enter an indoor fire scene without a hard hat and eye protection, and never enter an indoor fire scene without the ability to summon help should it be needed (i.e., radio, alarm, or a good set of lungs). Bright flashlights are essential, with spare charged batteries on hand. A good electronic flash is a must for photography, and your author recommends a good monopod over a tripod when documenting indoor fire scenes. The nice thing about a monopod is that, when used with an off-camera shutter release, the investigator can hoist the camera overhead to capture a good view of the entire floor of a room. Your author also recommends a camera that has a good LCD since taking photographs while wearing a breathing or filter apparatus is challenging without one. Your author carries with him a tapered mouth shovel, a fire rake, a Halligan, a small trowel, and a strong whisk broom for clearing debris. Fire scenes are problematic, dangerous, and challenging. Be certain to have health and safety protocols in place that are strictly followed.

Fire Investigations

Arriving on the Scene

The fire scene investigation scientific methodology begins the moment the investigator arrives on the scene. Once at the scene, immediately document the environmental conditions, which include the temperature, humidity, and winds, as well as your initial observations. Be sure to have your camera at the ready and begin taking photographs as quickly as possible (Fig. 14.1). Consider also having a video camera to document firefighting efforts. This video can later be used to confirm observations made after entering the scene. Also, although not likely to occur in the correctional setting, a video of a fire scene in progress may be essential to the analysis of a fire scene when the fire has consumed the entire structure. Video is also a good method of capturing elements of the fire that may not initially be noted when first on the scene, such as the behavior of the fire, the spread of the fire, and areas where the fire is concentrated or difficult to extinguish.

Locate the incident commander of the disturbance and the commander of the firefighting response. These individuals will be exceedingly busy, but it is best just to let them know that you are on the scene. Following this, locate the first responders and witnesses to the early stages of the fire to get statements of

Figure 14.1 Firefighters venting a roof.

their observations. Ask probative questions to determine if there was an odor of gasoline or chemicals in an area where those products were not generally stored. Inquire as to whether there was the sound of a low-pressure "whomp" or if they heard or saw an explosion. Ask the witnesses if they noticed fire spreading on the floor or if the fire spread unusually fast and downward, or if they noticed a bright yellow or orange flame with thick, black smoke. Perhaps the most important question to ask is if they saw someone fleeing the area with burns to their hands, face, legs, clothing, or hair. This person may be a suspect, a victim, or a witness, however, regardless of their role, they are likely in serious need of medical attention and must be found. Establish a fire scene perimeter using caution or crime scene tape, being a crime scene entry and exit log, and post-scene security. Once this is accomplished, the fire investigator should find a convenient place to stage their equipment, prepare their protective gear, and await the all-clear to enter the structure.

Entering the Fire Scene

Once the all-clear has been given by fire personnel, it is best to confer with the firefighters to ascertain in which area of the structure the most water was required to extinguish the flames. This information may provide an advanced warning regarding the portions of the structure that may have the most structural damage caused by heavy streams of water. Your author begins the scene inspection from the exterior of the building, assessing the building for evidence of forced entry, inspecting the area for discarded accelerant containers, noting and documenting smoke damage, and examining debris that may have been shoveled out of windows by firefighters. Look for surveillance cameras on the exterior of the structure, as well as on nearby structures that may have captured the initial stages of the fire or persons or vehicles leaving the scene before the fire was discovered. Follow your agencies' protocols for documenting the fire scene using photography and diagramming. Comprehensive notetaking is crucial during the investigation, and carrying a small digital recorder is preferable to a pen and pad when inspecting a fire scene as it keeps your hands free for other tasks and is less likely to be smudged by soot or a scene that may still be wet.

Searching the Scene

Begin your interior scene inspection starting with the area of least damage, working your way to the areas of greater damage while making an overall inspection of the fire scene to determine the extent of the damage and to look for the origin of the fire. The logic behind this progression of inspection was

Fire Investigations

the belief that fire always burned the hottest at its point of origin, and therefore the most damage would be found at the area of fire origin. Although still a general methodology, it may not always be the case. Fuels, draft (ventilation), building construction, or numerous other factors may cause a fire to burn hotter and longer than in the area where it began. For instance, grass fires tend to burn away from the point of origin, especially if there is wind or if fuel is more abundant in areas that are not available where the fire started. Your author investigated a recent fatal residential fire wherein the hall bathroom received the most damage; however, the fire had actually started in a bedroom that was separated by a wall. The reason the bathroom had received the most damage was because the kitchen and dining room, which were separated by the other wall, had very high ceilings with skylights. Windows opened in the bedroom and bathroom provided the draft necessary to draw the fire upward toward the compromised skylights. The fire made a small breach in the wall separating the bathroom and kitchen creating a chimney effect in the bathroom. Your author begins the search in the area of least damage because it is safer to do so. As I progress, I have a better sense of the spread of the fire and the stability of the structure.

As you begin your search, pay particular attention to floors, when possible, looking for signs of an accelerant substance that was used to start or spread the fire (Fig. 14.2A and B). These signs appear as an irregularly shaped burn pattern, also called ignitable liquid pour patterns, that often connect one room to another. Vapor detectors, also known as sniffers, are handheld electronic devices that can detect and separate hydrocarbon molecules from accelerant vapors. These tools are handy and relatively inexpensive to have in your fire investigation tool chest. Keep in mind that just because an accelerant was detected does not necessarily mean that an accelerant was used to start the fire or to make the fire grow and spread. Some common floor coverings or other household products, when consumed by fire, will leave behind a residue that

Figure 14.2 A and B Vehicle fires started by placing a can of gelatin ethanol chafing fuel underneath the driver's side running board. Note the extensive fire damage to the exterior of the driver's side doors. The dark burn pattern is a combination of the chafing fuel spreading away from its container and mixing with the liquefied plastic from the running board.

may have the appearance of an accelerant. Also, flammable chemicals tend to be stored closer to the floor and may spread across the floor when the containers in which they are kept are upset or compromised by excessive heat or flame.

Burn Patterns

Once you are finished looking at the ground, you will dedicate the majority of your inspection to looking at the walls and ceilings with the goal of discovering the burn patterns noted in this chapter. It should be noted that the patterns described in this chapter pertain to structure fires and may not apply to vegetation or vehicle fires.

The Classic "V" Pattern

When a fire burns against a wall, the hot gases from the fire form a shape that resembles a "V" on the wall. The "V" will point toward the origin of the fire like the tip of an arrow (Figs. 14.3 and 14.4). Should the fire start further away from the wall, the pattern will resemble a "U" shape, with a circular pattern

Figure 14.3 Although obscured by smoke, the other half of the "V" pattern pointed toward the origin of the fire, an unattended barbeque grill overturned by a gust of wind.

Fire Investigations

Figure 14.4 The classic "V" pattern of an arson fire of a house under construction. Sawdust had been piled into the corner of the building and ignited using a spray can and a lighter as a makeshift flamethrower.

on the ceiling above. A "U" pattern may also appear higher on a wall should the fire be extinguished before the "V" shape can fully form.

Alligatoring Burn Pattern

In wooden structures, areas of charring that look like something resembling alligator skin, or large blisters, may indicate that a rapid and intense heat was present in that area (Fig. 14.5). The presence of alligatoring does not necessarily mean that accelerant liquid was used; rather it is an indication that the fire burned in this area with intense heat and fast-moving flames. Considerations should be given to ventilation, the type of fuel surrounding the area, or the physical construction of the structure.

Figure 14.5 Alligatoring burn pattern on a vaulted ceiling from a fatal house fire.

Clean Burn Patterns

Clean burn patterns are quite often found in fire scenes in jails or prisons because of the extensive use of concrete or other non-combustible construction materials. A clean burn pattern occurs on a surface where deposited soot or charring has been burned away completely by a fire that is burning with intense heat directly underneath the pattern, leaving an area that appears clean (light grey or white) that is bordered by soot or char (Figs. 14.6 and 14.7).

Figure 14.6 Clean burn pattern on highly fire-rated sheet rock on the ceiling of a fatal house fire. Note the alligatoring pattern on the wood beams.

Fire Investigations

Figure 14.7 In this photograph the clean burn pattern is primarily on the concrete post with small areas on a concrete beam and concrete ceiling in a prison laundry room fire.

Spalling

Another fire burn pattern encountered in the jail or prison fire scene is the spalling burn pattern because of the extensive use of concrete as a construction material. Spalling occurs when extreme heat weakens the surface of

Figure 14.8 Spalling on the concrete ceiling in a prison laundry room fire.

the concrete leaving it scarred, pitted, or chipped (Fig. 14.8). Spalling can be found on concrete or masonry floors, walls, or ceilings.

Smoke Deposits

Smoke deposits may be present in areas where the temperature of the surface is cooler, and the fire has yet to consume the deposits. Smoke deposits may primarily be found on walls and ceilings and may provide the investigator with an understanding of ventilation conditions (draft) that may have contributed to the behavior of the fire (Figs. 14.9–14.11).

Fire Investigations 215

Figure 14.9 Smoke deposits surrounding a ventilator that, although turned off, continued to spin by the heat of the fire.

Figure 14.10 Smoke deposits from a bedroom window in a fatal house fire.

Figure 14.11 Smoke with a clear delineation mark at the mid-point of the wall. Also, note the smoke stains on the glass.

Chimney Effect

The chimney effect, mentioned earlier, can occur when the construction of certain areas of a building provides a tall space for the rising of heated gas and flames, often resulting in extensive damage and charring inside of that area; especially if there is a vent or skylight at the top of the structure. In a jail or prison, the best example of this would be in a stairwell or elevator shaft. Consider the chimney in a house as it draws air from an opening near the floor and vents it through an opening on the roof. The charring will likely be heavier toward the top of the space.

The Effects of Ventilation on Fire Patterns

Anyone who has had to deal with the aftermath of a housing unit riot or disturbance where chemical agents were deployed to restore order, knows the concept of positive-airflow ventilation for removing the lingering gas and introducing fresh air into the building. The process involves opening doors on opposite ends of the building, placing one large fan at one side blowing air into the building, and another large fan at the other blowing air outward.

This produces the effect of moving the air in one direction exhausting the gas and introducing fresh air. Air currents affect the behavior of fires as well. If a fire is burning in a building that is sealed, thus restricting the amount of air available, the fire will burn itself out as soon as the oxygen is depleted. However, if a door or a window is open, the fire will continue to spread. A few years ago, your author investigated several arson-related fires set in two-story abandoned farmhouses. The arsonist had a fair understanding of fire dynamics. He would door-kick the front door, open the first-floor windows and one window at the top of the stairs, and use an accelerant at the base of the stairs. As the heat rose, it pulled in air from the first-floor windows up the stairs and out the single second-floor window, which caused the fire to spread quickly upward. Using this information, we reinforced the front doors of the remaining houses and used plywood to cover the windows. This did not immediately stop the arsonist, but it slowed down his efforts sufficiently to be caught. The suspect was a transient who claimed the fires were accidentally set from a "warming fire" that got away from him. Your author was able to explain to the prosecutor that the fires were deliberately set using an accelerant and in a manner to use ventilation to ensure the spread of the fire. He was prosecuted for the crimes. In previous years, your author was tasked with investigating a prison laundry room fire, as seen in some of the photographs in this chapter. The area of origin was discovered to be underneath a concrete pillar, where a plastic cart had been parked by an inmate laundry worker. The cart had been filled with grey wool blankets recently removed from the industrial dryer. It was clear that this was the place where the fire started, but the question was how, and was it an accident or a deliberate act? The result of the investigation revealed that the fire occurred on the last day before a three-day holiday weekend. The inmate worker who was the lead man for the drying stage of the process had decided to make it a four-day weekend and failed to report to work. His job was covered by an inexperienced inmate worker. The inexperienced worker had improperly set the temperature on the dryer and did not follow the proper procedure for hand separating the wool blankets once they were removed from the machine. Instead, he dumped all the blankets together in a plastic cart and wheeled the cart to an area near a roll-up door to cool. However, before the blankets could be sufficiently cooled, the staff closed all the doors and left for the long weekend. One thin, well-worn, blanket smoldered until reaching an ignition temperature, which caused the configuration (Figs. 14.12–14.5). To verify this theory, your author requested the supervisor of the laundry facility to replicate the drying phase with the improper temperature settings to dry very thin, well-worn, wool blankets. The temperature was achieved to reasonably believe that the blankets would reach an ignition point. The cause of the fire was accidental in nature owing to an unfortunate series of events.

Figure 14.12 The industrial dryer at the prison

Figure 14.13 The remnants of the plastic cart (in the blue bucket) with the metal carts containing blankets that were parked nearby.

Fire Investigations

Figure 14.14 The hole cut into the roll-up door by the firefighting personnel in order to direct a stream of water onto the fire. It should be noted that all locks were too hot to insert a Folger Adams key from the inside of the facility, so access had to be made from the loading dock.

Figure 14.15 Fortunately, the majority of the damage was caused by the smoke. Laundry operations were restored in a week.

Interview Techniques in the Correctional Setting 15

There is no environment that will prove more challenging than a prison or jail to an investigator who is trying to get eyewitness statements from a reticent inmate population. Still, it can be done, provided you respect the prison politics to which the inmates are subjected by other inmates. I would still "canvas the neighborhood" following a homicide. If the incident occurred in a cell block, while I was in the preliminary stages of analyzing the crime scene, I routinely asked the inmates in the cells that overlooked the scene what they may have seen or heard. I restricted the time that I spent in front of each cell to just a few minutes, only enough time to find out if the inmate saw or heard anything and if they were willing to talk to me later in private. If a homicide occurred in a cell, I always asked the inmates in the neighboring cells, on both sides and the tiers above and below, if they heard anything unusual. Generally, I received an answer something to the effect, "I heard arguing," or, "It sounded like they were moving the bunks around," which leads to the follow-up question, "Do you remember about what time that was?" The response might be, "It was halfway through The Price Is Right," but that is sufficient to give you a plausible timeline.

Some facilities conduct mass fact-finding interviews to determine if an incident that may have happened between a few inmates might escalate into a facility-wide riot or a series of retaliatory attacks. This happens most often when incidents occur that are either between the races or between rival gangs or are of such importance that they might jeopardize the safety and security of the institution. These interviews are usually conducted by counselors or administrators and are done while the facility is on lockdown status. Inmates are brought out of their cells one at a time and taken to an interview room that is not in view of the other inmates. This is a good opportunity for the investigator to interview inmates who have expressed a willingness to provide information or inmates who were identified as being present when the incident occurred. However, it is best to coordinate with the other interviewers regarding the identities of those inmates who are to be interviewed by the investigators so that they are not interviewed more than once; also, it is important to establish a restriction on the amount of time that the inmate will be out of his cell as not to be detained in the interview room any more or less time than the inmate before or after. This is to prevent the perception that the inmate is cooperating and providing information. Therefore, if the interviewers decide that 8–10 minutes is sufficient for the interview, then each inmate should remain in the interview room for that length of time regardless of whether they are providing information or not. If more than eight minutes is required for the interview, the inmate should still be released back to his cell at the end of the allotted time with arrangements that he will be interviewed at a later date and in a manner that would not be readily apparent that the inmate was providing information to staff. It is important that you provide for the safety of your witnesses and therefore you do not want to give the impression to the other inmates that your witness is providing information.

Sometimes it is not how you ask the question, but how you do not ask. I have found that an inmate may not tell you who the suspect was out of a group of inmates who were present when another inmate was stabbed, but the inmate might tell you who it was not. So, it might be better to show an inmate a group of five inmates present at the stabbing and ask, "So, of these guys, who did not stab the guy?" The inmate might be more willing to identify the inmates who did not participate in the assault and thereby identify the suspect by default. That way he can go back to his housing unit or cell and say, "Hey, I told them you did not do it."

The prison where I worked had an inmate stabbed through the right earlobe. The victim was seated at a table in the back of the housing unit, playing cards with three other inmates, when the assailant walked up to him from behind, leaned over, and jabbed the weapon into the side of his head. The tip of the weapon managed to pierce the area directly behind the victim's earlobe and severed the tributary vein to the jugular. After being stabbed, the victim stood up from the table, projecting blood as he turned, and walked to the front of the housing unit where he found the tier officers, leaving projected bloodstains as he went. The officers immediately called an emergency over the radio and secured the housing unit's front door, thus restricting the movement of the inmates who were in the housing unit at the time of the incident. All inmates in the housing unit who were not in their cells were required to assume a prone position until such time as they could be checked for injuries or bloodstains on their hands or garments. The victim actually died en route to the hospital but was brought back to life due to the efforts of the life-flight medical personnel. He was rushed into surgery and the doctors at the hospital trauma unit were able to control the bleeding and save his life. In all, there were 39 inmates present outside of their cells in the housing unit at the time of the incident. After processing the crime scene, my partner and I interviewed the three other inmates who were at the table. Conveniently, they all were either looking in the wrong direction or had forgotten to bring their glasses to the table.

We decided to place the three in the Administrative Segregation Unit with the purpose of protecting them from the suspect who was still at large. This provided us with the opportunity to interview them later, at length and in private. We then reported to the hospital to take a statement from the victim who was by that time out of surgery and in recovery. Although it was apparent that the victim knew the identity of the assailant, he was less than cooperative with our investigation. We expressed our concerns that the facility would have to go on a prolonged lockdown if the suspect was of a different race. Perhaps not wanting to return to a prison that was on a prolonged full lockdown, the victim stated that he had seen the assailant ascend the rear housing unit staircase and noted that he was of the same race as himself. This admission opened the door for us to extract a partial description; an African American male, approximately 6' tall, 230 pounds, with salt & pepper hair and a slight gray and black beard. We were able to get the same vague description from two of the other inmates who were seated at the table at the time of the stabbing.

With this information, I was able to use the diagram drawn by the crime scene scribe of the position and identities of the 39 inmates present in the dayroom to identify four inmates who fit the description. During the housing unit mass interview process, I was able to double-alibi three of the possible suspects. This left one strong suspect who only had one alibi, his own when he claimed to be in the showers at the time of the stabbing. Again, I was able to place him at the foot of the front housing unit staircase using the diagram drawn by the scribe. When presented with this information, he stated that he meant to say he had stepped out of the shower and was standing by the staircase. Again, with the diagram in hand, I individually interviewed the two inmates who were documented as having been in the shower when the inmate movement was halted. At first, I did not ask them if our suspect was in the shower, rather if they could verify the presence of the other inmate who was documented there. Individually, each one confirmed that they were the only two inmates in the shower. I then asked them if they could confirm the presence of the suspect. Both inmates stated that the suspect had left the showers 10–15 minutes prior to the stabbing; giving him sufficient time to perform the deed and reach the front of the housing unit at the time the alarm was sounded.

Using this information, my partner and I moved the suspect to the Administrative Segregation Unit and conducted a Miranda interview. The suspect waived his rights and elected to make a statement. He admitted to the stabbing, stating that the victim had stolen a small, black & white television set worth about $20.00. In a heartfelt interview, the suspect stated that his mother had recently passed and that he had no family members left. He was the inmate that other inmates would go to in order to purchase small electronic items he had obtained from those who had either transferred to other facilities or been paroled, unable to take their televisions or radios because they were not officially on their property inventories.

Watching television had also become his only pleasure. Once the victim took the small television without paying him the required $20.00; the suspect informed us that he had become so angry that he plotted to kill him. He found a piece of glass in his cell window lower pane that he was able to remove and fashion into a short stabbing weapon and hid it in the shower area. He came in from his work assignment, quickly showered, retrieved the weapon, and proceeded to the back of the housing unit, where he knew he would find the victim in his usual card-playing seat. He stabbed him, ascended the back staircase, and walked down the tier parallel to the movement of the victim, broke the glass weapon into small pieces, discarded it into a garbage can, and descended the front staircase, where he was required to assume a prone position. He stated, "I had to kill him. If I hadn't, everyone would just walk away with all of my electronics. I couldn't sell anything." To confirm his story, I asked him to draw a picture of the weapon and the shape of the glass that he had procured from his cell. We then went back to his cell and matched the drawing to the missing piece of glass from the lower windowpane. After submitting the case to the District Attorney's Office for their consideration, my partner and I delivered the suspect's television set to his Administrative Segregation Unit cell; we felt some empathy for the inmate. The prosecutor was reluctant to file charges, but after a conference with my partner and myself, she filed the charges of attempted homicide. The suspect accepted a plea agreement for 12 years.

In most states, the criminal proceedings evidence codes allow for the protection of information obtained from confidential sources. Unfortunately, this does not always guarantee that the identity of the informant will not be discovered by the inmate offender, as often times the information provided in and of itself will reveal the identity of the source. Let's face it: if the cellmate of the offender was the only one privileged to the details regarding a criminal event, it is no stretch of the imagination for the suspect to figure out who provided the information. Furthermore, the identity of the confidential witness will always be revealed to the attorneys involved in the courtroom proceedings. It is up to the ethical standards of the attorney whether or not confidentiality will be maintained. I have been on the stand when a defense attorney attempted to reveal the source of the confidential informant through a process of elimination series of questions. I have also been on the stand when the defense asked a question that would have required the revelation of the identity of the witness and the prosecutor did not object to the question. I directed the question to the judge stating that responding to the question would reveal information already agreed upon by the court that would be withheld.

Therefore, I never guarantee an inmate absolute protection as a confidential source if the matter be prosecuted in court. I can, to some extent, guarantee them protection if the matter is resolved administratively through the departmental disciplinary process.

As a prison investigator, it is far more important that the facts of the case are discovered and that the matter is thoroughly and fairly investigated. It is then up to the investigator or attorney from the prosecutor's office to ascertain if the witness will be willing to testify in court.

It is possible to get eyewitness information from the inmate population provided you are aware that their cooperation, or even perceived cooperation, might jeopardize their safety and that of the institution. If measures are taken to safeguard their protection, and if the investigator is sympathetic to the concerns of the inmate and of prison politics to which he is subjected, it is still possible to obtain credible eyewitness testimony. My best advice to any investigator intent upon interviewing a convicted felon is to be genuine and sincere. Inmates can spot a phony a mile away.

One final story on the subject occurred just before your author retired from prison. I was sitting at my desk when the telephone rang. It was a detective sergeant from the Los Angeles County Sheriff's Department, Homicide Division. He was working on a cold-case homicide from 1978. The female clerk of a gas station convenience store had been robbed, kidnapped, raped, and murdered in a remote, mountainous region of Los Angeles County. The detective sergeant inherited the case early in his career, but he was preparing for retirement and wanted to make one final effort to solve the crime. New techniques in the recovery of DNA evidence were attempted, and finally, after almost four decades, a DNA profile was developed, and a search of the national DNA database provided the sergeant with a name; an inmate housed at our prison whom I will identify with the alias Inmate Barry Smith. The sergeant requested my assistance with arranging a visit to the institution and the collection of a confirmatory DNA buccal swab by the issuance of a search warrant. I agreed to be his liaison and the arrangements were quickly made for the following week. Before disconnecting, I asked the sergeant if he would provide me with some of the details of his investigation to see if I could be of assistance in gathering information. He reluctantly provided me with just the very basic information of what had happened. I then asked him if I could provide what I referred to as an intelligence gathering sortie to gather background information on Inmate Smith's incarceration history and pertinent information about his current conduct and associations. This would include a review of the file kept by the department, a review of his visiting history and approved and rejected visiting applications, the review of incoming and outgoing correspondence, and the monitoring of telephone calls from the institution to family and associates outside of the prison. The sergeant agreed, and I went to work finding out as much as I could about Inmate Smith. I discovered he was serving his third prison sentence, this time for armed robbery, that he was in his early 60s, was due to parole in six months, had been participating in a religious-based self-help therapy group at the prison, was estranged from his son, but was on good terms with his sister, and had written two books. One book was on prison poetry and the second was an autobiography. I ordered both books from an online vendor. Although the book of poetry was not my cup of tea, I found the autobiography quite interesting. I discovered that he was one of the founding members of an infamous street gang in the Los Angeles area, and I discovered a great deal about his youthful activities that included drug trafficking and other drug-related misadventures. I read his correspondence and listened to the telephone calls with his sister. During one call, the sister informed him that she would be up to the prison for a visit during the upcoming weekend. I arranged for an extra shift working in the visiting room, and I assigned the pair a table that was within earshot of the podium where I was posted. I overheard their conversation and determined that the sister was devoutly religious and that the self-help therapy Inmate Smith was receiving had a profound impact on his outlook for the future. On the day the sergeant arrived at the institution, I escorted him to the building where we conducted clandestine meetings with inmates. Inmate Smith was led into the room and the sergeant served the warrant. He carefully read the warrant and agreed to provide the requisite buccal swabs. After this was accomplished, Barry asked the sergeant, "What's this all about?" The sergeant said that he was working on a cold-case homicide from 1978 but was not prepared to speak with Barry at this time. He did ask Barry, "If this DNA does match the DNA from the crime scene, would you be willing to talk to me?" Barry dropped his head for a moment, looked up, and said, "Yes, but not here. Take me down south (to Los Angeles) and I might talk to you." Barry was returned to a holding cell, and I escorted the sergeant to his vehicle. We had agreed to meet later that night to go over the information that I had gathered. I asked the sergeant if he had any objections to my talking to Barry about "life in general." The sergeant had no objection provided I did not talk about the investigation or any of the details of the crime. I assured him that was not my attention and I returned to the place of the initial contact. Barry was escorted back into the room, and I asked him if he would like to talk about his well-being and progress with the self-help program. He had no objection, and we had a 45-minute discussion about life, books, what makes the character of the individual, and religion. The conversation was light, genuine, and frank. At one point, I placed my hand on his shoulder and said, "Barry, I do not care what you may have done in the past. I do not care for what you are doing in the present. What matters to me is what you will do in the future. You have the rare ability to help all these young men who are struggling with decisions they have made and are about to make." Barry looked at me and said, "I have demons inside of me. They have always been there. They have made me do things. They have ruined my marriage and my relationship with my son. I awake at night screaming because of these demons." I extended my right hand with my two fingers extended, tapped him on the chest, and said, "Barry, don't you think it is time to kill those demons?" He looked at me and said, "Do you think you can get that sergeant back here?" I called the sergeant and asked him to return to the institution. When he arrived, my partner escorted him back to the interview room. The sergeant sat down, started his voice recorder, and being mindful of the Miranda Advisement said, "You wanted to talk to me?" Barry looked at him, tapped the file folder in front of the sergeant, and said, "That one, I know that one. I did that one. Now let me tell you about the five you don't know about." It was then that I realized that the person with whom I had spent the past hour talking with was in fact a serial killer. Barry provided detailed information about the five murders he had committed, the location of the bodies that had not been found, and an agreement to continue his cooperation once he was returned to Los Angeles County.

While accompanying the sergeant to his car, he asked, "How did you do that?" I told him that we just had a heartfelt conversation, not an interrogation or interview. It was just two adult men talking about characters and books. Most important of all is the quality of genuine empathy for their well-being. If you say you do not care about their horrible past, you must be genuine in that sentiment. An inmate can spot a fake a mile away. Several months later, a letter addressed to me had come from Barry post-marked at the Los Angeles County Jail. The letter informed me that he had continued his cooperation, assisted with the unknown homicides, and had met with the now-adult children of the 1978 murder victim. The children had forgiven him. In closing, the letter bore this final remark: "The demons are dead." I wish I had kept that letter.

Essential Report Writing 16

Whenever I am asked to help new officers in the skill of writing effective reports, my response is invariably always the same: "Could they write before you hired them?" As the saying goes, if it is predictable, it is definitely preventable. As the nation's school system abandons its standards for grammar, spelling, and punctuation, and artificial intelligence can hinder personal development, law enforcement agencies have had to settle for lower standards in this field as well. When I joined my agency more than three decades ago, the entrance exam was weighted heavily on verbal, grammatical, and mathematic skills, and the exam was given a numbered grade. The higher your score, the more likely you are to get the job. Today, the entrance exam is scored pass or fail. Someone with great verbal skills has the same chance of getting the position as someone who does not understand even the basics of punctuation, spelling, and grammar. This new philosophy in hiring might work if the academies hired grammarians to instruct the recruits, but we all know this is not happening. To make matters worse, our report writers are being supervised by people who do not have sound report-writing skills themselves. These are the same people who are approving the report as acceptable even though the report may contain glaring grammatical errors. Think of the nightmare the poor deputy district attorneys must have attempting to prosecute a crime with police reports that are badly written, horribly punctuated, and grossly misspelled.

Apathy

When it comes to modern life, we see an apathy concerning proper grammar, spelling, and punctuation. Newspapers go to press with blatant grammatical errors. Textbooks also show signs of ineffective proofreading. Do not even get me started on the internet. Paying attention to the small details and giving your work that extra effort demonstrates professionalism and intelligence. Text messaging, blogging, posting, and chatting have destroyed what remained of our verbal acumen. I see police reports that are written in text-type language, and it kills me.

One of the most common mistakes that I see officers make is that they write as they talk. What generally happens with this form of writing is that punctuation disappears completely, and the report becomes one very long run-on sentence. If punctuation does not disappear entirely, it is supplemented with an inordinate number of commas.

First and Foremost

First and foremost, you need to learn how to type. This skill is being lost in our younger generation. Do not get me wrong, I do see youthful people tapping away at computer keyboards and cellular telephone touch pads with incredible speed; however, they sacrifice accuracy, spelling, and punctuation. Several – ok, many decades ago – I spent an hour every day clacking away on an old Royal manual typewriter under the tutelage of Brother Onorato, SJ. A passing grade was 45 words per minute. That was considered a good speed in the pre-word processor/PC era and an acceptable speed for college work. While working at my agency's headquarters, I managed to boost my speed to 85 words per minute. I believe that this is the acceptable speed for modern-day applications. My sister types at a blistering 130 words per minute. She and I had a talk about this as I was preparing for this book. We came to a startling conclusion: We both have the keyboard memorized and each letter of every word that enters our thought process is automatically transformed into its letter position on the keyboard. In other words, if I am thinking of the word "break," I automatically think "b" is lower center, "r" is at 11 o'clock (left hand) upper keyboard, "e" is at 11 o'clock (left hand) next to the "r," "a" is far left keyboard middle row (left hand), and "k" is at two o'clock middle keyboard (right hand). You would be amazed at how fast your brain can process this information. Having achieved this, you rarely have to look at the keyboard and your eyes remain on the screen, which allows you to compose more efficiently in your head. It also allows you to correct your errors while you are typing instead of after you have finished. Now, let's get this through your thick skull: You have four fingers and one thumb on each hand, and they all work independently of each other. Therefore, there is no reason at all for hunting and pecking. Furthermore, the keys never change their location on the keyboard so there is never a reason to look around for that elusive letter. If you own a computer, there is no reason why you cannot improve your typing skills as there are plenty of inexpensive typing software programs on the market, some of which make games out of typing exercises. I am told "Typing of The Dead: Overkill" is a PC software download that allows the user to improve their typing skills while dispatching the ubiquitous zombies. Once again, it is up to you to put that extra effort into improving these skills and increasing your professionalism.

Essential Report Writing

The English language is structured for a reason. The reader should not have to suffer for your failure to get the basic concept of composition. The reader should not have to read a sentence more than once to understand what you, the writer, are trying to convey. It may not be fair, but you will be judged on your efforts. That is just the way it is and there is no reason why it should not be that way. In a jury trial, your credibility as a competent law enforcement official will hinge upon three things: your appearance, your presentation, and the quality of your report. Improper grammar in your report will reflect upon your competency as an investigator or reporting employee. It will also reflect upon your intelligence as an investigator. The grammar in your report will reflect upon your aptitude and your skills of critical thinking as an investigator. Most of all, improper grammar will have an adverse effect on the way you represent your department or agency. There was a time when that mattered.

Here is where you will benefit from my experience: I have testified a lot. I have testified in everything from complex narcotic-related conspiracy-type investigations to homicide investigations and investigations involving intricate forensic analysis. If the defense attorney cannot challenge the evidence, they will always challenge the evidence collector or analyst. It is their job to make you, the expert, look like the biggest Barney Fife in the world. If you think that your report is not fair game, you are grossly mistaken. I once had a defense attorney find one typographical error in a 16-page search warrant and hammer me for 10 minutes in front of the jury regarding that error. Throughout the entire trial, he continued to bring up this one little mistake to the extent that he even included it in his closing argument. It was grueling. In the end, it did not matter because the jury found his client guilty, but his strategy could have worked had I had a lot of grammatical mistakes in my warrant and reports.

Some of you are going to hate this third bit of advice I am about to give: READ! Read as many books as you possibly can. It does not matter what you read, just read, but make sure it is an author who has a keen understanding of the language. I always have a book on the nightstand, and I try to read a chapter every night before going to sleep. My preferred books in my youth were the Agatha Christie murder mysteries. These days my book selection tends to be related to military history or forensics.

Now that I have abandoned the environment of the prison for a municipal police agency, I have had a realization of a fourth, albeit more modern, hindrance to good report writing: technology. Unlike in the correctional setting where there may be the luxury of additional staff who can provide coverage for an officer who needs to spend an hour or two writing a report, police agencies need speed. An officer who spends an hour or two writing a report is an officer not handling calls for service or being proactive in the prevention of crime. Dictation software has made its way into the law enforcement world. These tools do speed things up a bit, but we are far from that age of artificial intelligence where a computer program can tell the difference between the word "led" and the word "lead" or the difference between "their" and "there" and sometimes "they're." In other words, the computer program is only as accurate as the proofreader. These days, I write highly analytical reports that require a skillful amount of precision to convey significantly important forensic information. I am doubtful artificially intelligent dictation software is quite up to handling bloodstain pattern analysis. We will see what the next decade may bring. I fear this topic will be reconsidered in the next edition of this book, which will likely be dictated in its entirety to a computer or written by artificial intelligence. The next bit of technological kit that has had a dramatic impact on report writing, both good and bad, is the body worn camera (BWC). The problem is not with the BWC itself, because they have contributed much in the way of accurately memorializing a law enforcement contact, but in the reliance upon them by younger officers to replace the art of good notetaking with the convenience of digital video and audio recordings. And so, as I sit in my office or laboratory, I can hear officers in the report writing room replaying the same few minutes of BWC footage over and over, and over again. This goes on for hours. So, a report that would have taken perhaps 20 minutes to write using proper contemporaneous notes often takes two hours or more. I find it infuriating.

For my final complaint, I will partially place the blame on the supervisors who are approving the reports written by the officers. However, far too often, reports with criminal charges are submitted for prosecution that are absent any narrative addressing the elements of the crime being charged. For example, the elements of the crime of terrorist threats include the words "reasonable and sustained fear." Yet in the entire body of the report, never once is it mentioned if the recipient of the threat felt in any way threatened and in fear. My advice to the new report writer is to familiarize yourself with the laws you intend to charge, to understand the elements of that crime, and to be certain the elements are clearly stated in your report. Otherwise, you will be frustrated by the constant rejection of criminal charges against the people you are arresting.

So, What Exactly Is a Report?

Pure and simple, a report is a written statement providing a permanent record of your actions, observations, and discoveries. Nearly every official action you take, participate in, or observe will ultimately result in a written report.

Essential Report Writing

It is the documentation of what you did, what you saw, what you smelled, what you heard, and what was told to you by eyewitnesses. And yes, like it or not, punctuation, spelling, and grammar ARE important. Notice I said that a report is a record of YOUR actions, observations, and discoveries. In this regard, reports generated using artificial intelligence may look great, but they are not a representation of your actions, nor could they ever. I can only imagine how an attorney for the defense would use that to their advantage before a jury when they discover you did not write your own report. Woe betide the investigator who uses artificial intelligence to write a search warrant. In my humble opinion, using artificial intelligence to do your work for you is a clear indication that you have abandoned any hope of striving to be the very best at your profession.

Positive Identification

One thing for certain is that you will, at some point, be asked to identify the defendant in court. True, it very likely is the guy sitting next to the defense attorney, but you wrote that report three years ago, how can you be certain that is the guy you saw committing the crime? Well, it should be in your report. Now we all know how things work out. You are one of 40 people that responded to the incident. You cuff up the suspect and escort him to a holding cell or patrol car. You turn him over to the custody of another officer and you return to your assignment. Hours later, you get a call from your lieutenant asking for a report. Of course, you did not write down the name of the inmate or any other identifying information. So, what do you do? "Hey, lieutenant, what was the guy's name?" There is nothing worse than finding out three years later while you are in the middle of your testimony before a jury that the lieutenant gave you the wrong name. So, who is to blame for that little debacle? Well, frankly you are to blame. Even if you did take the time to get the guy's name as you were putting him in the back seat of the car or escorted him to the infirmary, you can bet that the defense attorney is going to ask you a follow-up question: "How did you establish his identity?" "I asked him," just is not good enough. Very likely you are not going to remember how you identified the suspect. That is why it is imperative that you personally take the initiative to positively identify the suspect(s), victim(s), and witnesses involved in the incident using the photograph as it appears on an official document, or some other verifiable source AND you make a notation of this in your report.

- "I identified Inmate Jones using the photograph as it appears on his departmental issued identification card."

The Nuts and Bolts of Your Report

Your report must be a complete accounting of the occurrence, the parties involved (suspects/victims/witnesses/responders), the evidence collected, the statements made, the things heard, smelled, and seen, the elements of the crime, or lack thereof, and the subsequent investigation.

Notetaking

A notebook should be part of your uniform and you should make good use of that notebook. It is a good idea to develop a system of abbreviations that can speed up your entries, especially if you are recording statements of witnesses. Remember, if you are not documenting an exact statement from a witness in your report, there is no need to use quotations. Remember that your notebook can be subpoenaed as evidence. So, always be professional in your notebook entries, and never throw your notebooks away.

Fairness

As I said, the reporting officer is only interested in documenting the facts. The competent investigator is interested only in discovering the truth. It is not your job to be a judge or jury. The objective investigator looks for the evidence that will not only prove guilt but also exonerate the innocent. Always avoid the use of words that may produce connotations that cloud the true meaning of the facts. Do not use descriptive terms that tend to exaggerate what was actually observed by witnesses. Using language like, "The callous nature of the crime would indicate that the attacker had a grudge," or, "the gaping wound was hideously large," shows bias and a lack of objectivity.

Abbreviations

If you intend to use an abbreviation or acronym throughout your report, you must first inform the reader what the abbreviation or acronym means: "I forwarded the details of the occurrence to the Investigative Services Unit (ISU). ISU will forward the complaint to the District Attorney's Office for disposition." The abbreviation or acronym should follow the formal title parenthetically.

Completeness

All essential facts are to be included so as not to require additional information. The facts recorded must be relevant to the report. Do not, however, sacrifice completeness for the sake of being concise. If it is necessary to be wordy in order to have an exact description of an event, then it is better to be wordy.

Formalities

Do not be a lazy writer. Never abbreviate law enforcement titles (i.e., Sgt., Lt., Capt., etc.). This is the crutch of the lazy writer. Always use the formal title of law enforcement personnel first and then use the more casual title in the remaining text. Therefore, when first introducing a person to the report, use their formal title, such as Correctional Captain J. Smith. Following that introduction, you may refer to this person subsequently as Captain Smith. Never refer to a person by last name only. This is a journalistic technique that has no place in report writing.

The Chronological Narrative

The narrative form of writing begins at the point at which the writer becomes involved in the action. The narrative ends at the point where the writer's action is completed.

Therefore, the opening statement in the paragraph introduces the writer, gives a brief description of the incident or offense being charged, and begins the narrative.

> "On June 18, 2016, at approximately 0735 hours, while assigned as an Investigative Officer with the Correctional Training Facility (CTF), Security & Investigations Unit, I was dispatched to the Central Facility Maintenance area, Carpenter's Shop, following a report of a breaking-and-entering, and the theft of tools. Upon my arrival, I was met by T. Escobar, Carpenter III, who informed me that a window leading into the shop had been broken, and someone had manipulated the window latch and entered the shop. That person then stole three tools. Mr. Escobar led me to Toolbox #3 and showed me that tool #13, a pair of anvil pliers, was missing from the shadow board. The padlock to Tool Box #3 had been broken and was lying on the floor along with a miter-gauge from a nearby table saw. I noted a pry bar (tool #21 from Toolbox #3) was on the floor near the steps leading to Tool Room #105, the door frame of which had been pried open …"

Please avoid beginning each sentence with, "I then …"

Your Report in Court

Always consider the questions that you will be asked by attorneys during courtroom proceedings while writing your report. For example, let us examine this passage from an actual report:

- While conducting a security check, I observed Inmate Smith standing between bunks 13 and 14. He was holding something in his hand. I ordered him to show me what he was holding in his hand. Inmate Smith refused to show me what was in his hand and said that he didn't have anything in his hand. When I approached him, he opened his hand and an item fell to the floor. I told him to step away from the object. Instead, he kicked it underneath bunk 13. After placing him in handcuffs, I looked underneath bunk 13 and discovered six small clear plastic bindles inside of some toilet paper. The bindles appeared to contain green leafy matter, which later tested positive for suspected marijuana.

These are the questions I would ask as an attorney for the defense:

- You said you were conducting a security check. Can you explain a security check to the jury? What type of housing unit was this? Was it a dormitory or a cell block?
- What was the lighting like in the dormitory?
- Approximately how far away were you from my client when you observed his hands?
- You stated these were bunk beds with one bed above another. Is bunk 13 below bunk 14 or is it bunk 13 low and 13 up? Was my client assigned to any of those bunks?
- How tall is my client? How tall is the top bunk? If my client is 5′ 9″ and the top bunk is 6′ off the ground, how were you able to see my client's hands?
- You said my client was holding something in his hand. In which hand was he holding this item? Would you like to refer to your report to refresh your memory? It is not in your report. What is the purpose of a report? Would you agree that knowing which hand the alleged object is being held would be an important detail to document in a report?
- How was the alleged object being held? Was it held in a hand that is clenched or open?
- Did you give my client a direct or lawful order to show you what was in his hand or was it a casual request? Did you neglect to include that detail in your report as well?

- You stated the "object" fell to the floor, but you offered no description of the object. Did you see the object fall without being able to provide any details whatsoever?
- You stated that my client "kicked" the object under the bunk when you instructed him to "step away." Is it possible while stepping back that the object was inadvertently nudged under the bunk?
- After placing my client in handcuffs, did you escort him from the area, or was my defenseless client, his hands cuffed behind his back, left vulnerable to assault by the other inmates while you were on your hands and knees looking under the bunk or did you leave the area before you looked under the bunk?
- You stated that you found five plastic bindles wrapped in toilet paper underneath the lower bunk. Since you could not describe the object that allegedly fell from my client's hand, how do you know if those bindles were already under the bunk before you even approached my client?

Now let us fix the report:

- At approximately 1130 hours, while assigned as Dormitory Officer #2, I conducted a welfare check of the inmates assigned to the North Dormitory. As I walked down the first row of bunk beds, I observed Inmate Smith standing between bunks 13 upper and lower and bunks 14 upper and lower. These bunks are spaced approximately 6′ apart and jut outward from the wall. As I approached, I observed Inmate Smith, who was standing in the space between the bunks, look at me and place his right hand behind his back. Upon reaching the open space between the bunks and with a clear and unobstructed view, I instructed Inmate Smith to show me his hands. At first, Inmate Smith, who was facing me, refused to remove his right hand from behind his back until I gave him a direct order. Inmate Smith moved his right hand from behind his back but kept it down by his side. I observed that his right hand was partially clenched with a white paper object being visible between the thumb and forefinger. I asked Inmate Smith to show me what was in his hand, to which he stated that nothing was in his hand as he opened his left hand. I ordered him to show me what he was holding in his right hand. Inmate Smith refused to show me what was in his hand and said that he didn't have anything in his hand. When I advanced by a few steps to detain him, Inmate Smith opened his hand and the white-in-color object fell to the floor. I instructed him to step away from the object. Instead, he looked at me, looked down, and kicked the object underneath bunk 13 with purpose with the tip of his right foot. I instructed him to place his hands behind his back, to which he complied, and I placed him in handcuffs. I summoned my partner to escort Inmate Smith to the front podium until escort officers arrived to take Inmate Smith to the Central Services holding cell. I remained at the bunks and looked underneath bunk 13 where I discovered six small clear plastic bindles wrapped in several sheets of toilet paper. No other item resembling the object that I observed fall to the ground was underneath the bunk. The only other objects underneath the bunk were a cardboard box containing a pair of black tennis shoes. Upon examination, I determined the five clear plastic bindles appeared to contain green leafy matter, which later tested positive for suspected marijuana with a combined net weight of approximately five grams, with a prison value of approximately $450.00 to $500.00.

The first report was the report that was challenged in court successfully with the jury returning a verdict of not guilty. The officer who faced the difficult questioning by the defense attorney was devastated that the jury believed the inmate's story over his. Following the trial, I asked the officer to relate the events as they happened during the incident, which had occurred nearly two years before the trial. The officer related to me the details outlined in the second or fixed report. I asked him how he was certain of these events, and he said, "I remember it as if it happened yesterday." I told him that the mistake he made was to defend a poorly written report. He should have abandoned the report and testified only by his memory. If the defense asked why a certain detail was not in the report, simply reply that you remember the event as if it was yesterday and that ends any defense reference to the report. Of course, it is far better to have written a thorough and detailed report to begin with.

Use Photographs in Your Report

Your author is a proponent of using photographs within the body of the report to clarify important information. If you are documenting a bullet hole in the fender of a car, provide a written description of the bullet hole and provide a thumbnail photograph to confirm the description so that there is no confusion like this (Fig. 16.1):

"Defect AA2 is a perforated bullet hole on the lower left rear taillight lens. Horizontal trajectory was determined by trajectory rod to be 55 degrees traveling right to left with a downward trajectory of approximately 1 degree. The bullet was not recovered."

Essential Report Writing 237

Figure 16.1 Documentation using photography: Photograph of the perforated bullet hole in the taillight lens.

Forensic Reports

Crime scene reports are more detailed than any other incident report because subsequent analysis by other forensic specialists such as bloodstain pattern analysts, shooting scene or crime scene reconstruction specialists, and entomologists may rely upon the condition of the crime scene immediately following the event. As an example, a bloodstain pattern examiner may need to know the environmental condition of the crime scene to understand the drying time of the blood documented in the scene. An arson investigator may need to know the ambient temperature, wind direction, and percentage of humidity to understand the behavior and spread of a fire. I document this information, which is handily found in the weather application on my cellular telephone, immediately upon reaching the crime scene, and I document this information in the introduction of the report like this:

"On December 29, 2022, at approximately 1900 hours, I responded to 1503 Red Bluff Avenue to provide mutual aid from the Greenfield Police Department, Forensic Services Unit, following a stabbing incident resulting in an officer-involved shooting. I arrived on scene at 2015 hours. The ambient outside temperature upon my arrival was 48 degrees Fahrenheit, with no detectable winds, with 80% humidity. Outdoor scene lighting was provided by overhead lamps, vehicles headlights, and supplemented with handheld flashlights. Although sufficient for scene inspection and evidence detection, electronic flash was required for photographic documentation purposes. The crime scene perimeter had been established prior to my arrival on scene."

Crime scene reports should also contain the following paragraphs:

The Introduction

The introduction paragraph informs the reader the date, time, and location of the crime scene. It also includes how you were notified to respond to the crime scene, your title and agency information, and your time of arrival.

Environmental Condition

The environmental conditions of the crime scene include the previously discussed weather conditions if the scene is outdoors, or the environmental conditions of an interior location. In indoor settings, this might include the ambient temperature, lighting conditions, whether doors or windows were open, or if an air conditioner or heater was running.

Initial Observations

Initial observations include all the details of the crime scene upon the first inspection. This may include information regarding the crime scene perimeter, the presence of a decedent, the presence of fired cartridge shell casings, the presence of weapons and their conditions, the need to preserve perishable or transient evidence, evidence of emergency medical attention, and any other observation related to items of evidence first noted in the scene.

The Body of the Report

The body of the report is a detailed presentation of everything that was done to properly preserve, document, and process the crime scene, and the collection and disposition of the evidence discovered within the crime scene. This may include efforts to enhance latent evidence in the scene or any other procedural effort to identify or visualize trace evidence. This may also include information pertinent to bloodstain pattern analysis or any other impression evidence in the scene.

Evidence Inventory

Before closing the report, please include an itemized inventory of the evidence that you collected and its disposition. It is frustrating as a forensic analyst to read through a dozen reports from a shooting incident and seeing that evidence was collected, but is only referenced as "Five shell casings were collected from the scene." It is helpful to include an inventory of the evidence in one convenient place in your report like this:

> While processing the crime scene, I collected the following items of evidence:
> Item #1 – One Remington Peters brand 9mm Luger brass fired cartridge casing
> Item #2 – One Federal Cartridge brand 9mm Luger aluminum fired cartridge casing
> Item #3 – One Winchester brand 9mm Luger brass fired cartridge casing
> Item #4 – One Remington Peters brand .40 S&W caliber brass fired cartridge casing
> Item #5 – One CCI brand .40 S&W caliber aluminum brass fired cartridge casing

All items of evidence were processed into long-term evidence storage at the Greenfield Police Department.

Your Final Report

Once you have submitted your final report, no changes to that document should occur. Corrections and additional information should be provided as a supplemental report. Never make a change to your report after the original has become part of discovery in court proceedings.

In Summary

If you follow the advice that I have presented in this document, you should have no problem writing reports that will establish a permanent record of the facts of an incident or investigation. So, in summary:

> Learn to type
> Punctuation, spelling, and grammar ARE important
> Be accurate, detailed, concise, and complete
> Be fair, objective, and impartial
> PROOFREAD YOUR WORK MORE THAN ONCE!

Remember, if you have someone proofread your report, make sure they have a good foundation in grammar, spelling, punctuation, and effective report writing skills themselves.

EXAMPLE REPORT

On April 17, 2016, at approximately 1810 hours, while assigned as an Investigative Officer with the Security and Investigations Unit, I received a telephone call from the North Facility Watch Commander instructing me to respond to the "A" Facility to process a crime scene following the attempted homicide of Inmate Aguilar, F-1226X, WB-242L, by his cellmate, Inmate Fonseca, F-8332X, WB-242U. I arrived at the "A" Facility at approximately 1915 hours along with Investigative Officer A. Yerby. Upon our arrival, I was informed that Inmate Fonseca was being escorted to the "A" Facility Medical Clinic for evaluation. Officer Yerby and I met with the escorting officers and accompanied them and Inmate Fonseca to the clinic where I collected blood specimen swabs from under the nail of his right middle finger, on his left forehead area, and on his left thumbnail. I positively identified Inmate Fonseca using the photograph as it appeared on his form CTF-260 Bed Card. Officer Yerby photographed Inmate Fonseca using a digital camera. Inmate Aguilar had been transported to an outside hospital prior to my arrival at the institution. Senior Registered Nurse M. Anderson informed me that the decision was made to send Inmate Aguilar to the outside hospital because of two deep tissue stab wounds to his upper back. At approximately 1945 hours, Officer Yerby and I arrived at Whitney Hall and the crime scene at cell "B" 242. This cell is on the Second Tier, Yard Side, approximately three cells south of the front staircase. The cell had been sealed by responding staff and isolated by yellow caution tape. Correctional Officer J. Hewlett informed me that the cell had been closed immediately following the removal of the two inmates and that responding personnel did not enter the crime scene.

I took possession of the crime scene, obtained a key set, and opened the cell door. The cell floor was covered with a large amount of dried reddish fluid consistent with human blood. This fluid was also present on the four walls, door, lower bunk metal sheet, and toilet/sink fixture. No bloodstains were noted on the upper bunk metal sheet or mattress or ceiling. The ambient temperature of the cell was approximately 72°F, and the cell window was open. Relative humidity within the cell was approximately 76%. The cell had a north-east orientation when standing in the open doorway, facing inward. Of note was the lack of a light bulb in the ceiling mogul and the lack of a fluorescent tube in the bunk light fixture, both of which had been broken during the incident. A light bulb had to be procured from a nearby vacant cell before an inspection of the crime scene could be made. The mattress on each bunk had been rolled and placed against each respective south-east wall. Each locker suspended on the upper south-west and north-west walls contained minimal property. No television or radio was present in the cell and the only entertainment appeared to be from a number of paperback books on the cell writing desk and in the locker containing the property of Inmate Fonseca. The hot water tap on the sink was defective and ran continuously into the toilet bowl, which appeared to drain internally in a manner to maintain equilibrium. An inmate-made improvised stabbing weapon was noted in the bowl of the toilet.

I photographed the crime scene using a digital camera equipped with flash in its entirety as it was found by me. Following this, I placed evidence markers to represent individual items of evidence. I placed marker #1 to represent the stabbing weapon in the toilet. I placed evidence marker #2 to represent a bloodstained T-shirt that was discovered in the space between the toilet/sink fixture and the south-east cell wall. I photo-documented various bloodletting events in the crime scene, including shoe-print impressions, impact spatter, cast-off and cessation cast-off patterns, and a large heart-shaped void on the cell floor near the foot of the lower bunk. I retrieved the stabbing weapon from the toilet bowl and noted that it was constructed from a plastic toothbrush, blue in color, that had been tempered by the repeated application of heat with the handle end twisted into a sharpened point with a handle fashioned from strips torn from a garment resembling the waist portion of a pair of boxer shorts. The overall length of the weapon was approximately 5 ½" with a blade measuring approximately 13/4" in length. I collected this weapon as item DJD#1. Upon inspection of the bloodstained T-shirt, I noted a hole consistent with having been caused by a stabbing weapon on the upper right rear back panel, and a smaller hole on the upper right rear collar. I collected this shirt as evidence item DJD#2. I determined that there was insufficient lighting to map the bloodstain evidence in the cell. Therefore, I elected to secure the cell until the morning of the following day when ambient lighting would be more conducive to proper bloodstain pattern analysis and documentation. I closed the cell window, locked the door, and placed evidence tape along the door and jamb. I also placed a locking mechanism "boot" over the keyhole and placed a security padlock for which I alone maintained the key on the boot to prevent tampering with the scene. At approximately 2050 hours, I returned to the Security and Investigations Unit and downloaded the digital images into the Digital Image Evidence Computer.

While processing the crime scene, I processed the following items of evidence:

> Item DJD#1 – One inmate-manufactured improvised stabbing weapon, hardened and sharpened plastic, blue in color with a cloth handle, recovered from the toilet.

Item DJD#2 – One bloodstained Hanes brand T-shirt, medium in size, white in color, with holes consistent with a stabbing assault, recovered from the space between the toilet/sink fixture and south-east cell wall.

Item DJD#3 – Two blood specimen swabs collected from the right middle fingernail of Inmate Aguilar.

Item DJD#4 – Two blood specimen swabs collected from the left forehead of Inmate Aguilar.

Item DJD#5 – Two blood specimen swabs collected from the left thumbnail of Inmate Aguilar.

All items of evidence were processed into long-term evidence storage at the Security and Investigations Unit.

Courtroom Testimony 17

This chapter is based on the American "common law" legal system and may not apply in countries with distinctly different legal systems.

A Powerful Responsibility

The accepted etymology of the word testimony reflects that it is of Latin origin. Old English usage of the word is recorded in the 15th-century meaning, "proof or demonstration of some fact, evidence, or piece of evidence"; with an early 16th-century legal definition of a "declaration or sworn statement of a witness," with thanks to Etymonline.com. Your author prefers to think of courtroom testimony as the presentation of information that supports only the truths or facts of a matter for lawful consideration.

The testimony of a crime scene investigator or analyst in courtroom proceedings is a powerful responsibility that must be undertaken with the utmost professionalism, ethical integrity, and unbiased objective attention to the factual presentation of the evidence based solely on scientific methodologies and sound protocols, policies, and practices. Your author cannot stress enough that forensic witnesses must be aware of their own limitations and the limitations related to the significance of the evidence being presented and that any conclusion rendered is within the scope of their area of expertise and about conclusions that they have given careful, logical, and objective consideration. Furthermore, the forensic witness must never misrepresent their qualifications or certifications. An incident comes to mind when an investigator at a nearby prison continued to represent herself as a certified crime scene investigator during testimony until amid a jury trial for a very serious matter, the defense council asked her to produce proof of certification. She produced a certificate of completion of a basic crime scene investigation training course. In fairness to the investigator, one could see where the confusion might exist, but there is a tremendous difference between being certified in your field of expertise, which generally requires a demonstration of skills and competencies through an examination process, and merely completing a single training course.

Preparation for Testimony

Once you receive your subpoena to appear in court, contact the attorney who is requesting your testimony or the court's subpoena coordinator and let them know if you are available to testify on the requested date or if there is a genuine conflict that might require a continuance. Make sure that you are aware of the courtroom number and where that courtroom is located within the courthouse. The attorney will request a pre-trial conference or interview to go over your testimony. In most jurisdictions, it is acceptable for the prosecutor to have this conference with witnesses. If the defense asks you on the stand if you had discussed your testimony with the prosecutor prior to trial, answer in the affirmative. The defense will attempt to imply that there is improper coercion between you and the prosecutor, but there is nothing unusual or improper about discussing your testimony with an attorney before trial; in fact, if subpoenaed by the defense, they would insist upon a pre-trial briefing as well. Review your report to refresh your memory and, if necessary, highlight or mark certain areas of the report containing details that might be important to your testimony so that you can find the information quickly when you are on the stand. Every second you take searching your report for an important detail will seem like an eternity. Mentally practice your testimony, especially regarding knowledge, training, experience, and job duties.

Try to find out the layout of the courtroom, especially which side the witness box is located, where the jury sits, and where the clerk and recorder are sitting. In most courtrooms, the prosecutor will sit nearest the jury, and that is the side on which you will raise your hand and take the oath to tell the truth. Remember that in most jurisdictions, in a jury trial, the defendant is not restrained unless there is a motion prior to trial to have some form of undetectable restrain mechanism applied. This may be of particular note in the correctional setting, as some defendants seated in the courtroom have already been convicted of multiple violent offenses.

On the day of the trial, be certain that your appearance will convey to the jury a sense of professional confidence. If your approved dress code is that of a duty uniform, be sure to find your best-fitting, cleanest uniform. If your uniform includes a hat, be sure to remove it before entering the courtroom. Do not wear sunglasses in the courtroom. If you own a pair of prescription sunglasses, then you also own a pair of regular prescription glasses. Polish your shoes and shine your badge.

If your dress code requires you to wear a business suit, be sure to wear a well-pressed, well-tailored suit of current fashion. Polyester has been out of style for 30 years. Do not wear a suit that is most suitable for a nightclub or an evening in the town. Men should be clean shaved and well-groomed and should always wear a jacket and conservative tie with a business suit. Tattoos seem to be the fashion with modern-day law enforcement personnel, but efforts should be made to cover tattoos that might sway the jury. Let us face it, if the testifying officer has more tattoos on his hands, face, and neck than the defendant inmate, the jury might be inclined to believe the inmate's testimony over the officer's. This might not be fair, but it is reality and I have witnessed this firsthand. Just remember that you are representing not only yourself and your professionalism but also your agency, your fellow officers, and your competence as a peace officer or investigator.

Arriving at the Courthouse

Drive to the courthouse in a safe and courteous manner. Do not antagonize other motorists near or around the courthouse. You risk inviting the ire of citizens who may be selected for the very jury you are about to testify before. The same is true for parking illegally or J-walking in proximity to the courthouse. A jury member who witnesses a peace officer in violation of municipal ordinances and vehicle codes may disregard even the best testimony owing to their expectation that we are not only entrusted to uphold the laws but also obey them ourselves.

Waiting Outside of the Courtroom

Remain quiet and professional while waiting outside of the courtroom. Do not use your cellular telephone, chew gum, or use tobacco products. If you must use your cellular telephone, step outside or find a quiet place. Speak quietly and do not use vulgar language. Do not speak loudly or in an unprofessional manner while waiting outside of the courtroom. Do not speak to the members of the jury as they enter and exit the courtroom. Do not speak at length to people in the restroom as they might be members of the jury. Do not use crude, vulgar, or profane language ever! Do not discuss the case or your testimony with other people who still must testify. Be very careful in this, because many defense attorneys have employees or defense witnesses who are also waiting outside and may report your interactions with other witnesses to the judge. If the jury takes a recess outside of the courtroom, politely excuse yourself and walk to an area on the other side of the hall and wait for them to return to the courtroom before you return to the benches outside of the courtroom.

Taking the Stand

Even the most seasoned expert witness gets nervous when they take the stand. Let us face it, there is a lot riding on your testimony. The guilt or innocence of the accused may be decided by your testimony. Perjury, whether purposeful or by accident, may adversely affect your career. To reduce anxiety, it is best to concentrate on those things that give you confidence and to control your breathing to reduce nervous feelings. Arrive at the courthouse early enough to find parking and casually walk to the courthouse. Be certain that your cellular telephone is set to silent or turned off before you enter the courtroom.

Organization is the best way to reduce anxiety. Have your reports in a folder that is tabbed and that looks professional. I have seen detectives arrive at court with a banker's box filled with scattered papers and every time a question was asked, the detective had to dig through this collection of papers to find his desired report. It was embarrassing to watch.

Sit up straight in the chair with both feet planted firmly on the floor and avoid rocking or swiveling. Speak clearly into the microphone and speak slowly enough for the court recorder to document your testimony. Whenever possible, when asked a question, provide your answer directly to the jury. When I am asked a question by either the prosecutor or defense attorney that requires a lengthy or descriptive response, I make eye contact with the attorney first and then I turn to the jury and answer in a way that the average citizen can understand. Always remain cheerful, but do not be condescending.

Before testifying as an expert witness, you may be asked questions by the prosecutor, the defense attorney, or the judge to determine if you have the experience, training, and expertise in a specific field like narcotics or forensics. The judge will determine if you meet the necessary requirements, according to the decisions of either *Frye* or *Daubert* rulings, to proceed with your testimony. It is always a good idea to provide the prosecutor and defense attorney with a copy of your *curriculum vitae* listing your training, experience, and qualifications.

Here is a little trick that I learned a long time ago: when a word or name that is difficult to spell, like phenolphthalein, comes up in your testimony, say the word, interrupt your testimony, and spell the word for the court recorder. This accomplishes more than just making the recorder happy. Not only will the jury think you are very thoughtful for spelling the word for the recorder, but also the defense attorney will recognize that you have testified before and may not be as confident about challenging your testimony.

There are two ways that you are allowed to testify in courtroom proceedings: by memory and by memory refresh. Keep your report on your lap or on the shelf in front of you in a folder or binder to prevent it from being rolled up or damaged. Remember that the defense attorney has a right to obtain a copy of anything that you brought to court. Ask for permission to refer to your report to refresh your memory. If permission is granted, review your report, find the information, and then place the report back on your lap face down and respond from memory.

Be sure to address the court as "your Honor" or "Judge." When the attorney asks you a question, take a short pause before answering. This gives the other attorney an opportunity to object to the question. It also gives you an opportunity to think of your response before answering. If there is an objection, wait for the judge to either sustain the object, which means that you do not have to answer the question, or overrule the objection, which means you must answer. You may have to ask the attorney to repeat the question. Avoid making quick answers and think carefully about your responses. Avoid using highly technical terms or prison jargon. Remember that the jury has probably never set foot in a prison or jail. They do not know that "the Hole" really means the Administrative Segregation Unit, that "ISU" may stand for the Investigative Services Unit, or that a shiv or shank is an inmate-manufactured stabbing weapon. You may have to describe things like control booths, sallyports, food-ports, etc. Do not lower your language to that of the defendant. Avoid referring to inmates as "Homies" or "bro," or "cuz," or any other colloquialism.

The court recorder cannot record a head nod, shoulder shrug, grunt, uh, huh, or nah; clearly say yes or no. The court recorder also cannot record two people talking at the same time. Listen to the question, respond to the question, and wait for the next question. Do not fill silent pauses with additional information. If there is a pause in questioning, it is likely not because they are waiting for you to provide additional details, but more likely the attorney is organizing their thoughts. If you do not understand the question, ask for it to be rephrased. If you do not know the answer to a question or cannot remember, say so. Never make up an answer. Never tell a lie because you think it will improve the testimony. If you realize that you have made a mistake in your testimony, inform the court, and correct the mistake before you leave the stand.

One tactic used by attorneys is to ask questions that must be answered with either a "yes" or a "no" response, at times with great determination and emphatic tone. In these circumstances, answering "yes" or "no" may be misleading to the jury if those responses are not qualified with additional testimony. Therefore, it is incumbent upon the forensic witness to inform the judge that additional comment is required as to eliminate any confusion that might exist and to properly represent the evidence.

Be respectful to the prosecutor, defense attorney, judge, and defendant. Do not roll your eyes to questions from the defense attorney. Do not get argumentative or show disdain towards their questioning. One defense tactic is to ask you questions in a manner that will cause you to lose your temper, thereby diminishing the effectiveness of your testimony. Remain calm, polite, and professional. When a defense attorney cannot attack the evidence, they will attack the evidence collector or the evidence analyst. This is to be expected.

Remain cheerful, polite, and respectful, and have confidence in the evidence you have collected or analyzed and in the job you have done.

When asked to handle evidence in court, ask for a pair of gloves, or have a pair in your pocket beforehand. Ask the bailiff for a pair of scissors to open the package. Find a spot on the envelope that hasn't been previously cut or sealed with evidence tape. Remove the evidence, examine it, and then hold it up for the judge and jury to see. The prosecutor will give an item of evidence a prosecution exhibit number and the defense may give another item of evidence a defense exhibit number. Be sure to reference the item by its exhibit number. When finished, place the item back into the envelope and return it to the attorney. When asked to examine more than one item of evidence, ask the attorney to allow you to examine one item of evidence at a time. If this is not possible, be certain to keep the items separated and return them to the appropriate envelopes.

The first series of questions will come from the prosecutor as direct examination. Following this, the defense attorney will be allowed to ask questions as cross-examination. Just when you think you are done, the prosecutor always has the last line of questioning with the re-cross examination. The judge can also ask questions at any time. In some states, like Arizona, the jury can even ask questions through the judge.

Once you are done testifying, you will either be told that you are excused, which means you can leave, or you may be subject to recall, which means you have to remain outside until called to testify again. You may also be asked to return at a later time as a rebuttal witness.

The most important and unique aspect of testifying in court in matters relating to the correctional setting is that the jury, the attorneys, and perhaps even the judge have never been in a prison or jail and are unfamiliar with the environment, characteristics, and circumstances encountered there. Your testimony must be narrative and descriptive in order to paint a picture with your words. Terminology, functions, and events that are common to us are foreign concepts to the average civilian. For example, something as routine as a chow release for those of us employed in the correctional setting must be explained as a release of a certain number of inmates by tier, wing, or dormitory who file down a corridor or across an exercise yard to a dining hall, where they walk past a steam-line, receive a tray containing a balanced portion of food and then are seated by row at a series of metal tables.

The Conclusion

18

Each jail and prison is unique, and no single method of crime scene investigation works perfectly for them all. Jurisdictional concerns over the agency that is responsible for the processing of crime scenes or the investigation of criminal misconduct in the jail or prison must be worked out with the administration of each agency and the representatives of the county District Attorney or County Attorney, or authorities responsible for the prosecution of crimes in the custodial setting. Sadly too, there is no better target of litigation than jails and prisons. Unfortunately, the result of this litigation can often adversely affect the procedures and policies regarding the responsibilities of the first responders. Some agencies have been sued so many times over inmate deaths that it is the policy of those departments that CPR and rescue breathing must be initiated even in cases where an inmate is known to be dead, much to the chagrin of the County Coroner's Office or Medical Examiner's Office investigators and the sensibilities of the crime scene investigators and analysts regarding the preservation of evidence. Common sense and corrections simply are not the best of friends.

Furthermore, legislation can also have an impact on the local authorities and crime scene investigators. The Prison Rape Elimination Act signed into law by the Federal government under President G.W. Bush has influenced the way suspected custodial rape cases are handled. In an alleged sexual assault at my facility, the incident commander was so busy making notifications to the Headquarters personnel and coordinating efforts with county officials that calling the crime scene investigator was simply over-looked for two days. Although the clothing of the suspect and the victim was collected by the county officials, whatever evidence that may have been in the cell was lost as the suspect was allowed to return to the cell before the CSI team could make an examination for forensic evidence. Yet, as I always say, we learn from our mistakes and sometimes the mistakes must be repeated numerous times before the lesson is learned. That is why I strongly recommend that each facility, cell block unit office, watch commander's office, or captain's office must have a secure location for the placement of standardized protocols and procedures for every foreseeable incident. The procedures should be itemized, plainly written in language that is easy to understand and simple to follow, preferably with a checklist format attached. The procedures should be updated regularly and be current with the trends and discoveries in the forensic community.

It is recommended that those persons tasked with the processing or analysis of crime scenes have certifications earned through examinations administered by entities other than the employing agency. Training must be current and constant; and the technician or analyst must avail themselves of scientific studies, textbooks, journals, periodicals, and articles. In forensics, even the most experienced expert will always be a student.

Finally, I never recommend the "let someone else do it" mentality of crime scene investigations. If you request other agencies to come into your facility to process a crime scene, you are assuming that they are the "experts" when, in fact, you have no idea what their training, experience, and commitment to your scene really are. Build your own team and give them the training, supervision, equipment, and latitude that they need to get the scene processed correctly.

In closing this book, I would like to relate two stories, both of which occurred quite recently, and both of which demonstrate the importance of forensics in any criminal investigation.

An inmate was discovered on the bottom bunk of a two-man cell with an incised wound to his right neck. He had suffered massive blood loss but had yet experienced exsanguination. The manner of his discovery was by his cellmate, who had entered the cell during the scheduled unlock and observed the victim quivering. The victim's face and upper torso were blocked from view by a towel draped over a string, the towel providing a privacy screen. The cellmate pulled back the towel, observed the tremendous amount of blood that had collected on the mattress, pillow, blankets, and wall of the lower bunk, and immediately ran from the cell yelling, "Man down!" The tier officers promptly responded and summoned emergency medical assistance.

The victim was airlifted to a trauma center where his prognosis of survival was bleak. Suspicion had immediately fallen upon the cellmate as having slashed the victim's neck when he entered the cell. The cellmate was placed in handcuffs and escorted to a holding cell. Fortunately, I happened to be at the institution on my day off, covering a vacant shift in one of the visiting rooms and I overheard the emergency radio traffic. I notified the lieutenant who was in charge of the facility that I would respond to process the crime scene.

Upon my arrival, I conducted a field interview of the cellmate, who told me that he had entered the housing unit during the courtesy in-bound yard movement, ran up the stairs to his cell, and retrieved his shower products from the victim, who passed the items under the cell door. The cellmate then took a quick shower in order to get back to the cell in time for the scheduled unlock. Following his shower, he stood on the tier in front of his cell awaiting the manipulation of the bar mechanism that unlocked all cell doors on the tier. While waiting, he spoke with the inmate in the neighboring cell, who was also standing on the tier. Both inmates observed the victim lying on the lower bunk and assumed he had been asleep.

The Conclusion

When the bar dropped, the neighbor stepped into the neighboring cell and the cellmate stepped into his assigned cell. According to the cellmate, he was talking to the victim, who was lying on his bunk with a towel suspended on a string that hid the victim's upper torso from view. He received no reply. While putting away his shower products, he noticed a "quivering" movement and feared that his cellmate was having a stroke or seizure. He pulled back the towel, saw the blood loss and, "ran from the cell screaming." I thanked him for his testimony and promised a quick investigation. Before leaving, I asked him to hold up his hands. I noted a tan line indicating the absence of a watch on his left wrist.

I proceeded to the crime scene and met with one of our new on-duty investigators, who I designated as the crime scene photographer. After his preliminary photographs were taken, I entered the cell, making sure to first scan the cell floor with a soft flashlight at oblique angles. In doing so, I noted an absence of blood evidence on the floor. I examined the ceiling, north, east, and west walls, writing desk, and toilet/sink assembly; all of which were absent blood evidence. No razor blades or inmate-manufactured slashing-type weapons were present in the toilet, sink, and garbage bag or visible in the crime scene. I then examined the lower bunk and discovered pooled blood on the mattress, pillow, blankets, and space between the mattress and south wall. The blood-letting event was passive in nature. No spatter was noted on the wall that supported the pillow or the bottom of the upper bunk. Of note was a circular transfer and swipe pattern on the south wall proximal to the blood-letting event (Fig. 18.1).

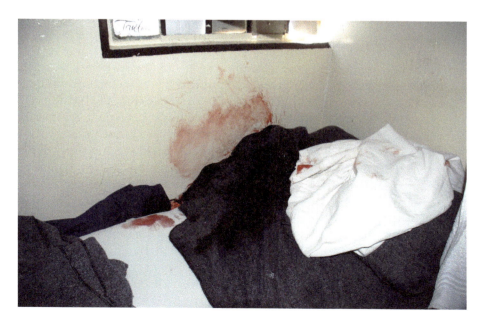

Figure 18.1 The deliberately made circular bloodstain pattern on the cell wall.

One bloodstained safety razor blade was noted in the gap between the mattress and the south wall embedded in a clot of blood. A second blood-soaked razor blade was discovered tucked between the layers of the blood-soaked blanket. After examining the blood-letting event, I was convinced that the victim had attempted suicide. The doubting lieutenant arrived at the cell and our new on-duty investigator envisioned a theory of how the cellmate had entered the cell, found the victim sleeping, slashed his throat, and ran from the cell to raise the alarm so as to draw attention away from himself as the suspect. Of course, the blood evidence contradicted this conclusion. The passive blood-letting occurred on the right-hand side of the bunk at the level of the neck, shoulder, and right arm of the victim. The lack of spatter indicated that the victim did not struggle, which would be expected even if suddenly roused from sleep. Surely the suspect would not take the time to conceal one of the razor blades within the folds of a blanket. No blood was noted on the cellmate. Being right-handed would have made it more likely that the front or left side of the victim's neck would have been cut. But most obvious to me was the circular pattern of transfer and wipes on the wall. Had the transfer and wipes been the result of a struggle, I would not have expected to see a circular uniformity of the pattern, but rather random transfers, wipes, and swipes. I had seen these patterns before in incised suicide attempts.

During the slow blood-letting process of a self-inflicted incised wound, many inmates who are confined to a small portion of the cell will often times play with the blood, as if finger-painting with an arm, or a finger, and I determined that the pattern was made deliberately by moving the blood-stained right forearm up and down in a repeated brushing manner. Furthermore, the amount of blood loss indicated that the victim bled for a period of time beyond that of the cellmate entering the cell and subsequently summoning assistance. I also spoke with the inmate in the neighboring cell, who confirmed the cellmate's story. I recommended the release of the cellmate from the holding cell, a recommendation that was reluctantly accepted by the lieutenant. The victim recovered from his injury and later admitted to the suicide attempt. A suicide letter was also found between the pages of a book during an inventory of his property. I mention this story because we often forget that it is always just as important to find evidence that exonerates a suspect as it is to prove his guilt.

The second story did not occur at the prison, but in a local city. I had just provided a 40-hour CSI for Patrol class to detectives and officers from the local law enforcement agencies. About three weeks later, while briefing for a gang enforcement operation, I was approached by the detective and two patrol officers from one of the local agencies. They were all beaming with broad smiles. "Uncle Dog," greeted the detective, "You are going to be proud of us." He then related the story of how shortly after attending the class he received a call to respond to a breaking and entering at a residence.

The Conclusion

Although he and one of the patrol officers arrived at the house too late to apprehend the suspects, the second patrol officer noticed a suspicious vehicle occupied by three youths leaving the area. He pulled the vehicle over, detained the occupants of the car, and summoned the detective and patrol officer to his location. When the detective arrived, he noticed small black fibers on the hands of one of the occupants. He also noted vegetation, seeds, and leaves on the pants of the same occupant. Using an evidence collection kit that I had assembled for him, the detective collected the fibers and vegetation, taking great care to preserve each item of transfer evidence in small evidence envelopes. The detective instructed the patrol officers to detain the occupants until such time as he could examine the residence for evidence.

As the detective exited his vehicle in front of the residence, he noted a hedge that separated the house from the neighboring house. He noted the hedge had the same leaves and seed material that he had found on the suspect's pants. He then looked inside the hedge and found electronic items and jewelry that had been hidden. He also found a pair of black cloth gloves. He collected all the discovered items into evidence and proceeded back to the detained vehicle and occupants. He placed all the suspects under arrest and transported them to the police department. When faced with the forensic analysis of the scene and the physical evidence collected that linked them to the crime, all the suspects admitted their culpability in the crime.

Edmond Locard's Principle of Evidence Exchange, which postulated that when two objects come in contact, there is an exchange of material from one to the other, is very much still valid today. They had learned from the class to be observant and to pay close attention to the smallest of details. I was indeed proud of these officers.

Glossary

A

ABFO Scale: Designed by the American Board of Forensic Odontology, the ABFO No.2 scale is an "L"-shaped scale with a white background, with either inches or metric measurements, designed for the photographic documentation of bite marks. These scales are perfect for the photographic documentation of wounds.

Abrasion: The removal of the epidermis layer of skin by scraping due to friction against a hard surface.

Accidental discharge: The discharge of a firearm when the weapon discharges because of wear, improper design, mechanical fault or defect, or alteration without the process of pulling the trigger (Hueske).

Administrative Segregation Unit: A cell block or housing unit used for housing inmates with either safety or disciplinary concerns. Movement in this housing unit is generally restricted and controlled.

AFIS: The Automated Fingerprint Identification System is a computer-based biometric system that stores and analyzes fingerprint data.

Alligatoring: A burn pattern that look like something resembling alligator skin, or large blisters, that may indicate that a rapid and intense heat was present in that area

Alternate Light Source: A light source that emits high-intensity ultraviolet, visible, and infrared lights used to search for evidence that is difficult to see with white light or the human eye.

American common law system: A body of unwritten laws based on legal precedents called *stare decisis* as established by the courts.

Amido Black: An amino acid staining dye method used in forensic investigations to detect fingerprints deposited with blood. Amido black stains the proteins in blood a blue-black color ($C_{22}H_{14}N_6Na_2O_9S_2$).

Angle of deflection: The angle between the muzzle of a firearm at discharge to the target impact (Hueske).

Angle-finder: A useful digital or mechanical tool used for measuring the vertical angle of a bullet defect.

Angle of ricochet: The angle of the altered path of a bullet or shot pellet from an impacted surface (Hueske).

Anoxia: The complete deprivation of oxygen to the brain.

Ardrox: A fluorescent spray that is designed for enhancing latent prints that have been developed with cyanoacrylate

Area of convergence (bloodstain): The area containing the intersections generated by lines drawn through the long axes of individual stains that indicates in two dimensions the location of the blood source (SWGStain).

Area of convergence (shooting): The two-dimension intersection of lines drawn by matching fracture lines in safety glass in a shooting incident.

Artery: Tubular branching muscular-walled vessels that carry oxygenated blood from the heart through the body to organs and tissues.

Asphyxia: The partial deprivation of oxygen to the body that may result in hypoxia.

Avulsive laceration: An injury where the impacting force strikes the skin at an angle causing the skin to slip or rip.

B

Back-spatter pattern: A bloodstain pattern resulting from blood drops that traveled in the opposite direction of the external force applied; associated with an entrance wound created by a projectile (SWGStain).

Ballistics: The forensic study of bullets or other projectiles in flight (Hueske).

Baseline: The tape-measure line in diagramming starting at a fixed point and a known compass direction used as a basis for other intersecting measurements.

Basic Yellow 40: A fluorescent yellow dye stain used with an Alternate Light Source to visually enhance fingerprints developed by cyanoacrylate ester fuming.

Battery: The condition of a weapon when it is ready to fire (Hueske).

Bird's Eye View: A form of diagram where the two-dimensional depiction of the crime scene is from above and looking down with a zoomed-out perspective.

Bloodstain Pattern Analysis: Bloodstain Pattern Analysis is the interpretation of bloodstains found at a crime scene in order to understand or reconstruct the actions that caused the bloodshed.

Bluestar™: A very sensitive latent bloodstain reagent that produces an intense blue chemiluminescence.

Bolt-action: A firearm with a breech that is in line with the bore and requires manual manipulation to load, cock, fire (typically the release of a firing pin), and extract a cartridge and cartridge case (Hueske).

Bore: The internal aspect of a barrel beyond the chamber (Hueske).

Breech: The opening in a firearm where cartridges are loaded into the chamber (Hueske).

Glossary 257

Buccal swabs: A cotton or other applicator-tipped swab used to collect cells from the inside of a person's cheek for DNA confirmatory testing. The word "buccal" means "cheek" or "mouth" and is pronounced as "buckle."

Bullet: The projectile component of a cartridge (Hueske).

Bullet defect: A suitable term for a bullet or pellet hole (Hueske).

Bullet jacket: The metallic outer skin of a bullet (Hueske).

Bullet wipe: A combination of grease and soot surrounding the margins of a bullet defect caused by the progression of a bullet (Hueske).

C

Caliber: The cross-sectional diameter of the interior of a barrel from land to land. This is also the cross-sectional diameter of a bullet (Hueske).

Cartridge: The complete components of a round of ammunition including a cartridge casing, primer, propellant, and bullet. A cartridge should never be defined as a "bullet" in your report (Hueske).

Cartridge case: The metal or paper container that holds the propellant, bullet, and primer (Hueske).

Casting: A process that uses a casting material like dental die stone to create a 3D model of an impression found at a crime scene.

Cast-off pattern: A bloodstain pattern resulting from blood drops released from an object due to its motion.

Center-fire cartridge: A cartridge that has a primer pocket in the center of the headstamp where a primer is seated (Hueske).

Cessation cast-off pattern: A bloodstain pattern resulting from blood drops released from an object due to its rapid deceleration.

Chamber: The cavity attached to the barrel that is constructed to fit a particular cartridge, into which is loaded in order for it to be fired. Revolvers will have multiple chambers (Hueske).

Chamber marks: The transferred striations, impressions, or indentations on a cartridge casing from the imperfections within the chamber walls. These marks are significant of individual characteristics (Hueske).

Chimney effect: The dynamic effect of fire caused by the upward movement of air in structural areas that are tall, like elevator shafts or stairwells, causing super-heated gases to rise, thus pulling air in from lower areas resulting in intense burn patterns towards the upper level of the structure.

Chop wounds: A deep, gaping wound caused by a heavy weapon like a hatchet or axe.

Clean burn pattern: A burn pattern that occurs on noncombustible surfaces when the soot or smoke deposits are burned off leaving a light grey or white surface.

Clip: A device used to load ammunition into a magazine (Hueske).
Close contact shot: A shot fired with the muzzle of the firearm pressed against a target (Hueske).
Clinical photographs: Non-prejudicial photographs taken of wounds that show only the wound without blood, painful expressions, or any other image that will cause a sympathetic response by the judge, jury, or attorneys.
Close-up photographs: Photographs taken with the intent to provide detailed images of an item of evidence. The object will appear larger than normal size and centered in the frame. A scale is necessary for comparative purposes.
CODIS: An acronym for the Combined DNA Index System, which is a computer software program that operates local, state, and national databases of DNA profiles from convicted offenders, unsolved crime scene evidence, and missing persons (Bureau of Justice Statistics).
Compound fracture: A broken bone that protrudes from the skin.
Contusion: A contusion, also known as a bruise, is a type of tissue hematoma that occurs when small blood vessels under the skin burst and leak blood into the surrounding tissues.
Concentric fractures: Circular fractures of glass radiating outward from a bullet impact (Hueske).
Conchoidal fractures: Fracture lines that are visible in broken glass when viewed from the side that allow for the determination of the direction of the applied force (Hueske).
Coomassie Blue: An enhancement chemical used to dye blood-contaminated fingerprints on porous or non-porous surfaces, which produce bright blue visible prints ($C_{45}H_{44}N_3NaO_7S_2$).
Cyanoacrylate ester fuming: A chemical development method that uses esters from cyanoacrylate adhesives to detect latent fingerprints on non-porous surfaces.
Cylinder gas deposit: The deposition of soot on surfaces of a firearm where a gap exists between the cylinder and the barrel. This is most commonly associated with revolvers (Hueske).

D

Datum: The fixed point of the baseline where the tape measure begins at zero.
Dead-Line: To make a jail or prison cell mandatorily vacant for maintenance or security reasons.
Diagramming: The process of creating a two-dimensional depiction of the crime scene using accurate measurements.
Dithiooxamide: A chemically specific chromophore test for the presence of copper ($C_2H_4N_2S_2$).

Glossary

DNA: Deoxyribonucleic acid is a polymer composed of two polynucleotide chains that wrap around each other to form a double helix, which carries genetic information.

Dog dots: Circular and colorful self-adhesive stickers that are used in crime scene mapping to ensure that photographs are taken parallel to the film plane.

Double action: A firearm with a trigger mechanism that cocks and releases the hammer without the need for manual cocking (Hueske).

Double-barrel: Commonly, a shotgun with barrels arranged side-by-side or over-under; however, pistols and rifles with two barrels may also be referred to as double-barreled.

Drip trail: A bloodstain pattern resulting from the movement of a source of drip stains between two points (SWGStain).

E

Edge characteristic: A physical feature of the periphery of a bloodstain (SWGStain).

Ejection: The removal, whether manual or automatic, of the fired cartridge casing from the breech to facilitate a reload (Hueske).

Ejection pattern: A clustering of ejected fired cartridge cases that may assist in determining the direction a firearm was discharged from a given position (Hueske).

Ejector marks: Small marks left on the soft metal of a cartridge case or shotshell as it is being ejected from the breech (Hueske).

Evi-Vac System: A forensic vacuum cleaner that captures trace evidence in a sterile container.

External ballistics: Also called exterior ballistics, the forensic discipline associated with bullets upon leaving the barrel of a fired firearm (Hueske).

Exploded view diagram: A two-dimensional visual depiction of a crime scene where the ceiling and walls are connected but laid flat.

Expectoration pattern: A bloodstain pattern resulting from blood forced by airflow out of the nose, mouth, or a wound (SWGStain).

Exsanguination: A significant loss of blood from the body to no longer sustain life.

F

Firing pin: The mechanism that strikes a primer and causes a discharge of the cartridge (Hueske).

Firing pin impression: The three-dimensional impression left on the primer by the firing pin (Hueske).

First Responder: A person with specialized training and authority who is among the first to arrive at an incident or emergency.

Flash suppressor: A device attached to the muzzle of firearm to reduce flash upon firing (Hueske).

Flow pattern: A bloodstain pattern resulting from the movement of a volume of blood on a surface due to gravity or movement of the target (SWGStain).

Footwear impression: A detailed impression of a shoeprint either in two-dimension as a transfer or in three-dimension as a molded deposit in a soft material.

Forcing cone: A transition between the chamber and the barrel that aligns the bore with the chamber (Hueske).

Forward spatter pattern: A bloodstain pattern resulting from blood drops that traveled in the same direction as the impact force (SWGStain).

Fractures: A complete or partial break in a bone.

Function testing: The process of testing a firearm to determine operability (Hueske).

G

Gassing: A felonious battery by the intentional placing, throwing, or projecting of human bodily fluids, excrement, or other bodily substances on correctional personnel.

Gas operated: A firearm that utilizes gas from the discharge of a cartridge to cycle additional cartridges into the breech and chamber (Hueske).

Gauge: In a shotgun, the gauge is the number of pellets or shot by size that equal to one pound (Hueske).

Grid pattern search: A search technique whereby large areas are reduced to smaller areas that can be easily searched by fewer people. This technique can also be used in smaller areas where it is necessary to locate and document minute trace evidence.

Grooves: The helical grooves in the interior of the barrel that prove stabilizing spin on a fired bullet (Hueske).

Gunshot Residue (GSR): Residue associated with the primer and propellant upon firing (Hueske).

H

Hammer: The mechanism that delivers energy to the firing pin (Hueske).

Handgun: Any weapon that is designed to be held by hand without support (Hueske).

Hexagon OBTI Immunochromatographic Rapid Test™: A two-part presumptive screening test to determine if a blood specimen is consistent with the human species.

Horizontal: Parallel to the plane of the horizon

Hungarian Red: An aqueous solution used to enhance fingerprint deposits in blood when used with an Alternate Light Source (between 520nm-560nm).

I

Impact spatter pattern: A bloodstain pattern resulting from an object striking liquid blood SWGStain).

Incised wounds: Also known as a cut or slash, is a clean, straight cut in the skin caused by a sharp object with a sharp edge or tip that leaves a wound that is generally longer than it is wide or deep.

In-Custody deaths: Any death of a person in the custody of another.

Infrared Imaging: A photographic technology that captures images of the IR spectrum (750nm +/-) which is invisible to the human eye. It is useful to detect bodily fluids or GSR on dark colored fabrics.

Inmate manufactured improvised handheld weapon: A common object that has been altered by an inmate to increase its potential as a weapon, or the assembly of objects that can be used as weapon that is small enough to be held in a hand. A "shank" or "shiv" is a specific term used for a stabbing-type weapon.

Internal ballistics: The forensic science that deals with the firearm prior to the bullet exiting the barrel (Hueske).

International Association of Bloodstain Pattern Analysts (IABPA): Founded in 1983 by Professor Herbert MacDonell, an organization of forensic experts specializing in the science of bloodstain pattern analysis (iabpa.org).

International Association of Arson Investigators (IAAI): Formed in 1949 and chartered in 1951, an organization dedicated to support fire, arson, and explosive investigation professionals through leadership in education, training, professional development, certification, networking, advocacy, and the provision of resources (firearson.com).

International Association for Identification (IAI): Founded in 1915 by Harry H. Caldwell of the Oakland Police Department in California, the IAI is the oldest and largest association for forensic practitioners, which also maintains certification programs in numerous forensic disciplines including bloodstain pattern analysis, crime scene investigations, and latent print examination, amongst others (theiai.org).

Indeterminate range: A shot fired from a distance that cannot be determined.

Intermediate range: A shot fired when the muzzle of the weapon is held away from the body at the time of discharge yet is sufficiently close to cause powder "tattooing" and stippling (Hueske)

Interview: In law enforcement, a structured formal conversation, based on inherent protections, intended upon eliciting specific information from a suspect, witness, or victim.

J

Jail: A place of confinement for a person held in lawful custody.

Jugular vein: A paired venous structure that collects blood from the brain, superficial regions of the face, and neck, and delivers it to the right atrium of the heart. The jugular veins are not protected by bone or cartilage (NIH).

K

Keyholing: A bullet impact that resembles a keyhole the result of a bullet that tumbles or wobbles in flight (Hueske).

L

Laceration: A blunt-force injury produced by a shearing or crushing force, such as caused by a fist, a lock-in-a-sock, a broom handle, or an impact-type weapon.

Langer's lines: Also called cleavage lines, Langer's lines were first described by Karl Langer in 1861, and are skin tension lines.

Lansberry's liquid: Also known as ridge builder, Lansberry's liquid is applied to friction ridge skin to produce better exemplar (inked) ridge print impressions where other efforts have failed.

Latent: Invisible to the human eye.

Lateral angle of deflection: The deflection of a bullet to the right or the left from its original trajectory as the result of a ricochet.

Lead card: In crime scene photography, the lead card is a placard that provides useful information in a photograph that includes the date, time, case number, and name of the photographer, etc. The lead card was essential in film emulsion crime scene photography as it provided details of what photographs were on the film roll. It is still used by many law enforcement agencies.

Leuco Malachite Green (LMG): A presumptive test for blood that can also be used to visually enhance blood prints. The reaction to blood will produce a greenish-blue result. LMG is a known carcinogen and therefore personal protective equipment must be used.

Leuco-Crystal Violet (LCV): Also known as Aqueous LCV, a reduced form of gentian violet, it is a highly sensitive formula to visually enhance blood prints. The reaction to blood will produce a vibrant violet result.

Glossary

Lever action: A firearm that uses a lever to open, close, or cycle cartridges into the breech (Hueske).

Ligature: In forensic pathology, a device used to externally constrict the throat causing the deprivation of oxygen.

Ligature marks: Contusions on the neck created by a ligature.

Ligature strangulation: The act of strangulation with the use of a cord, rope, wire, or other cord-like device.

Line of sight: The imaginary line from the sights of a firearm to a target.

Lividity: The settling of the blood in the lower portions of the body dependent on gravity after death resulting in a reddish-purple discoloration of the skin.

Long gun: A firearm designed to be supported by the shoulder (Hueske).

M

Magazine: The internal or detachable box that contains a supply of ammunition that is fed into the chamber of a firearm (Hueske).

Manual strangulation: The external constriction of the throat using the hands, fingers, arms, or other articulable body parts resulting in a deprivation of oxygen.

Mapping: A process of identifying, measuring, and documenting important items of evidence in a crime scene; especially used in bloodstain pattern analysis and shooting scene investigations.

Microcrystalline drug test kits: An empirical presumptive test for drugs in which there is a chemical reaction between a narcotic or controlled substance and a reagent that yields a crystal formation that can be observed as a color change.

Mid-Range photography: Also known as evidence-establishing photographs, mid-range or medium-view photographs record the position of items of evidence in relation to other items of evidence and their position within the crime scene.

Mini-Forensic laboratory: A small criminalistics laboratory at a jail, prison, or other law enforcement agency that provides a degree of forensic services, such as trace evidence discovery, latent ridge print development, evidentiary photography, serial number recovery,

Mist pattern: A bloodstain pattern resulting from blood reduced to a spray of micro-drops as a result of the force applied (SWGStain).

Molded: Also known as a plastic impression, a molded impression is an impression deposited in wax, mud, dirt, or any soft, rubbery surface.

Mutual Aid: An agreement between two or more law enforcement or criminal justice entities to provide support regardless of jurisdiction.

Muzzle: The open end of the barrel (Hueske).

Muzzle blast: The explosive shockwave at the muzzle as the result of combustion of propellants after discharge (Hueske).
Muzzle imprint: An abrasion in the skin resembling the muzzle of a firearm following a close or near contact shot (Hueske).
Muzzle velocity: The speed of a bullet at the moment of exiting the barrel (Hueske).

N

N-95 mask: A respiratory protective device designed to achieve a very close facial fit and very efficient filtration of airborne particles (FDA).
Near contact shot: A shot fired from a firearm where the muzzle of the firearm is not firmly pressed against the target but exhibits a small gap between the muzzle and the target (Hueske).
NIBIN: The National Integrated Ballistic Information Network (NIBIN) is the only national network that allows for the capture and comparison of ballistic evidence to aid in solving and preventing violent crimes involving firearms (ATF).
Ninhydrin: A chemical reagent used to process ridge print impressions on porous materials. Ninhydrin reacts with amino acids, which produces a deep purple impression called Ruhemann's purple.

O

Oblique: Held at a slant or angle.
Overall photographs: Also known as scene establishing photographs, overall or over-view photographs document the entirety of the crime scene, its location, and its boundaries.

P

Parallel photographs: Photographs taken with the lens parallel to the evidence in an effort to reduce or eliminate distortion.
Patent: Impression evidence that can be seen with the human eye without the need for enhancements.
Pellet: Small round shot used in shotgun shells (Hueske).
Penetration: A bullet that enters a target but remains within the last substrate it impacted (Hueske).
Perforation: A bullet that remains within the last substrate it impacts (Hueske).
Perspective photographs: Crime scene photographs taken with the photographer standing at full height (natural perspective) or at the same height as the person who did the action and with the camera lens set to mimic what the human eye may see.

Glossary

Phenolphthalein: A presumptive test for the presence of blood. It reacts to the heme molecule and produces a bright pink positive result.

Pinch-point: The first impact point of a ricochet (Hueske).

Point of origin (bloodstain): Also referred to by area of origin, the three-dimensional location from which spatter originated.

Point of origin (fire): A place where a fire first started.

Pooled blood: A bloodstain pattern resulting from an accumulation of liquid blood on a surface (SWGStain).

Powder stippling: Powder particles are the result of the discharge of a cartridge that impacts the skin causing small abrasions that are imbedded into the skin (also known as tattooing) (Hueske).

Prejudicial photographs: Photographs that may play on the emotions of the judge or jury and therefore, outweigh their probative value.

Primer: A cup containing a shock-sensitive propellant containing lead, antimony, and barium, that is seated in the base of a cartridge when struck produces the ignition process of the cartridge propellant (Hueske).

Prison Rape Elimination Act: The Prison Rape Elimination Act (PREA) of 2003 is the first United States federal law intended to deter the sexual assault of prisoners. The bill was signed into law on September 4, 2003 (NIJ).

Projected bloodstain pattern: A bloodstain pattern resulting from the ejection of a volume of blood under pressure.

Propellant: The combustible unit of a cartridge or shotgun shell (Hueske).

R

Radial fracture (forensic pathology): Also known as a distal radius fracture or wrist fracture, a break in the radius bone near the wrist.

Radial fracture (shooting): Fracture lines in glass that radiate outward from a bullet impact site (Hueske).

Ready bag: A duffel bag containing personal protective equipment like latex gloves, N-95 masks, eye protection, and Tyvek coveralls.

Rectangular diagramming: A crime scene diagramming method using two perpendiculars to measure objects and items of evidence.

Revolver: A firearm that uses a rotating cylinder to hold and fire cartridges (Hueske).

Rhodamine 6G: A fluorescing dye used to enhance latent fingerprints developed on non-porous surfaces with cyanoacrylate ester fuming and when used with a laser or Alternate Light Source.

Ricochet: A bullet that has altered its original trajectory by skipping, bouncing, or deflecting off of a surface but maintains its integrity (Hueske).

Ricochet crease: An indentation or furrow in a surface caused by a bullet striking a surface but being deflected without penetration of perforation (Hueske).
Rifling: Spiral grooves cut into the interior of a barrel consisting of lands and grooves that provide spin for the bullet as it travels the length of the barrel.
Rifling twist: The direction of the rotation of rifling (right or left) in which the grooves are cut (Hueske).
Rigor mortis: The stiffening of joints and muscles by the depletion of adenosine triphosphate following death.
Rough sketch: A rough, hand-drawn sketch of a crime scene noting important objects and items of evidence.

S

Safety glass: Glass that uses layers of transparent coatings to prevent glass from shattering into shards with sharp edges and is commonly found on the doors of automobiles.
Same plane photographs: A photographic technique where a scale is placed on the same plane as the object being photographed in order to produce examination quality photographs minimizing distortions.
Scene perimeter: The designated demarcation of the scene of a crime separated from its boundaries.
Semi-automatic: A firearm that automatically fires, ejects, and loads cartridges in its chamber after every shot fired and with each pulling of a trigger (Hueske).
Shell casing: A suitable term for a cartridge casing (Hueske).
Shotgun shell: A rimmed, cylindrical (straight-walled) cartridge used in shotguns (Hueske).
Skin Print Black™: A magnetic carbon-free powder developed by Doje's Forensic Supplies for developing fingerprints on skin.
Slug: A single projectile loaded into a shotgun shell (Hueske).
Small Particle Reagent: An aqueous development medium used for latent ridge print impressions deposited on wet, non-porous surfaces including glass, plastic, metals, and adhesive sides of tape.
Smoke deposits: Carbon deposited on surfaces as a byproduct of fire.
Sodium Rhodizonate: A presumptive test used to detect the presence of lead.
Spalling: The chipping off of pieces or layers of concrete, masonry, or brick when exposed to extreme temperatures in a fire.
Spatter: A bloodstain resulting from a blood drop dispersed through the air due to an external force applied to a source of liquid blood (SWGStain).

Glossary

Stab wounds: A penetrating trauma to the skin that results from a knife or a similar pointed object with an injury that is deeper than it is wide.
Sticky-Side tape formula: An aqueous solution used for developing ridge print impressions on the adhesive side of the tape.
Strangulation: The obstruction of blood vessels and airflow in the neck by constriction of the throat that may result in asphyxia.
Swipe bloodstain pattern: A bloodstain pattern resulting from the transfer of blood from a blood-bearing surface onto another surface, with characteristics that indicate relative motion between the two surfaces.

T

Tempered glass: A type of safety glass produced by controlled thermal or chemical treatments to increase its strength and is commonly used in vehicles (Hueske).
Trace evidence: Any type of evidence that is so small that it can be easily transferred or exchanged between two surfaces without being noticed and may need magnification or other enhancement techniques to locate and document.
Trajectory: The flight path of a bullet or shot after leaving the barrel (Hueske).
Trajectory rod: A plastic, metal, wood, or fiberglass rod inserted into a bullet defect presenting two points of reference and used to determine the vertical and horizontal angles of impact (Hueske).
Transfer bloodstain pattern: A bloodstain resulting from contact between a blood-bearing surface and another surface (SWGStain).
Transfer bloodstain impression: A bloodstain pattern resulting from contact between a blood-bearing surface and another surface leaving behind a distinct shape of the bloodstained object.
Triangulation diagramming: A measurement method that uses two or more permanent fixed positions forming a triangle in a crime scene to record the location of an item of evidence.

U

Unintentional discharge: The discharge of a firearm through human interaction with the trigger when the action was not intended.

V

"V" notch: In full or partial suspension hanging, the ligature may, upon finding a point of suspension, produce a mark on the neck that resembles an inverted "V" around the neck.
"V" pattern: Also known as a classic "V" burn pattern, a pattern produced by the fire burning up and away from the point of origin.

Vertical flight path: At right angles to the horizontal plane, the vertical flight path of a bullet will determine if the bullet was traveling upward or downward upon impact with a surface.

Void bloodstain pattern: An absence of blood from an otherwise continuous bloodstain pattern.

W

Wave castoff: As a drop of blood impacts a target at an angle, the direction of travel is determined by the "tail" or "cast off" caused by inertia.

Wipe bloodstain pattern: An absence of blood in an otherwise continuous bloodstain or bloodstain pattern.

Z

Zero-edge protractor: A protractor with a flat edge that crime scene investigators use to determine the horizontal, and vertical, angle of impact (Hueske).

Zone of possibility: In shooting scene reconstruction, the zone of possibility is the determination of the likely position of a shooter or shooters based on bullet defect analysis, trajectory analysis, shell casing ejection pattern analysis, and the understanding a firearm may not be in a fixed position (Hueske).

Index

Note: – *Italicized* page references refer to the figures.

A

Abbreviations in report writing, 232
Abrasions, 108–111, 114, 119
Acceleration injuries, 120; *see also* Head injuries
Accidental discharge
    defined, 95
    vs. unintentional discharge, 95
Acid fuchsin, 183
Administrative Segregation Unit (ASU), 67–68, 137, 151, 205, 222–223, 247
Adventures of Don Quixote de la Mancha (Cervantes), 119
AED pads, 17
Aerial view, 63, *64–65*
AFFF, *see* Aqueous film-forming foam
Alligatoring burn pattern, 211–212, *212*
Alternate light source (ALS), 3, 25, 31, 41, 78, *164*, 176
American Board of Forensic Odontology (ABFO) scale, 55, *162*
American common law system, 243
Amido black, 31, 41, 183
Angle-finder, 85–86, 97
Angle of deflection, 86
Angle of impact, 85–86, 90–94, 97–103, 129, 133
    from elevated positions, 91–94
    by measuring the defect, 100–102
    of ricochets, 102–103
    using a trajectory rod, 97–100
Angle of ricochet, 86
Aqueous film-forming foam (AFFF), 206
Aqueous LCV, *see* Leucocrystal Violet (LCV)
Ardrox, 181
Area of convergence
    bloodstain, 40
    shooting, 96, *96*
Artery, 143, 151, 153, *153*
Asphyxia, 148, 204

Assembly Bill 999 (AB999), 77
Assistant to lead, 22–23
Association for Crime Scene Reconstruction, 7
Automated fingerprint database, 180
Avulsive laceration, 113, *113*

B

Ba'athist Iraq, 8
Back spatter pattern, 133
Ballistics, 87, 88
Baseline method, 67–71, *68*, *70*
Basic yellow, 181
Battery, 87
Bevel, Tom, 6, 128
Biological evidence, 77–78, 190–192, 194–195, 198–199
    collection, 190–194
    dried flaked blood, 193
    dried human, 195
    gloves, 191–192
    masks, 192
    from suspects, 198–199
    touch DNA, 192–193
    types, 190
    from victim, 198–199
    wet bloodstained items, 194
Bird's eye view, 62, *62*, 73
Bite marks, 17, 199
Blood
    evidence, 20, 31, 80, 146, 164, 169, 174, 251–252
    -letting event, 81–82, 128, *131*, *136*, *142*, 142–144, 146, 251–252
    specimen, 145, 173–174, 193, 240, 242
    transfers, 81, 169
Bloodied evidence, 194–198; *see also* Evidence
Bloodstain
    circular pattern, *251*
    collection, 193
    impressions, 161

269

mapping, 24, 30, 39–40, 131, *132*, *133*
pattern analysis, 6, 22, 40, 128, *128*, 230, 238, 241
pattern analysts, 23, 25, 128, 130, 237
Bloodstain pattern analysis (Gardner and Bevel), 6, 128
Bloodstain pattern evidence, 128–146; *see also* Evidence
cast-off, 137–139
cessation cast-off, 137–139
collecting specimen, 144–145
drip trail, 141
flow, 141–142
impact spatter, 133–135
mapping, 131, *132*, 133
overview, 128–133
pooled blood, 142–143
projected bloodstains, 143
scenario, 146
transfer and transfer impressions, 139–140
void patterns, 135–136
Bloodstain Patterns (MacDonell), 6
Blood testing, 198–200
bite marks, 199
buccal swabs, 198
fingernail scrapings, 198–199
observations, 199
presumptive drugs testing, 199–200
of victim/suspects, 198–199
Bluestar, 31, 41, 146, *146*
Body worn camera (BWC), 230
Bolt action, 87
Bore, 87–88
Brady v. Maryland (1963), 11
Breech, 87–89
Buccal swabs, 33, 195, 198, 225
Bullet; *see also* Shooting incidents
core, 87
defect, 61, 85, 87, 90, 94, *95*, *96*, 100, 133, 135, *135*
defined, 87
documenting, 94–95
hole, 85, 236, *237*
jacket, 87
penetration, 95
perforation, 95
trajectory, 98
wipe, 87
Burn patterns
alligatoring, 211–212, *212*
classic "V" pattern, 210–211

clean, *212*, 212–213, *213*
spalling, 213–214, *214*
Bush, G.W., 249
Butcher paper, 14, 28, 75, 77–79, 166, *185*, 185–186, 195–197
BWC, *see* Body worn camera (BWC)

C

Cagney, Jimmy, 86
Caliber, 86, 87
California Department of Corrections & Rehabilitation, 77
California Government Code Section 27491.2, 46
California Penal Codes, 44, 73
California Vehicle Codes, 10, 12n1
Captains, 5, 203, 249
Carotid artery, 151; *see also* Artery
Cartridge, 87–90
case, 87–88
casings, 103–106
center fire, 87
fired, 106–107, 238–239
unfired, 103–106
Casting, 31, 161–162, *163*, 175
Cast-off pattern, 81, 130, 132, 137–139, *139*, 241
Center fire cartridges, 87
Cervantes, Miguel de, 119
Cessation cast-off pattern, 132, 137–139, *138*, 241
Chain of custody, 14–15, 19, 24, 157, 194–195, 202–203
Challenges, 1–4
in court, 42, 75, 196, 236
to investigators, 2–3, 195
trace evidence as, 195
Chamber
fuming, 178–180, 185, 192–193
laminar-flow PCR, 187, *187*
marks, 87
ninhydrin, 185
Chimney effect, 209, 216
Choking, 149; *see also* Strangulation
Chop wounds, 126–127, *127*
Christie, Agatha, 229
Chronological narrative, 233
Classic "V" pattern, *see* "V" pattern
Clean burn patterns, *212*, 212–213, *213*
Clinical photograph, 56, *56*
Clip, 87

Index

Close contact shot, 87
Close-up photographs, 54
Cold-case homicide, 224–225
Collection
    biological evidence, 190–194
    bloodstain, 193
    devices, 192
    of evidence, 23, 40–41
    gassing incident, 73–74
    specimen, 74–75, 128, 144–145, 191, 203
Completeness, report writing, 232–233
Comprehensive notetaking, 208
Computer-assisted mapping systems, 24–25
Concentric fractures, 87
Conchoidal fractures, 87
Condoms, 77–79, 195
Conduct initial observations, 34–36
Confirmatory Drugs Testing, 202
Conjunctivae petechiae, 150
Constitution of State of California, 9
Contact sheets, 57
Contamination, 14, 17, 42
Contrecoup injuries, 120–121; *see also* Head injuries
Control scene, 35
Contusions, 21, 108–112, 114, 119, 169
Coomassie blue, 31, 41, 183
Coroner's Office, 20–21, 36, 46–47, 49, 182, 249
Correctional medical personnel, 16–18
Courtroom testimony, 50, 59, 243–248
    arriving at courthouse, 245
    preparation, 244–245
    responsibility, 243–245
    taking stand, 245–248
Craniectomy, 121
Craniotomy, *see* Craniectomy
Crime scene investigation (CSI)
    analyst, 5–6, 21–22, 39–43, 60, 135, 164, 184
    baseline form, 71
    documentation of, 39, 50
    during escapes, 80–82
    preservation, 44–46
    shooting incidents, 83–86, 91–107
    team, 20–21, 23–24, 35–36, 38, 192
    use-of-force incidents, 82–83
Crime Scene Photography (Robinson), 6
Criminalistics: An Introduction to Forensic Science (Saferstein), 6
CSI inventory, *see* Inventory
Curriculum vitae, 246

Custodial officers, 1, 190
Custodial setting, 1–3, 5, 13, 45, 47, 85
    advantage, 83–84
    microcrystalline test kits, 200
    problem, 2
    scene contamination, 42
    sketches used in, 62
    suspects, 56
    witness, 13
Cyanoacrylate ester fuming, 31, 104, 179–181, *180*, 185, 192–193
Cyano-Shot™, 179
Cylinder gap deposit, 87
Cystoliths, 202

D

Datum, 29, 37, 39, 61, 72
Daubert rulings, 246
Dead-line, 42, 151
Deadly force shooting incidents, 84–86; *see also* Shooting incidents
Debriefing
    formal, 43
    on-scene, 42
The decedent, 36–37, 44–45, 48–49, 137, *152*, *153*, 168–169
Deceleration injuries, 120; *see also* Head injuries
Deoxyribonucleic acid (DNA)
    analysis, 130, 166, 174–175, 186
    buccal swab, 224
    collection kit, 33
    contamination, 47
    of crime scene team, 1
    database, 203, 224
    the decedent, 174
    discovery of, 1
    evidence, 1, 17–18, 75, 82, 165, 188, 193, 196–197, 199, 224
    profile, 203, 224
    specimen, *17*, 97, 182, 187
    swabs, 37, 48, 175
    touch, 104, 189
    typing, 40, 43, 176, 179, 181, 190, 192, 194, 198, 203
    veritable cornucopia of, 1
Deploy additional resources, 34–36
Diagramming, 20, 27–29, 37, 39, 170, 208; *see also* Sketching
    kit, 29
    prior to start, 60

protocols and procedures, 60–61
rectangle method, 67–71
technician, 24–25, 39
things to remember, 60–61
triangulation method, 67–71, *69*
Digital image protocols, 57–58
Digital video images, 59
DiMaio, Dominick, 6, 108, 120, 121
DiMaio, Vincent, 6, 108, 120, 121
District Attorney's Office, 17–18, 22, 76, 223, 232
Dithiooxamide test, 88
DNA, *see* Deoxyribonucleic acid
Documentation of crime scene, 39, 50
Documenting bullet, 94–95
Dog dots, 94
Doje's Skin Print Black™, 176, 182
Double action, 88
Double-barrel, 88
Double glove, 18, 191
Dried flaked blood, 193
Drip trail, 132, 141, *141*
Drying cabinets, 14, *15*, 194
Duqenois–Levine method, 201–202
 chain of custody, 202–203
 confirmatory drugs testing, 202
Dust impressions, 161–162, *163*; *see also* Impressions

E

Einstein, Albert, 11
Ejection, 88, 90
Ejector marks, 88
Electrostatic Dust Print Lifter, 162
Elevation view, 62
Environmental condition, 35–36, 39, 207, 237–238
Escape, 47, 80–82, 86, 103, 176, 204–205
Establishing photographs, 51–52, 54
Ethics, 8–12
Evidence
 biological, 77–78, 190–192, 194–195, 198–199
 blood, 20, 31, 80, 146, 164, 169, 174, 251–252
 bloodied, 194–198
 collection kit, 30
 collection of, 23, 40–41
 collector, 24, 191, 229, 247
 dealing with, 190–203
 gathering, 36–37
 inventory, 187, 239
 markers, 22, 27–28, 29, 39, 51, 60–61, 241
 processing, 43
 recovery kit, 32
Evidence Technology Magazine, 6
Evident Crime Scene Product's PathFinder™, 162
Evidentiary photographs, 23–24, 38, 54–55, 161, 186
Evident's Wet Powder, 181
Evi-Vac system, 37, 78
Exploded view, 62–63, *63*
Exsanguination, 47, 151, 250
Exterior ballistics, 88
Extraction removal techniques, 77

F

Facial petechiae, *see* Conjunctivae petechiae
Fairness, 232, 243
Faro ScanStation, 61
Femoral artery, 151; *see also* Artery
Final report, 71, 239–242
Fingernail scrapings, 78, 198–199
Fingerprint evidence, 176–189; *see also* Evidence
 cyanoacrylate ester, 179–181
 mini-forensic laboratory, 184–188
 ninhydrin, 177–179
 overview, 176–177
 ridge print impressions in blood, 183–184
 scenario, 188–189
 skin print black, 182
 small particle reagent, 182–183
 sticky-side tape, 181–182
Fingerprint impressions, 48–49, 176, 182, 192
Fire & Arson Investigator Journal, 205
Fired bullets, 103–105, 106–107
Firefighting efforts, 195, 205–207
Fire investigations, 204–219
 alligatoring burn pattern, 211–212, *212*
 arriving on scene, 207–208
 burn patterns, 210
 chimney effect, 216
 classic "V" pattern, 210–211
 clean burn patterns, 212–213, *213*
 effects of ventilation on fire patterns, 216–219
 entering fire scene, 208
 overview, 204–206

Index

searching, 208–210
smoke deposits, 214–216
spalling, 213–214, *214*
Fire investigator certification program, 205
Fire Investigator Health and Safety Best Practices, Third Edition, 205
Firing pin, defined, 88
Firing pin impression, defined, 88
First assessment, conduct, 40
First responder
    conferring with, 35
    duties of, 4
    individual, 1
    priority of, 44
    report of, 46
    responsibilities of, 13–16, 44–45, 249
Flash suppressor, 88
Flow pattern, 132, 141, *142*
Folger Adams key, *219*
Footwear evidence, 155–175; *see also* Evidence
    bloodstained footwear, 155, 162, 164, *165*, 167, *167*, *170*, 172
    bloodstained shoe print, 161, *164*
    molded impressions, 161
    photographing, *159–160*
    scenario, 166–175
Footwear impression, 1, 80, 155, *159*, 162–164, 167, *167*, 169, 172, 183; *see also* Impressions
Forcing cone, 88
Forensic camera kit, 32
Forensic Certification Management Board Operations Manual, 28–29
Forensic Magazine, 6
Forensic pathology, 108–127
    abrasions, 108–111
    chop wounds, 126–127
    contusions, 108–111
    fractures, 122–126
    head injuries, 119–122
    incised wounds, 115–119
    lacerations, 112–113
    overview, 108
    stab wounds, 114–115
Forensic Pathology (DiMaio), 6, 108
Forensic reports, 237–239
    body of report, 238
    environmental condition, 238
    evidence inventory, 239
    initial observations, 238
    introduction, 238

Forensics Source Sticky-Side Powder Kit, 181
Forensic vacuums, 195
Formal debriefing, 43
Formalities, 233
Forward spatter pattern, 133, *135*
Fractures
    brawler's, 122, 126
    comminuted, 122
    compound, 122
    facial, 122–124, *124*, 125
    focal, 122–123
    maxilla, *124*
    transverse, 123, *123*
    wrist, 125
Frye rulings, 246
Fuming chamber, 178–180, 185, 192–193
Function testing, 88

G

Gardner, Ross, 6, 34, 128
Gas operated, 88
Gassing incident, 73–79
    collection, 73–74
    evidence collection kit inventory, 76
    sexual assault, 76–79
    skin contact, 75
    swabbing, 74
Gauge, 88, 233
Geberth, Vernon, 6
Gentry, Jeffrey, 128
Global positioning systems, 61
Gloves, 191–192
Grid-pattern sketch method, 70, *71*
Grooves, 88, 90
GSR, *see* Gunshot residue
Gulf War, 8
Gunshot residue (GSR), 30, 88, 90

H

Hammer, 88, 104, 188–189
Handbook of Forensic Photography (Weiss), 6
Handgun, 88, 104, 188–189
Head injuries, 119–122
    contrecoup injuries, 120–121
    subdural hematoma, 120
    traumatic brain swelling, 121
Hexagon OBTI Immunochromatographic Rapid Test method, 130, 137, 172

Index

Homicide
    category, 149
    investigation, 6, 20, 165, 194, 229
    victim, 149, 151
Horizontal angles of impact, 85, 90–92, *97*, 100
Horizontal trajectory, 236
Hot shots, 148
Hueske, Edward, 6, 86
Hungarian red, 41, *164*, 183

I

IAAI, *see* International Association of Arson Investigators
IABPA, *see* International Association for Bloodstain Pattern Examiners
Ice-pick type weapon, 114–115, *115*
Ignitable liquid pour patterns, 209
Impact spatter pattern, 132–135, *134*, *135*, 241
Impressions
    bloodstain, 161
    dust, 161–162, *163*
    evidence casting kit, 31
    fingerprint, 48–49, 176, 182, 192
    firing pin, 88
    footwear, 1, 80, 155, *159*, 162–164, 167, *167*, 169, 172, 183
    molded, 56, 161
    ridge print, 183–184
    textbook, 17
    transfer bloodstain, 81, 132, 139–140, *170*, *173*
Incidents
    deadly force shooting, 84–86
    gassing, 73–79
    less-lethal shooting, 84
    major, 16, 23, 27–28
    non-major, 26
    use-of-force, 82–83
    warning shot, 84
Incised wounds, 108, 115–119, 126, 151–154, 250, 252
In-custody death, 46–49
Indentations, 87, 90, 102, 195
Industrial dryer, 217, *218*
Infrared imaging, 83, *83*
Initial notification and response, 34
Initial observations, 34–36, 41, 204, 207, 238
Inkless Shoe Print™ kit, 164
Inmate-manufactured weapons, 1, 55, 114, 117, 119, 179, 181, 193

Intermediate range, 88
Internal ballistics, 88
International Association for Bloodstain Pattern Examiners (IABPA), 7
International Association for Identification (IAI), 6–7, 29, 128
International Association of Arson Investigators (IAAI), 205
International Association of Chiefs of Police, 8
Interview
    fact-finding, 220
    field, 250
    Miranda, 222
    room, 220–221, 226
    techniques, 220–226
    video-documented, 59
Inventory, 26–33
    alternate light source kit, 31
    blood evidence enhancement, 31
    bloodstain mapping kit, 30
    diagramming kit, 29
    DNA collection kit, 33
    evidence collection kit, 30
    evidence marker kit, 29
    evidence recovery kit, 32
    forensic camera kit, 32
    impression evidence casting kit, 31
    latent print development kit, 31
    measuring kit, 29
    personal protective equipment ready bag, 33
    photographic lighting kit, 32
    shooting scene kit, 29–30
Investigative Services Unit (ISU), 199, 232, 247
Investigators, 5–12
    challenges to, 2–3, 195
    ethics, 8–12
    lead, 21–23
    moral character, 8–12
    primary ambition of, 19
    responsibilities of, 18–21, 28–29
    trained, 5
    training for, 6
Irregularly shaped burn pattern, 209
ISU, *see* Investigative Services Unit

J

Jailhouse justice, 2
Jewelry boxes, 106

Index

Journal of Forensic Identification, 6
Jugular vein, 151–152, *154*
Julia Child approach, 177

K

Kastle-Meyer, *see* Phenolphthalein
Keyholing, 88

L

Lacerations, 20–21, 108, *112*, 112–114, 113, *113*, 117, 119
Laminar-flow PCR downdraft chamber, 187, *187*
Laminated glass, 89
Langer's lines, 114
Lansberry's liquid, *see* Ridge builder lotion
Larger photographic L-scales, 55
Latent print development kit, 31
Lateral angle of deflection, 89
Law enforcement officers, 9–10, 46
LCV, *see* Leucocrystal Violet
Lead card, 52, *52*
Leadership, defined, 8
Lead investigator, 21–23
Leica ScanStation, 61
Lentini, John J., 205
Less-lethal shooting incidents, 84; *see also* Shooting incidents
Leucocrystal Violet (LCV), 183
Leuco Malachite Green (LMG), 30, 130, 198
Lever action, 89
Lieutenants, 5, 82
Ligature, 148–150
  marks, 149, *150*
  strangulation, 149, *150*
Line of sight, 89
Lividity, 37, 47, 111
Livor mortis, 111, *111*
LMG, *see* Leuco Malachite Green
Locard, Edmond, 253
Long gun, 89, 191
Los Angeles County Sheriff's Department, Homicide Division, 224

M

MacDonell, Herbert, 6
Magazine, 89, 189; *see also* Bullet
  follower, 89
  safety, 89

Magnetic brushes, 31, 176
Major incident, 16, 23, 27–28
Major occurrence, 27
Man-made disaster, 28
Manual strangulation, 148–149
Mapping, 24, 28, 30, 39–40, 55, 129, 131
  bloodstain, 24, 30, 40, 131, *132*, *133*
  computer-assisted, 24–25
  techniques, *133*
Markers, 55
  drop, 22
  evidence, 22, 27–28, 39, 51, 60–61, 241
  genetic, 190
  placement of, 23
Marquis Reagent, 200–201
Masks, 18, 33, 77, 105, 144, 191–193
Mass casualty, 28, 204
Maxilla fracture, *124*
Measuring crime scene, *see* Sketching
Measuring kit, 29
Mecke Reagent, 201
Medical distress, 20
Medical emergencies, 3, 16
Medical episode, 3
Medical Examiner's (ME) Office, 36–37, 47–48, 108, 249
Microcrystalline test kits
  Marquis Reagent, 200–201
  Mecke Reagent, 201
  Scott's Reagent, 201
Microphotography, 38
Mid-range evidence photographs, 53–54
Mini-forensic laboratory, 184–188
Mist pattern, 133, 135
Molded impression, 56, 161; *see also* Impressions
Moral character, 7, 8–12
Mutual aid, 2, 53, 82–83, 166, 188, 205, 237
Muzzle, 86–89, 91–92
  blast, 89
  imprint, 89
  velocity, 89

N

N-95 mask, 18, 33, 77, 144, 192
Narcan (Naloxone), 148
National Fire Protection Association's NFPA 921 Guide to Fire and Bomb Investigations, 205
National Integrated Ballistic Information Network (NIBIN), 104–106

National PREA Resource Center, 76–77
Near contact shot, 89
NFPA1321 Standards for Fire Investigation Units, 205
NIBIN, *see* National Integrated Ballistic Information Network
Ninhydrin, 176, 177–179, *178*, 185; *see also* Ruhemann's purple
Non-major incident, 26–27
Non-sworn personnel, 6
Normal program, 3, 8
Notetaking, 208, 230, 232

O

Oblique lighting, 35–36, 156, 159, 161, *162*, *163*, 176, 192, 251
On-scene debriefing of CSI team, 42
Open fracture, 122
Overall photographs, 51–52, 54

P

Para-military organization, 5
Patent, 189, *189*
Patterned contusions, 109
Patterns, *see* specific patterns
Peavey, Lynn, 161, *162*, 164, 179, 200
Pellet, 86–89, 94
Pellet defects, 94–95
Penetration, 102
    defined, 89
    vs. perforation, 95
Perforation, 102, *135*
    defined, 89
    vs. penetration, 89
Perimeter, 9, 22, 35–36, 41
    inside, 53–55
    outer, 45, 81, 205
    outside, 53–55
    scene, 19, 22, 35–36, 41, 45, 53, 208, 238
Periphery, 41–42
Personal protective equipment ready bag, 32
Perspective photographs, 51
Phenolphthalein, 30, 130, 137, 246
    color test, 198
    test method (Kastle-Meyer), 172–173
Photographer, 22, 23–24, 35, 37–38, 51–53, 55–56, 251
Photographic lighting kit, 32
Photography
    clinical, 56, *56*
    close-up, 23, 54–55
    conditions at the scene, 50
    crime scene, 37–39, 50–55
    digital image protocols, 57–58
    digital video images, 59
    establishing, 51–52, 54
    evidentiary, 23–24, 38, 54–55, 161, 186
    injuries, 55–56
    inside perimeters, 53–55
    lead card, 52, *52*
    mid-range, 54
    outside perimeters, 53–55
    overall, 51–52, 54
    perspective, 51
    prejudicial, 56
    in report, 236–237
    same plane, 24, 38, *54*, 54–55, 159, *159*, *162*
    suggested protocols, 49–50
    video cameras, 59
    video evidence, 58–59
Pinch-point, 89, 103, *103*
Pistorius, Oscar, 18
Pitchess Motion, 11
Plastic cart, 217, *218*
Plot plan, 61–63, *64–65*
Pocket Rod, 30, 131
Point of origin
    bloodstain, 40
    fire, 209
Pooled blood, 142–143, 169, *170*, 251
Portable lighting equipment, 3
Poser 6™ software programs, 67, *67*
Positive identification, 16, 48–49, 231
Powder stippling, 89
Practical Analysis and Reconstruction of Shooting Incidents (Hueske), 6, 86
Practical Crime Scene Processing and Investigation (Gardner), 34
Prejudicial photograph, 56
Presumptive testing, 39–40, 130, *144*, 144–145, 172–173, 198–200
Primer, 87–89
Principle of Evidence Exchange, 253
Prison Rape Elimination Act (PREA), 76–77, 249
Privacy Rule of Health Insurance Portability and Accountability Act of 1996, 78
Processing evidence, 43; *see also* Report writing
Processing methodology and checklists

Index

bloodstain pattern mapping, 39–40
collection of evidence, 40–41
the decedent, 36–37
deploy additional resources, 34–36
documentation of crime scene, 39
first assessment, 40
formal debriefing, 43
initial notification and response, 34
initial observations, 34–36
on-scene debriefing, 42
photographing, 37–39
processing evidence and report writing, 43
scene periphery, 41–42
second assessment, 41
securing or releasing scene, 42
Projected bloodstain pattern, 143, *143*, 221
Proof sheets, *see* Contact sheets
Propellant, 87–90
Protocols and procedures, 44–79
diagramming, 60–61
gassing incident, 73–79
in-custody death, 46–49
markers, 55
measuring crime scene, 62–73
photography, 49–59
preservation, 44–46
scales, 55
sketching, 60–61, 62–73
Punch Pro™ software programs, 67, *67*
Pythagoras, 92, 94

R

Radial artery, 151, 153, *153*; *see also* Artery
Radial fracture, 89
Ready bag, 18, 33
Rectangle diagramming method, 67–71
Report writing, 6, 43, 57, 86, 108, 227–242
abbreviations, 232
apathy, 227–228
chronological narrative, 233
completeness, 232–233
in court, 234–237
described, 230–231
fairness, 232
final report, 239–242
first and foremost, 228–230
forensic reports, 237–239
formalities, 233
notetaking, 232
photographs, 236, *237*
positive identification, 231

Response classification system, 26–33
major incident/occurrence, 27–28
man-made disaster, 28
mass casualty, 28
non-major incident, 26–27
Responsibilities, 13–25
of analyst, 21–22
of assistant to lead, 22–23
of crime scene team, 21
diagram technician, 24–25
evidence collector, 24
of first responder, 13–16
of investigator, 18–22
of medical personnel, 16–18
other specialist, 25
photographer, 23–24
scribe, 23
Revolver, 87–89, 148
Rhodamine 6G, 181
Ricochet, 89, *102*, 102–103
angle of, 86
crease, 90, 102
Ridge builder lotion, 49
Ridge print impressions in blood, 183–184
Rifling, defined, 90
Rifling twist, defined, 90
Rigor mortis, 37, 47, 149
Robinson, Edgar G., 6, 86
Roosevelt, Eleanor, 11
Rough sketch, 39, 71, 72–73
Ruhemann's purple, 177; *see also* Ninhydrin

S

Saferstein, Richard, 6, 200, 202
Safety glass, 90, 96, 193
Same plane photographs, 24, 38, *54*, 54–55, 159, *159*, 162
Scales, 24, 27–31, 38–40, *54*, 55
adhesive-backed, 131
American Board of Forensic Odontology (ABFO), 55
photographic, 22, 29–31, 94, 174
use of, 38
ScenePD 6 Pro diagram, *66*
Scene perimeter, 19, 22, 35–36, 41, 45, 53, 208, 238
Schwarzkopf, H. Norman, 8
Scientific Protocols for Fire Investigation (Lentin), 205
Scott, L. J., 201
Scott's Reagent, 201

Index

Scribe, 20, 23, 222
Second assessment, conduct, 41
Securing or releasing scene, 42
Self-inflicted incised wounds, 151–154, 252
Semen-stained sock examination, *79*
Semi-automatic firearm, 90
Sergeant, 5–6, 82, 188–189, 224–226
Sexual assault, 16, 76–79, 249
Shell casing, 72–73, 84–85, 90, 104–105, 238–239
Shooting incidents
    angle of impact, *see* Angle of impact
    area of convergence, 96
    bullets collection/recovery, 103–105, 106–107
    calculation of distance, 91–94
    deadly force within secured perimeter, 84–86
    direction of ricochets, 102–103
    documenting bullet, 94–95
    fired cartridge casings, 103–105, 106–107
    less-lethal within secured perimeter, 84
    pellet defects, 94–95
    penetration *vs.* perforation, 95
    scene investigations, 86
    unfired cartridge casings/bullets collection, 103–105
    unintentional *vs.* accidental discharge, 95
    warning shot incidents, 84
Shooting scene kit, 29–30
Shot accountability, 90
Shotgun shell, 89–90, 107
Sirchie, 131, 145, 161–162, 179, 200
Sketching, 60–73; *see also* Diagramming
    baseline method, 67–71
    datum, 72
    forms, 71
    grid, *71*
    rectangle method, 67–71
    rough sketch, 72–73
    sketching forms, 71
    suggested protocols, 60–61
    triangulation method, 67–71
Skin contact, 75
Skin Print Black, 37, 176, 182
Slashing-stabbing type weapon, 117, *117*
Slashing type weapons, *116*, 117
Slashing type wounds, *see* Incised wounds
Slug, 90
Small particle reagent (SPR), 176, 182–183
Smoke deposits, 214–216, *215*, *216*
Sniffers, 209

Sodium rhodizonate, 30, 90
Soil samples, 195
Solemn oath, 9
Soot, 87, 90, 206, 208, 212
Spalling, 213–214, *214*
Spatter patterns, 130
Specimen
    blood, 145, 173–174, 193, 240, 242
    collection, 74–75, 128, 144–145, 191, 203
    DNA, *17*, 97, 182, 187
    dry-swab, 193
Spin stabilization, 90
SPR, *see* Small particle reagent
Stab wounds, 114–115, *115*, 125, 240
State of California, 9, 77
Steenkamp, Reeva, 18
Sternocleidomastoid muscle, 154
Sticky-side tape, *181*, 181–182
Strangulation
    by hanging, 148–151
    ligature, 149, *150*
    manual, 148–149
Subdural hematoma, 120; *see also* Head injuries
Suicide investigations, 147–154
    overview, 147–148
    self-inflicted incised wounds, 151–154
    strangulation by hanging, 148–151
Suicide watch, 147
SuperSticks, 131
Swabbing, 37, 40, 74, 177, 193, 203
Swipe bloodstain pattern, 251–252
Sworn personnel, 6

T

Tempered glass, 90
Testimony
    courtroom, 50, 59, 243–248
    eyewitness, 76, 224
    virtuous, 10
    word, 243
Textbook impression, 17; *see also* Impressions
Thompson Model 1927A1, 86
Thumbnail prints, *see* Contact sheets
Touch DNA, 18, 82, 104, 189, 192–193
Trace evidence, 37, 44, 190, 194–195, 198, 238; *see also* Evidence
Trajectory, 84–85, 89–91, 97–100, 101–102
    bullet, 98
    horizontal, 236

rod, 29, 85, 90–91, 97–101
vertical, 91
Transfer bloodstain impression, 81, 132, 139–140, *170*, *173*; *see also* Impressions
Transfer bloodstain pattern, 137, 139–140
Transverse fracture, 123, *123*
Traumatic brain swelling, 121; *see also* Head injuries
Triangulation diagramming method, 67–71, *69*
Tripods, 51, 54, 85, 130, 155–159, 162, 206

U

Unfired bullets, 103–105; *see also* Bullet
Unintentional discharge
   vs. accidental discharge, 95
   defined, 95
United States Fire Administration, 204
Use-of-force incidents, 82–83; *see also* Incidents

V

Vacuum Metal Deposition, 104
Vapor detectors, 209
Ventilation on fire patterns, effects of, 216–219
Vertical flight path, 99
Vertical trajectory, 91
Vested interest, 7
Video cameras, 59
Video evidence; *see also* Evidence

documentation, 59
objectives of, 58–59
procedures, 59
suggested protocols, 58–59
A Visual Guide to Bloodstain Analysis (Gentry), 128
"V" notch, 149, *150*
Void bloodstain patterns, 135–136, *136*
"V" pattern, *210*, 210–211, *211*

W

Warning shot incidents, 84; *see also* Incidents
Wave castoff, 133
Weapons
   ice-pick type, 114–115, *115*
   inmate-manufactured, 1, 55, 114, 117, 119, 179, 181, 193
   slashing-stabbing type, 117, *117*
   slashing type, *116*, 117
Weiss, Sanford, 6
Wet bloodstained items, 194
Wet Wop, 181
Wipe bloodstain pattern, 251–252
Wrapping technique, 196–198
Wrist fractures, 125

Z

Zero-edge protractor, 29, 85, 90, 92, *93*, *97*, *99*
Zone of possibility, 90
Zygomatic bone, 124